Harvard Historical Studies, 115

Published under the auspices
of the Department of History
from the income of the
Paul Revere Frothingham Bequest
Robert Louis Stroock Fund
Henry Warren Torrey Fund

FOREST RITES

The War of the Demoiselles in
Nineteenth-Century France

Peter Sahlins

Harvard University Press
Cambridge, Massachusetts
London, England
1994

Library of Congress Cataloging-in-Publication Data

Sahlins, Peter.
Forest rites : the War of the Demoiselles in nineteenth-century
France / Peter Sahlins.
p.   cm. — (Harvard historical studies ; 115)
Includes bibliographical references and index.
ISBN 0-674-30895-6 (cloth)
ISBN 0-674-30896-4 (pbk.)
1. War of the Demoiselles, France, 1829–1831.   2. Ariège (France)—
History.   3. Peasant uprisings—France—History—19th century.
4. Land tenure—Social aspects—France—Ariège.   5. Forests and
forestry—France—Ariège.   6. Peasantry—France—Ariège—Political
activity.   I. Title.   II. Series: Harvard historical studies ; v.
115.
DC256.8.S28   1994
944.06'2—dc20
93-49841
CIP

For Sooni, David, and Forest, Demoiselles all
And for my parents, always

CONTENTS

PREFACE

n early May 1829, strange reports surfaced from the forests of Saint-Lary in the Ariège Pyrenees, reports that quickly attracted the attention of local and national officials. Deep within the forests, a state forest inspector glimpsed "three women of a size much larger than is expected of this sex." The "women" chased him and three forest guards away as they sought to verify reports of sheep pasturing in prohibited areas of the royal forests. Over the next few days, bizarrely clad groups of peasants frightened off charcoal-makers in the employ of ironworks owners, burned guards' huts in the forests, and threatened innkeepers who agreed to lodge forest guards. It quickly became apparent to the authorities that the rebels in question were not women at all, but male peasants who, in defiance of the restrictions imposed by the National Forest Code of 1827—and the forest guards' claims of authority in enforcing that law—appeared "armed and disguised as women" to reclaim possession of their forests.

Thus began the "War of the Demoiselles," the "Ladies' War," which was to puzzle and annoy administrative and military officials and frustrate their efforts to understand and to repress it. Between 1829 and 1831—with sporadic reappearances until the late nineteenth century—bands of male peasants from the mountain communes of the Ariège, "armed and disguised as women," scared forest guards and charcoal-makers from the forest in this elaborate and peculiar war.

The peasants called themselves "Demoiselles," but it was a middle-class author's nostalgic recollections of the events in 1857, a generation after 1829, that not inappropriately named the events a "war."

After all, in 1829 some peasant rioters claimed "to be fighting a war against the forest guards," others donned military costumes, carried flags and other paraphernalia, and overall, the language of their revolt drew heavily on military metaphors. It was indeed a strange war, one which saw—at least between 1829 and 1831—no prisoners taken and no enemies killed. But it was no less clearly a war. Although the Demoiselles fought a dramatic and playful battle, the spoils were a matter of life and death for the peasants of the Ariège.

The mountain peasantry of the Ariège fought this festive rebellion to defend their possession of the forests against the dual and related forces of state-building and capitalism in nineteenth-century France. The peasants opposed the implementation of the 1827 National Forest Code, which systematically restricted forest use-rights essential to their agricultural and pastoral way of life. The confrontation of the local populations with the state forest administration forced another latent struggle to surface—between the local forest and ironworks owners (a class of rural notables) and the peasantry. In both cases, the battle was fought over the possession and use of the forests. In an age, not unlike our own, when natural resources were rapidly being depleted, social groups with opposing conceptions of and distinct interests in the forest came directly into conflict.

Throughout France, peasants revolted against the increasingly disruptive presence of the state and the market during the nineteenth century. But such resistance became especially charged in 1830. In July of that year, a three-day political revolution in Paris—the "Three Glorious Days"—ended the Restoration and began the July Monarchy, installing a slightly more liberal government under a new king, Louis-Philippe. While that political drama was played out in Paris, all over France peasants rioted against new taxes, rising prices, and restrictions of their rights to the forest. The War of the Demoiselles coincided with—indeed, it was a local version of—the political upheaval of the July Revolution of 1830.

But the War of the Demoiselles took a more dramatic form than other popular struggles throughout France, and since 1830, the events have inspired nearly a dozen dramatic works, including plays, novels, two films, and even a comic book. The peasant men wore their shirts untucked with a belt in order to take on the appearance of women, blackened their faces and hands, and occasionally wore animal skins. Armed with their agricultural tools, hatchets, and guns, they gathered in the forest at night to expel with great fanfare state forest guards and charcoal-makers.

The symbolism of the disguise and the elaborate, ritualized character of the events suggest that much more was at stake than can be adequately invoked by the words "rebellion," "revolt," or "uprising." Similar terms were used by those who sought to repress the rebellion, and they have been employed by subsequent historians as well. Yet only one set of meanings can be recovered from this perspective, from this view of such outsiders as state officials, forest administrators, and other members of the dominant classes. For however accurate or plausible, however sympathetic to the concerns of the local populations (just as many of the officials were), an account framed solely in terms of peasant rebellion against the forces of state-building and capitalism cannot grasp the cultural and symbolic dimensions of the revolt. More precisely, such an account cannot make sense of the specific historical and cultural contexts of these curiously attired rebellious male peasants, "armed and disguised as women."

In this book I seek to recover and interpret a peasant culture in revolt: a contested symbolic universe at a particular historical moment. I want to reconstruct the world in which the disguise and the drama of the War of the Demoiselles made sense. It is a local world, one region of the French Pyrenees during the nineteenth century, but it is also a more broadly understood one, encompassing peasant cultures in the Pyrenees, in France, and in Europe, from the sixteenth to the nineteenth century. These peasant cultures, now largely lost, can be reconstructed only with great difficulty and care, since the principal sources which historians have at their disposal—the archives of governments, theocracies, and armies, to recall Carlo Levi's words—tend to mask the meaning of events and cultural practices of local peasant society. In interpreting the culture from which the peasants drew their forms of protest, I will have recourse to these and to other sources, such as folkloric inquiries and judicial trials. Here, the voices of peasants can occasionally be heard, although they are always framed by and filtered through the linguistic and cultural categories of a dominant culture. Such is the challenge of making sense of these ill-fated and desperate wars, "incomprehensible to historians."

This book tells the tale of a dramatic peasant uprising in nineteenth-century France, but it also raises questions of anthropological and historical importance that reach well beyond the forests of the Ariège. Historiographically, one of my aims is to link two historical periods—the Old Regime and the nineteenth century—which too often remain artificially separated by the divide of the French Revolution. I reach back to the beginning of the early modern period, the sixteenth century, and forward to issues which are still very much alive today. Three histories, in particular, frame my account of the War of the Demoiselles: the environmental history of forest management and exploitation; the history of French popular cultures (specifically, of rural or village culture); and the history of political revolt and revolution.

It is perhaps appropriate, given the first of these contexts, to consider the structure and themes of this book by expanding on a metaphor of the forest used by the seventeenth-century French philosopher René Descartes. In *Discourse on Method,* first published in 1637, Descartes considered how best to follow a firm and resolute course of action in his practical life, as well as in his thought:

> In this I would imitate travelers who, finding themselves lost in a forest, ought not to wander this way or that, or, what is worse, remain in one place, but ought always walk as straight a line as they can in one direction, and not change course for feeble reasons, even if at the outset it was perhaps only chance that made them choose it; for by this means, if they are not going where they wish, they will finally arrive at least somewhere where they probably will be better off than in the middle of the forest. (1980, 13)

In fact, Descartes' manner of thinking—his path of logic founded on the straight lines of mathematical reason, out of the darkness of the forest—leads straight into the politics of the forest administration, first of the absolute monarchy, then of the bourgeois state in the nineteenth century. It leads to an abstract and rational "management" of forest space, the imposition of order on perceived chaos. But it also speaks directly to the inability of officials in 1829 to understand the War of the Demoiselles, using their own language of practical reason and instrumentality; and from there, the Cartesian inheritance, with its insistence on straight lines of argument and its focus on utility, also works to inhibit our own understanding of the events.

This book does not take a single path from the forest; on the contrary, it strikes out along several paths leading from deep within the forests of the Ariège to the wider worlds of culture and politics since the sixteenth century.

The first chapter describes the outbreak of the War of the Demoiselles. Here I ask questions about how the events were interpreted by those who sought to repress them. The limitations of Cartesian reasoning are revealed in the arguments by forest officials and historians alike, who, in the logics of practical reason and instrumentality, explain the disguise as women by showing the functions which it served. Three chapters follow, each one narrating the story as it unfolded between 1829 and 1831, while offering a different and complementary path out of the forests of the Ariège.

Chapter 2 presents the initial stage of the revolt, in the spring and summer of 1829, then delves deeper into the forests, attempting to reconstitute their meanings within peasant culture, while placing the War of the Demoiselles in the larger perspective of state forest management and local peasant culture since the seventeenth century. Chapter 3 considers the timing of the revolt from the summer of 1829 through the spring of 1830; it takes the path of peasant festive culture, assessing the symbolic and temporal intersection of festival and revolt in the War of the Demoiselles and in France more generally between the sixteenth and eighteenth centuries. Chapter 4 treats the revolt after the summer of 1830; it takes the path of political revolution, considering the exchanges of peasant and bourgeois cultures within and after the July Revolution of 1830.

The boundary of fiction and history has been tested in recent years by social and cultural historians of the popular classes in early modern Europe. Using extraordinarily rich and detailed sources—such as Inquisition records and criminal trial testimony—historians have been able to reconstruct and interpolate the mental worlds and choices of otherwise silent individuals. We thus know a great deal about a Friulan miller Menocchio, about an imposter-husband Arnauld du Tilh, the would-be Martin Guerre, and about a village of Cathar heretics in Montaillou. (Curiously, the last two stories, like that of the Demoiselles, are set in the pays de Foix.) Historians have been carefully listening to these voices, and silences, while also demonstrating to readers that their own reconstructions, the narrative frames of those voices, lie within the bounds of the historical record. Whereas modern historians have tended to listen for the distinct voices of individuals, this tale of nineteenth-century peasant communities in revolt concentrates on collective meanings construed and re-constructed from a fragmented, incomplete, and always inadequate record.

Each chapter in this book narrates an aspect of the War of the Demoiselles and explores a set of themes: about the revolt in space, in time, and in the political imagination. This book has no footnotes; important secondary authors are cited within the text. I have documented each chapter in a separate bibliographic essay which comments on archival sources and scholarly work. These essays may be read for a more complete understanding of the character and quality of the sources, and the ways in which specific interpretations were constructed. The Sources provide a complete bibliography of primary and secondary materials consulted in my research on the War of the Demoiselles.

Governments, Theocracies, and Armies are, of course, stronger than the scattered peasants. So the peasants have to resign themselves to being dominated, but they cannot feel as their own the glories and undertakings of a civilization that is radically their enemy. The only wars which touch their hearts are those in which they defend themselves against that civilization, against History and Government, Theocracy and Army. These wars they fought under their own black pennants, without military leadership or training and without hope, ill-fated wars that they were bound to lose, fierce and desperate wars, incomprehensible to historians.

Carlo Levi, *Christ Stopped at Eboli*

1. THE WAR OF THE DEMOISELLES

he first reports of peasant men "armed and disguised as women" in the royal forests of Saint-Lary were heard during early May 1829. In the nearby mountain villages of the district called the Castillonnais, several municipal councils were in the process of petitioning the courts to uphold the peasants' inherited rights to gather firewood, building materials, and to pasture animals in the royal forests, against the restrictions imposed by the 1827 Forest Code. But certain peasants of those same communes took matters into their own hands, chasing the royal guards and charcoal-makers from the forests. By the last week in May, bands of men in the forest appeared regularly in their distinctive garb, cutting wood in prohibited areas and freely pasturing their herds of sheep without regard for the restrictions established by the royal forest guards. On 22 May in the royal forest of Sentein, a large group of men "entirely disguised as women," gathering to the sound of a seashell, chased several forest guards from their houses with guns shot into the air, screams, threats, and invectives. On 26 May, bands of Demoiselles pillaged the houses of two particularly hated guards at Augirein, where they took all the wooden objects into the forests and burned them. The guards in the Bellongue complained to the prefect of their inability to find lodging: none of the innkeepers of the Castillonnais would house them, and for good reason. At Illartein, during the night of 27 June, and at Bordes, during the night of 7 July, the peasant rioters presented themselves as Demoiselles to the village innkeepers, warning them not to take in guards.

The rioting spread in the months of June and July throughout the valleys of the Castillonnais, to the southwestern part of the Ariège

department, to the Bellongue, Biros, and Batlongue valleys. The rioting then spread south, up to Ustou (following the traditional route
of summer transhumance of cattle); and to the west, over to several
communes of the neighboring department of the Haute-Garonne.
There, in the village of Fougaron on Sunday, 26 July, thirty-nine
Demoiselles entered a cabaret and ordered wine. Elaborately attired
and led by three costumed men calling themselves "The Captain,"
"The Executioner," and "The Priest," these disguised peasants later
went into the forest, where they destroyed five shelters erected by
the charcoal-makers. "What started as a game following the extreme
cowardice of the forest guards," wrote the colonel in charge of the
thirteenth legion of the royal constabulary, "is starting to get serious." The prefect called in military troops, yet not only could these
be used solely at the request of the local mayors—who were, according to a frustrated official, "all Demoiselles themselves"—but
they proved extremely ill-suited to the task.

The Demoiselles knew the lay of the land; they moved swiftly, often
at night, through the forests with which they were so familiar. The
soldiers, strangers to the region, lacked a knowledge of the terrain,
moved slowly in rigid formation, and were useless in preventing incidents. The forests protected the peasants from their enemies: as the
peasants of Seix had described it three centuries earlier, "The forests
are necessary since they constitute the protection and defense of the
district, since enemies, in the woods, can neither know nor see the
paths, but local people count on the paths and prevent their enemies
from coming by ambushes." In 1829, the role of soldiers and gendarmes was reduced to reporting the damage done by the Demoiselles. "The presence of soldiers at Saint-Lary has produced no effect,
nor [has it] in any of the neighboring communes," wrote the sub-
prefect of Saint-Girons. Besides the failure of tactics, frequent rivalries among the military command, political administration, and royal
constabulary prevented the presentation of a unified front.

In this moment of relative freedom of action during the early summer of 1829, the peasantry's repertoire of collective actions was
quickly established. In many cases, the Demoiselles would go about
the ordinary business of summer work, especially pasturing sheep in
the forests or on the high mountain pastures. When the guards sought
to restrict these activities, seizing stray animals or larger herds in areas of the forest declared "protected," small groups of Demoiselles
rallied to the call of seashells or cow horns and reclaimed their flocks.

Occasionally, larger groups would form, such as the two-dozen Demoiselles who gathered in the Bonac forest on 8 June, or the same number who, following a seizure of cows at Bordes on 30 May, drove out the forest guards. The Demoiselles used the same tactics against the charcoal-makers: on 8 July, seven or eight disguised peasants chased off the workers employed by Sr. Trinqué in Ustou, threatening them with certain death; and on the night of 16 July in Sentein, between thirty and forty peasants, "armed and dressed as women," expelled both guards and charcoal-makers from the forests. Using the familiar tactics of shooting guns into the air, shouting, and screaming invectives, they threatend their enemies with murder and mutilation while chasing them out of the forests.

For the principal objective of the rioters during this first moment of the revolt was the expulsion of their "enemies" from the royal and communal forests, their enemies being both the charcoal-makers, working in private and state forests, and the royal and private forest guards. (The Demoiselles were selective. When four gendarmes and a town official ran into fifty Demoiselles in the forest near Massat in February 1830, they were told to move on: "It's not you we're after, continue on your way, and nothing will happen to you, but if you disobey, it's your life.") Most of these charcoal-makers and guards had been recruited from the villages of the Ariège, the charcoal-makers most notably from the commune of Bosc. Yet they were invariably found working in communities not their own; the forest guards, especially, were always "foreigners," strangers to the village communities. The peasants called them *salamagnos* ("salamanders"), describing their distinctive uniform—green with a yellow shoulder band striped with green—and evoking other characteristics of that creature, including the way it camouflaged itself in bushes, and its legendary ability to survive fire.

At first, the higher authorities believed that it was specific guards who, because of their abusive exercise of authority, were being singled out. Indeed, the administrative archives of the Ariège are full of documentation of the guards' reign of extortion and terror over the local populations. In Massat, according to a contemporary memoir written by the adjunct-mayor, the forest guards did not even bother to pursue the peasants on the mountains. Situating themselves at the town limits, they threatened and extorted peasants returning from the forests with firewood. The guards were poorly paid, their salaries a function of the revenue generated in the leasing of forest lands; in

1829, a meager wage indeed. They were largely illiterate and had minimal knowledge of the National Forest Code they were assigned to enforce. "The poor conduct and partiality of the guards have brought on a considerable bad feeling." So concluded the forest commission named by the prefect in September 1830, summing up the relations between the local communities and these guards: "They seem to have inspired quite a terror, such that they are more respected than the municipal authority itself. They received or demanded gifts each year from families who had nothing. This supposed obligation, if not met, assured that sooner or later one of the family members would be the object of judicial pursuits." By this time, the authorities recognized what had long been the peasantry's goal: the removal not of particular, abusive guards, but of the entire forest administration from the mountain forests and the recovery of the forests for themselves. To reclaim "their" properties, the peasant rioters directed their wrath against the charcoal-makers in the employ of forest and forge owners who, like the guards, presented themselves as the immediate obstacle to their full enjoyment of the forest lands.

Scaring off the guards was only one way of reclaiming possession and control of the forest. At night, the Demoiselles also attacked and destroyed the guards' shelters in the forests. On the night of Sunday, 14 June, they vandalized a shelter built in the commune of Riverenet; and on the night of 24 June, they dismantled one in the royal forest of Castillon. Sometimes they even attacked the houses of the guards themselves, as on 12 July in Galey. Occasionally, they confronted the guards directly in the villages, as during the night of 18 July at Illartein. By early July, the Demoiselles struck with ease, and nothing seemed to stop them. When in August 1829 the prefect authorized pasturing in the forests for one year as a means of calming the local communities, he was only officially recognizing what was already being done.

By then, the name and reputation of the Demoiselles were well established. The term, adopted by local and national officials, was first used by the peasants themselves, and not without irony. For the word normally designated a young lady of honorable standing, and a peasant demoiselle was already something of a deliberate and self-conscious joke. All the more so as the peasants of the neighboring villages in Couserans had a saying, recorded in the mid-nineteenth century: "Dress up a weed and it can look like a demoiselle" ("Habillo ouo rouminguero que semblo ouo démaisèlo," quoted in Biros

1974, 259). So the male peasants of the Castillonnais "dressed up" in order to appear as young women in the summer of 1829.

Yet it is clear that they were not, technically, "dressed as women" at all. The male peasants did not, in fact, attempt to take on the identity of women, as might male transvestites. Rather, they adopted the abbreviated, caricatured signs of women without abandoning their masculine identity. As the prefect reported, "The disguise consists only in darkening the face with red or black, wearing a white shirt outside the clothes instead of leaving it tucked in, tightening the waist with a colored band, which gives the shirt the impression of a skirt, and finally placing on the head a handkerchief or a woman's headpiece." Thus in the marvelously simple act of disguise, the men took out the white wool shirt normally worn tucked into the trousers and allowed it to cover them to mid-thigh. Only rarely did the peasants actually wear women's clothes: in March 1830 at Miglos, one of the rioters wore "old-fashioned women's clothing," and in late April 1830 near Bosc a Demoiselle wore "a red skirt and his shirt outside, which reached down to his knees." Otherwise, there was little variation in the basic disguise, although the masks worn by the peasants were, by contrast, the object of great individual elaboration. Some Demoiselles painted their faces red and black in symmetrical patterns, as at Buzan in July 1829. Frequently the mask consisted of sheets of material draped over the face (Saint-Lary in 1830), handkerchiefs worn on the face, sometimes with three holes punched "to see and breathe" (at Aucazein and Buzan in 1829), or sheets of "light tracing paper" (Saint-Lary in 1830). Alternately, some Massat rioters in January 1830 wore sieves on their faces, attached with string. Others wore, on their heads, "a false face made of cardboard left over from the carnival festivities," handkerchiefs, woolen bonnets, sheep or fox skins, and, as the prefect noted, women's headpieces.

The "disguise as women," then, a phrase which was to echo throughout official correspondence, became a shorthand for invoking the distinctive dress of the rioting peasants. As such, the phrase masked a wide variety of costumes and paraphernalia, some of which was also drawn from the animal world. At Massat in January 1830, several Demoiselles had pigs' bristles stuck on their chins and lips. In Boussenac, the Demoiselles "covered their heads with the hides of sheep or foxes," according to the testimony of one villager. At Ustou, "a wolf's tail serving as a plume" was found in the house of a suspected rioter. Again, just as the peasants made an ironic self-reference to their honor by calling themselves Demoiselles, so too did they make a mocking reference to their reputation for savagery. In the early nineteenth century, Prefect Brun of the Ariège described the "savage and vindictive spirit" of the mountain peasant, "who shares three-quarters of his time with the bears and wolves with whom he engages [in] daily battles, and from whom he slowly catches the ferocious and disturbing character of these carnivorous animals." Partially disguising themselves as animals in 1829, the Demoiselles played out his worst fears.

But more important, though the male peasants presented themselves as caricatures of women, they nonetheless reinforced their masculinity by adopting military costumes, paraphernalia, and headgear. At Aulus, in June 1829, one peasant wore "a white casque, flat, ribboned with red." A tri-cornered hat was seen at Massat and Gudannes in 1830. A Demoiselle from Saint-Lary wore "a bonnet or casque which formed two horns on the top part," while others wore turbans. Military symbolism, in fact, was central to the disguise; occasionally, the Demoiselles carried something akin to flags, as at the Arnave ironworks in March 1831, or at Seix in April 1830, when they appeared "with a white cloth at the end of a stick in the form of a flag." In the social organization of the revolt, military titles and insignia proliferated, and "Captains," "Lieutenants," and "Generals" abounded. In a series of written threats—fourteen letters authored by self-proclaimed Demoiselles were made public between November 1829 and March 1831—the Demoiselles frequently signed themselves "Captains" or "Regimental Chiefs" while they made use of the military language of command. The Demoiselles claimed to be "fighting a war against the forest guards," according to a peasant from Sartou, near Massat, who was struck twice with a stick by the masked rioters for not joining them. And indeed, this strange war of partially disguised male rioters and forest guards continued for two and a half years.

Why did the peasants bother to disguise themselves at all? What was the meaning of the elaborate ritual drama enacted by the Demoiselles of the Ariège? And what was the significance of their rebellion? Historians of the War of the Demoiselles, in attempting to answer such questions, frequently tell plausible stories about the social and economic background of the revolt, its immediate causes in the 1827 Forest Code, and the functions which the disguise played in masking the identities of the rioters and establishing solidarity among them.

In the remainder of this chapter I offer another such account, introducing the society and economy of the mountain peasantry of the Ariège, and the "forces" acting upon it in 1829. In doing so, I hope to suggest some of the limitations of such a narrative, in particular its failure to address the substance and distinctiveness of a peasant culture whose values and beliefs defined and structured even the most mundane and instrumental forms of behavior. Officials in 1829, like past historians of the Demoiselles who stressed the practical and instrumental logic of peasants in revolt, tended to mask the cultural stakes at play.

The Village, the Forest, and the State in the Ariège

The Ariège river gave its name to the newly created department during the revolutionary refashioning of France in the winter of 1790. Until that point, the region that was to form an administrative unity was an area of vast social, geographical, and administrative diversity. Under the jurisdictional confusion of the Old Regime, three administrative entities had divided the lands of the Ariège: the Couserans, to the west, part of the royal jurisdiction of Comminges; the county of Foix, with its own provincial estates, but tied to the Intendancy of Roussillon, in the center; and the civil diocese of Mirepoix, to the east, part of the province of Languedoc. The entanglement of these and several smaller jurisdictions in 1789 was so great that to go from the towns of Foix to Saint-Girons, a distance of forty-four kilometers (twenty-seven miles), one had to cross six provincial boundaries.

The creation of the Ariège department in 1790 also united regions of important geographical, economic, and political differences. The Ariège was a kind of fracture zone where distinct economic and social structures came together. To the east, the feudal system was relatively entrenched, whereas to the west, the peasant communities lived under royal jurisdiction, and thus relatively free of seigneurial authority. To the east, the villages tended to be grouped in nucleated settlements and organized into large valley-communities—Gudannes, Massat, Miglos, Vicdessos—that exploited vast pastures and forest lands in common. To the west, dispersed settlements were more prevalent, and valley-communities were much smaller; indeed, they rarely consisted of more than several villages and hamlets grouped together—Moulis, Biros, Bethmale, and Bellongue together formed the Castillonnais. The west, the Couserans, had always been staunchly Catho-

Department of the Ariège

lic, and as such stood opposed to the pays de Foix in the east, where the Albigensian and later the Protestant heresies had taken root. The geographical, political, and historical diversity of the lands of the Ariège was extreme. Indeed, the appearance of the Demoiselles from one end of the department to the other, from the forests of Saint-Lary to Belesta, was testimony to the first real unity of the Ariège. It suggests the way in which arbitrary administrative boundaries could quickly, in the space of three decades, become meaningful frameworks of social and political identities.

More than a merger of geographical and jurisdictional differences, the Ariège department also brought together villages with distinctive regional cultures. To the east, the costumes, language, and customs of Languedoc predominated, whereas the western side of the department formed part of Gascony. Moreover, cultural and linguistic fragmentation of the mountainous zone was extreme, leading Maurice Chevalier, a disciplined observer in 1830, to note that "each valley of the Pyrenees . . . is a separate country, which, by a wealth of exclusively local nuances, has its own character and identity." Yet despite this diversity, the peasant communities that took part in the War of the Demoiselles shared a distinctive identity.

It was an identity founded on geography: the Demoiselles came from the mountainous, forested valleys of the northern slopes of the Pyrenees, valleys running curiously east and west from the Arize mountain south to the Spanish and Andorran boundaries. This mountain geography set them off from the villages of the fertile Lauragais plain covering the northern third of the department, whose market center and administrative capital was the town of Pamiers. The mountain communities of the Ariège had historically exchanged food, cattle, and people with the villages of the plain, for each represented a separate and complementary economy, social structure, and culture. ("Sheep go up, women go down" was a well-known proverb of the region, perhaps referring, at least since the nineteenth century, to the tendency of women to migrate to the plain to work as wet nurses and servants.) But the peasant communities that revolted in 1829 were those which shared a mode of production and way of life, combining agriculture and stockraising, centered around and in the forests.

In mid-nineteenth-century Ariège, the forests occupied roughly 150,000 hectares, about 30 percent of the territory, but nearly all of it situated in the mountainous districts of Saint-Girons and Foix, in the middle and upper valleys of the Pyrenees. More than half of this land, some 58 forests totaling 83,000 hectares, belonged to the state, which in the years after the French Revolution had "recovered" for itself much forest land previously in the hands of communities. About a fifth of the forests actually belonged to the communes, whereas the remainder—some 41,000 hectares—was privately owned, usually by the notable families who had bought or inherited the forests from the feudal lords during the property transfers of the Revolution.

Today these forests cover a larger terrain and consist primarily of replanted pine and deciduous growths. But in the mid-nineteenth century, the mountain forests were mostly beech, although some sessile oak existed at the lower elevations and some older pine growths could be found on the exposed north faces of the valley, extended up to 1700 meters in altitude. Bounded on the lowland side by arable fields and meadows, and above by the vast mountain pastures, the forests were a resource central to the peasant way of life. Unlike the forests of other regions of France, such as Brittany, the Alps, or even the eastern Pyrenees, the forests of the Ariège were too inaccessible to be exploited for wood sales, and with the exception of relatively small professional groups of charcoal-makers and, of course, the forest guards, no part of the population lived exclusively from the forests' resources.

Yet the mountain peasantry depended on the forests for its livelihood: the forests yielded firewood, building materials, agricultural tools, wooden shoes, soap for washing, torches for lighting, and some foodstuffs. And increasingly during the nineteenth century the forests provided a source of cash-cropping in the wood, firewood, and ashes (used in the manufacture of soap) sold on the local markets and in the towns of Foix, Saint-Girons, and Castillon.

The forest was a source of subsistence and of income, but, paradoxically, it was also an obstacle to the production of wealth. For the forests constantly threatened to encroach upon arable lands at the lower elevations, where a small subsistence culture of rye and potatoes formed the primary crops of the mountain communities. It was not fertile land—certainly not in the seventeenth century, when Louis de Froidour, the royal forest official, traveled through, describing "the poor and wicked quality of the lands." Agriculture still barely yielded at a ratio of three grains gathered to one sown in the early nineteenth century. The forest was the enemy of agriculture, and every year, especially as population pressure strained available agricultural resources, the peasants burnt back the forests.

At the same time, a certain amount of forest was necessary to the pastoral economy on which the nineteenth-century peasantry depended. For without the forests, as many were to note during the War of the Demoiselles, stockraising would be impossible, and without livestock manure and the income generated from raising cattle, the mountain peasantry would have been sooner forced to emigrate to the plain, as eventually was to happen after 1850.

In 1830, the prefect of the Ariège claimed that two-thirds of the mountain population depended on raising cattle or sheep for their very survival; stockraising long held a central place in the peasant society and culture of the Ariège Pyrenees. The poorest peasants might own a couple of sheep or a cow, essentially for local consumption and the fabrication of clothing. Peasants with larger herds raised sheep for sale at the fairs and markets that provided the towns of Languedoc and Gascony, as well as those on the Spanish side of the Pyrenees, with milk, butter, wool, and meat. It was not the peasants alone who had a vested interest in stockraising: the richer townspeople—notaries, doctors, and shopkeepers—contracted out herds to the poorer peasantry, and it was their capital that allowed the Ariège to support six annual fairs at Saint-Girons, seven at Castillon, and nine at Massat alone during the nineteenth century. The complementary interests of the peasantry and the small-town professional classes help to explain the initial solidarity of rich and poor inhabitants of the mountain districts in opposition to the 1827 Forest Code.

The forests were important to these livestock owners, both large and small. In the pastoral economy, the forests were essential pasture lands, especially in the critical months before the herds could ascend to the high pastures in the summer and when they went down to their winter homes in the granges. In this cycle of summer transhumance, the forests served as shelter from the sun and thunderstorms and provided essential nourishment, as the herds fed on the shoots and the forest undergrowth protected from the snow.

Around and in the forests, then, a complex mode of production—a sylvo-agro-pastoral system—had developed. The legal basis of this system of forest exploitation was named in the extensive use-rights, called *azempriu,* claimed by the nineteenth-century peasant communities. A series of medieval charters, mostly dating from the twelfth to the fourteenth century, as well as subsequent decisions of royal courts, had established and confirmed the rights of village communities to gather firewood, building materials, and to pasture animals in the royal and seigneurial forests. The earliest charters had been granted by the counts and viscounts of the great feudal domains of Couserans and Foix, and they gave the local inhabitants "free use" of the forests and mountains—as much in their interest, to attract and sustain feudal revenues, as in that of the peasants. Typical of these was the somewhat later grant made to the inhabitants of Massat, Oust, Ustou, Ercé, and Aulus by the seigneur viscount of Couserans, Odet de Lomagne, in 1446: "The said seigneur can not nor must not prohibit the inhabitants from using at their will the waters, pastures, or forests, in whatever way they wish."

The state was to call these "use-rights" *(droits d'usage),* as opposed to property rights, but such fine distinctions of the courts and ruling groups made little sense to the mountain peasantry. In the application of the 1669 Royal Forest Ordinance in the Pyrenees, Louis de Froidour agreed to maintain the communities' use-rights to firewood, building materials, and pastures—use-rights, he conceded, which were so considerable that "they amounted to a veritable property." "The inhabitants of these parts exploit the forests of His Majesty," he continued, "as if they were their own, giving to the said forests the names of their places as if they were communal lands."

During the War of the Demoiselles, the prefect reported that "public opinion perpetuated by tradition among the inhabitants holds that the forests are the property of the communities, and that no laws could be imposed to prohibit the exercise of their use-rights." The peasant communities claimed the right to take firewood and pasture in the forests within their boundaries, and some outside them. More important, they claimed to be able to exploit these forests according to their own practices of production, not those of the forest administration; and finally, they claimed the authority to exercise sovereignty over the forests, to police, in the Old Regime sense of the word as "administer," the forests by themselves.

The village communities, then, functioned during the Old Regime as corporate entities, controlling and managing their resources, theoretically for the benefit of all the constituent households. The heads of each household, numbering between thirty and two hundred in each village, sat on the local councils; officeholders were elected representatives (generally wealthier, established household heads). The councils, under the distant tutelage of royal officials, established a set of regulations designed to manage pasture and forest lands, stating the dates at which herds could enter the pastures, the areas which could be exploited for firewood, and imposing fines for delinquent animals. In the east, the management by the valley-community of collective resources overrode the disparity of pastures and wood among villages within the valley. The council employed its own forest guards and other officials—in Auzat, as many as thirty guards—to defend the communal enterprise against the abuses of pastoral individualism. In the Couserans, the policing and administration of communal resources took place more often at the village level, or within a grouping made up of a dominant village and its surrounding hamlets.

This communalist tradition, very much alive into the middle of the nineteenth century, was frequently undercut by oppositions among classes within the village. The village was an arena where the interests of a few "great households" of wealthier peasants opposed those of a growing agricultural proletariat, which relied increasingly on communal pasturing and forest rights for the livelihood of its members. But the communalist tradition remained a vital one throughout the Old Regime, especially as peasant communities and their councils entered into court battles with their own seigneurs and with the royal administration over the control and exploitation of the forests.

These struggles dated from the fourteenth century, but they began in earnest in the seventeenth century, when the rural nobility systematically increased its revenues from forest lands by establishing ironworks. The so-called Catalan forges proliferated, with their sophisticated if inefficient technology that relied on vast amounts of charcoal to produce iron. There were thirty-four ironworks in the Ariège river valley and five in Massat by 1669. In the interest of monopolizing the vast quantities of wood needed to make charcoal, local seigneurs sought to restrict the peasantry's use of the forests. The countess Sabran in Massat failed (for the most part) in court decisions of 1754, 1756, and 1761 to restrict the use-rights of local inhabitants, but during the eighteenth century her family appropriated a large quantity of forest lands. Elsewhere in the pays de Foix, wealthy seigneurs turned from their own exhausted lands to the royal forests in search of wood to supply the ironworks. (By contrast, in the regions of the Couserans to the west, where the War of the Demoiselles broke out in 1829, ironworks remained relatively few until the early nineteenth century, and their recent appearance was thus all the more intolerable.)

At the same time, the absolute monarchy in France undertook its first comprehensive attempt to manage forest lands in the interests of affirming political authority, acquiring revenue, and abolishing the "disorderly" practices of local modes of forest exploitation. Colbert's Forest Ordinance of 1669, invoking this "disorder" and claiming to "establish order and discipline" given both "the needs of private citizens and the necessities of war," intended to protect and exploit not only royal forests, but those of private proprietors and religious establishments as well. The royal ordinance prescribed a system of forest management that was to be applied universally across France. Yet during the ten years following the passage of the legislation, royal commissioners argued successfully for the lenient application of the ordinance. Louis de Froidour, the royal official who oversaw the implementation of the reform in the pays de Foix, argued that the king ought to "let go of the rigor of the new ordinance to accord the inhabitants the usufruct rights which they have enjoyed until now, as much for pasture as for the exploitation of the woods."

Froidour nonetheless passed a series of regulations which the village or valley councils, under royal or seigneurial tutelage, were responsible for enforcing. But in the course of the eighteenth century, the royal administration virtually abandoned any attempt to extract a profit from the forests of the Couserans and the pays de Foix, prohibited in doing so by the lack of navigable rivers and the difficulties of access to the high mountain forests. As we shall see, the peasant communities remained relatively untouched by the 1669 Ordinance.

The French Revolution, in a law of 25 December 1790, abolished the jurisdiction of the forest administration as part of its dismantling of the institutions of the Old Regime. In subsequent laws of 15 and 29 September 1791, the revolutionary government reestablished some general rules for the exploitation of state forest lands, but sanctioned the unfettered exploitation of private forest lands, in opposition to the "protectionism" (economic, not ecological) of the Colbert Ordinance. During the revolutionary decade, the peasants occupied the vacuum left by the absence of a state apparatus. In the mountain valleys, the shortage of arable land was severe, and the peasants seized on the failure of state authority and on antinoble sentiment to transform the forests into arable lands or to extend their previously restricted use-rights. They took possession of the state and communal forests.

From the point of view of outsiders, this revolutionary repossession of the forests—including their transformation into arable land and the multiplication of herds of pasturing sheep—was a mode of devastation. The destruction of France's forests during the Revolution is legendary. The romantic historian Jules Michelet waxed lyrical about such ruin:

> With the Revolution, all barriers fell: the impoverished population began together this work of destruction. They climbed, fire and spade in hand, to the eagles' nests; they farmed the ravines, suspended by a cord. Trees were sacrificed for the smallest things: they cut two pines to make a pair of sandals. At the same time, the small livestock, multiplied endlessly, established themselves in the forests, damaging the trees, the shrubs, the young sprouts, devouring all hope. (in Woronoff 1989, 44)

Hence the official myth of the peasant destruction of the forests, which took its distinctive shape and force from the revolutionary events of 1789. Yet from the communities' point of view, the experience of the Revolution gave birth to myths of a different kind, a popular republicanism that blurred the boundaries between Revolution and Old Regime.

It was not until 6 January 1801 (16 nivôse year IX) that the forest administration was reconstituted, and a series of subsequent laws ordered local communities to defend the titles to their usufruct rights to the new administration. The forest administration thus sought to recuperate forests in the hands of the peasantry; in the Ariège, this was the work of Etienne François Dralet (1757–1844), the lawyer turned district commissioner of the national forest administration, whose policy directives and ideological justifications gave shape to the Imperial Reformation in the Pyrenees.

In the Ariège, Dralet's first task was to recover the forest lands "usurped" by the mountain peasants since the 1669 Ordinance. In the thirteenth district, comprising the neighboring department of the Haute-Garonne and the western districts of the Ariège, Dralet was responsible for the addition of 50,000 hectares of royal forests in 19 separate judicial proceedings. Dralet ordered that those peasant use-rights that were recognized by the courts be maintained in these forests, yet he attempted to enforce the articles of the 1669 Ordinance that restricted pasturing rights in the forest—much to the dismay and anger of the local peasantry.

But Dralet and the Imperial Forest Administration went beyond its monarchical precedents by seeking to administer the forests as a profitable enterprise, granting concessions to private developers in order to generate revenue that would exceed the expenses of administration. Between 1807 and 1826, the state sold more than 800 hectares of forest lands, while between 1804 and 1813 alone, more than 950 hectares of forest land was rented out by the government to forge owners. But as was the case under the Old Regime, the inaccessible forests of the Ariège ultimately proved unprofitable in this regard— although for a moment, with wood prices escalating throughout France in the 1820s, the rural bourgeois owners of forests and ironworks in the Ariège did quite well.

The ironworks owners and the proprietors of forest lands emerged as two distinct groups after the French Revolution, although their interests were intimately linked in iron production. Only twelve of forty-three ironworks remained in the hands of noble families after the Revolution; the rest had been bought up by wealthy bourgeois, sometimes as confiscated estates, more frequently through marriage and the market forces. The great sylvo-pastoral domains of the Old Regime, such as the Sabran family's possessions in Massat, remained intact but fell into the hands of a new class of landowners—men such as Marrot at Moulis, Delpla and Roquemaurel at Massat, Lafont de Sentenac at Boussenac, and Trinqué at Ustou and Riverenet. Their only interest in the forests was in making charcoal to feed their ironworks.

As the number of ironworks in the department grew to fifty-seven by mid-century, their owners, concerned over the volatile iron markets and the escalating price of wood, increased production levels to three or four times those of the eighteenth century. As Dralet himself estimated, one forge required 1620 hectares of wood per year, and the "avarice" and "greed" with which the bourgeois owners of the more than 45 ironworks in the Ariège destroyed both private and state forests had left the peasant communities with little for their own needs by the time of the 1827 Forest Code. Already in 1802, the prefect warned that if the forty-two ironworks were destroying the forests, and "if their devastation isn't stopped, and if we don't work to replace the forests, three-fourths of the inhabitants will be forced to leave." Eventually, his prophecy would come true, as out-migration from the villages began in earnest after mid-century.

The forest owners restricted local use-rights to such a degree that, as one mayor reported to the prefect, "their conduct has generally made the peasants regret the passing of seigneurial despotism." It was a claim reiterated in the agricultural survey of 1848, which found that the peasants were much better off under the Old Regime than they had been since the Revolution. Such was the strange condition of the post-revolutionary peasantry in the Ariège, which looked back in longing to its seigneurs but also to a revolutionary moment which, when reenacted, would liberate the peasants from the present oppressive regime. The 1830 Revolution was to provide the occasion, as we shall see, to turn this myth into a reality.

If the Ariège peasants were suffering from wood shortage and assaults on their use-rights by greedy owners of forests and ironworks during the first half of the nineteenth century, they were also growing increasingly impoverished as a result of internal demographic pressures. Despite the Civil Code of 1804, which prescribed equal and partible inheritance, the mountain peasants developed a range of strategies to assure that the household and its properties remained largely intact in the hands of the eldest. Although some fragmentation of land plots did take place in the nineteenth century, many younger sons and nephews without land turned to stockraising as a full-time occupation. The number and size of herds in the Ariège substantially increased in the first decades of the century, if their quality decreased for want of resources. Seasonal agricultural work in Andorra and Spain provided the mountain peasants with a meager supplement to a subsistence economy, but now the population of the Ariège was dramatically rising and would soon reach its absolute limits.

From 1741 to 1846, the population quite simply doubled, rising 27.7 percent between 1801 and 1846, from 211,608 to 278,184 inhabitants. The fastest rate of growth—42.8 percent in those years, in the mountain district of Foix—was almost 1 percent a year! In 1846, the population density of the Ariège was 53 inhabitants/km^2; in the Couserans, it was 64; in the Batlongue valley, 70; in Massat, 87; and in the valley of Saurat, an unbelievable 125/km^2. The population growth most strongly affected the mountain communes, as births greatly exceeded deaths owing to the widespread (and widely decried) practice of men marrying young in order to avoid the draft. The growing population put pressure on agricultural lands: during the

French Revolution, according to the prefect LeBrun, the communal
lands of the mountain communities were "invaded" and turned into
arable lands, with dramatic and dangerous repercussions for the future. As the population increased, so did the importance of stockraising; and as this economic tie continued to link rich and poor peasants
within the community, it sharpened the conflict between the community and the forest and ironworks owners, especially in the valleys
of the Couserans.

It was in this context that the state passed and sought to implement
the 1827 Forest Code. On the one hand, the project, proposed in
1823, published and widely circulated in 1825, then debated and ap-
proved by the Chamber of Deputies in 1827, represented an attempt
to consolidate the earlier reforms of Colbert and Dralet. It continued
to insist, for example, on the necessity of reserving the best wood for
naval construction—a concern which had no relevance in the forests
of the Ariège. On the other hand, the extensive debates produced a
code in accordance with the "liberal" project, a monumental defense
of property rights. The Code argued that the 1669 Ordinance, which
was to have been applied on privately held lands, had restricted such
property rights too severely; more important, it decried local use-
rights, "which constitute, for public as well as private property, the
most formidable of dangers and the most fertile source of injury and
abuses."

The Forest Code and its accompanying ordinance of 1 August 1827
were aimed essentially at the "management" of royal and communal
forests, although owners of private forests in the Ariège saw their
own advantage in choosing to adopt the measures and means proposed, especially since the Code was directed toward abolishing local
use-rights and breaking the crucial linkage between the forests and
the pastoral economy. Article 61 gave the local communities two
years in which to prove, in a court of law, their use-rights to the
forest. This provision only produced in the Ariège a rash of largely
unsuccessful lawsuits as greedy lawyers from Foix and Saint-Girons
toured the mountain communes with wild claims, engaging the peasants in ruinous proceedings. Articles 67 and 69 gave the local forest
guards full responsibility in determining the timing, location, and number of cows the peasants could pasture, whereas articles 78 and
100 forbade villagers outright, in royal and communal forests, and
"notwithstanding titles to the contrary, to herd goats, ewes, or sheep
in the forests or the lands dependent on them, penalizing their propri-

etors with the maximum fine." They also provided a right to claim an indemnity "which will be regulated on a case-by-case basis in the courts."

Article 120 guaranteed the forest administration sole responsibility for determining each year which paths animals could cross through the forest and the amount of wood each community needed for firewood and new constructions. Each year, it was the local forest agents, appointed by the central administration, who would decide which areas were to be placed off-limits to the peasants. Residents of the communes themselves were forbidden to herd their own flocks (article 72) and had to use a communal shepherd appointed by the authorities. Article 75 required that "the users shall place bells around the necks of all animals admitted to pasturing, under the penalty of two francs fine for each animal found without a bell in the forests." This article alone, it was later suggested, "would dissolve all the savings of the mountain peasant families." The peasants were further prohibited from exploiting the smallest branch or growth without the authorization of the local forest guards (article 79), a practice which included firewood (article 81) and wood for construction (article 84).

In a general way, the 1827 Forest Code not only denied the peasantry their inherited rights, but also failed to recognize their current needs. The commune of Montaillou was authorized to cut "a sixth of the firewood it needs." The mayor of Belesta complained to the prefect that the wood assigned to the seven communes of the region would barely suffice for Belesta and Fougax alone. Moreover, the Code was virtually unenforceable, according to a forest agent in Saint-Girons, because of the size of the localities. For that district, there were sixty-four forest guards assigned to manage thirty thousand hectares of forest. "Perhaps created for all of France," a local official suggested, "the Code could absolutely not be applied in the Pyrenees": it was a "vicious, inexecutable system," claimed the governmental commission which reported in October 1830. And yet in the spring of 1829, the Code was applied with zeal, not only in the royal and communal forests, but in private ones as well.

Resistance and Revolt

Collective opposition to royal and private forest guards was an ancient tradition in the villages which came to form the Ariège, as it was in the Pyrenees more generally. Under the Old Regime, as long as the royal forest administration remained a distant and relatively tolerant authority, villagers tended to subvert its formal regulations, while frequently disputing among themselves their pasturing and firewood rights to the forest. The Couserans, to the west, had experienced one of the great waves of peasant antinoble and antistate revolt in the late sixteenth century, but as with the pays de Foix in the east, the peasants rebelled in the seventeenth and eighteenth centuries only when the monarchy occasionally attempted to restrict their rights to the forest. Such was the case in 1707 when the peasants of the pays de Foix forced the forest administration to abandon its project of dividing several forests between the communities and the state, restricting the former's rights to pasture. Yet it was only after the Revolution, with the stricter application of new forest legislation limiting pasturing rights and forcing village communities to take their wood in predesignated areas, that forest riots occurred with greater frequency.

The implementation of the laws of 1801 produced the only death of a forest guard which I have found recorded in the first half of the century, despite some historians' claims that murders of forest guards were frequent: in the commune of Sentenac, a guard was assassinated in the communal forest following weeks of threats and mutual antagonism. During other revolts in the first half of the nineteenth century, the peasants relied largely on invectives, threats, and their ability to periodically scare off the guards. In early May 1806, fifteen men and women from the commune of Oust rose up against a forest guard who had seized six cows in an area of the royal forest from which the peasants were prohibited from entering. "Armed, the ones with hatchets, the others with sticks," he testified, "they forced me to give back the cows, threatening to kill me." Other confrontations took place when forest guards confiscated herds of cattle, only to have peasants recapture them with threats. In August 1820, twelve men near Boussenac, "armed with hatchets and throwing rocks," tried to reclaim thirty sheep seized by the forest guards. In the forests of La Barguilhère during August 1828, thirty villagers arrived on the mountain to assist their shepherds, from whom a herd had been seized.

Larger uprisings, too, occasionally resulted from conflicts between forest guards and local populations. On 17 July 1807, François Soumlis and four other guards seized eighteen sheep illegally pastured in the mountains near Massat. They sequestered the herd in an inn of neighboring Riverenet; fifteen minutes later, "two hundred men and women armed with hatchets demanded, shouting loudly, that the guards be slaughtered." The crowd started to break down the door. The innkeeper fled out a side window, but was caught and beaten. The tactics are remarkably similar to those used by the Demoiselles, except for the crucial facts that none of the peasants was disguised, and that women were present—indeed, they were on the front lines. Although, as we shall see, the disguise occasionally appeared elsewhere in forest riots in the Pyrenees, it does not seem to have been part of the repertoire of collective actions in the villages of the Ariège before the revolt of the Demoiselles.

The years following the passage of the 1827 Forest Code proved to be different. In December 1828, as the Code was being phased in, the prefect reported to the interior minister that "the inhabitants show their great displeasure, menacing the guards; they would be quite easily disposed to unite in large numbers to scare them off, thus profiting from the fear which they have inspired in order to commit forest crimes with greater ease." In January 1829, forest guards in the Castillonnais met with some resistance during house searches for wood cut without permission. A large crowd threatened the mayor as he tried to protect the forest guards. In early May 1829, the commune of Moulis complained to the prefect that many of its titles which proved its use-rights to the royal forests, and which had to be presented to the courts prior to August, were burnt or lost, but that in any case "the government is too fair to take away a right which it has until today recognized." But just at that time, as forest guards began to enforce the Code, those strange reports surfaced in the commune of Saint-Lary. Resistance to the guards was "openly undertaken," and the male peasants appeared in the forest, "armed and disguised as women."

Explaining the Disguise

The disguise puzzled the authorities, but they quickly came up with a logical explanation for the male peasants' dress. The political, military, and judicial authorities at both the national and the local levels put forth a remarkably consistent explanation. For them, the disguise had a distinctly utilitarian character. First and foremost, the disguise as women concealed individual identities, allowing peasants to commit with impunity transgressions against the persons and property of the forest guards and charcoal-makers. Just as forest guards testified consistently to that effect, so too did the explanation emerge at the highest levels of authority. Thus in February 1830, it was concluded at a conference held in Toulouse between the prefect, the military commander, and the state prosecutor that "the men who masked themselves did so to commit with impunity crimes in the royal forests . . . Their only goal was and is to abrogate the jurisdiction of the forest administration."

But even for the authorities, the significance of the disguise was not fully explained in its ability to hide individual identities. In addition, wearing the costume was a sign that the person did not act in isolation: the disguise served to identify and group together the peasantry in a unified undertaking. Thus the prefectoral decree of 28 February 1830 condemned the "association" of Demoiselles: "Considering that this association, the existence of which has already been recognized by the courts, seems to have adopted a disguise found the whole length of these criminal scenes, and which has become the insignia of the association, this insignia will from now on sufficiently identify he who wears it as a member of the guilty group, which will place him in flagrant transgression of the laws." The authorities saw the mask and costume as a sign that denoted participation in an "association": the rioters were therefore subject to the articles of the penal code (265–268) that defined the presence of an "insurrectionary" group.

Moreover, the fact of "association" posited the existence of clearly defined leadership and group hierarchy. The obsession of the authorities with leaders, the "moving forces" of the association, frequently prejudged the events themselves. Thus the royal district attorney of Toulouse, with a consistently tough-minded approach, wrote that "these groups are quite strongly organized since, in one instant, at the request of a single man, a numerous group quickly assembles; armed, equipped, and disguised, it moves quite easily where he wants it to go."

We should not be too quick to deny that either of these two functions of the disguise was important during the War of the Demoiselles. After all, individuals did use masks to conceal their individual identities. In 1842, a forest guard testified that some Demoiselles "masked their faces as soon as they saw me coming." The same reaction of the rioters was noted at Massat in February 1830. And at Saint-Lary, in the attack on the charcoal-makers on 6 April 1830,

Pierre Lapierre Cyprien had his face "covered with a bit of linen, which the wind whipped up, but which he had the care to tighten down when we looked at him closely."

Yet it is true that the disguise was hardly an effective one. Not only did sweat wash off the black coloring, but several Demoiselles (in Saint-Lary and Massat) were later identified by traces of black left on their collars, hands, and faces. And more than one victim of the rioters testified that "they were so little disguised that someone from the region could easily have recognized them all."

As to the second function of the disguise—the identification of the rioters as part of an organized association—this too was both true and misleading. The leadership and hierarchy which the authorities saw in the rioting was in part an illusion produced by the proliferation of military symbols and the rioters' adoption of the language of military command. But it was true that the costume served to signify the unity of the peasant communities despite their overwhelming differences. After all, the mountain villages were worlds unto themselves, whose identities were frequently defined in opposition to their neighbors'. Villagers tended overwhelmingly to marry among themselves, as demonstrated in a sampling of marriage acts from the civil registers of the 1820s: less than 5 percent of the marriages took place between spouses from outside the village where the marriage was celebrated (generally that of the bride), and nearly all of these "foreigners" were from the adjoining villages in the valley. In accordance with the wisdom of popular proverbs from the region, the Ariège peasants married as close to home as possible.

Moreover, linguistic and cultural differences between neighboring valleys were highly marked. Several of the Demoiselles in 1830 in Esplas were known to be from Massat because part of their clothing distinguished them from the local villagers. And among several examples of linguistic differentiation, there was the case of a woman at Aucazein who testified against the Demoiselles, having recognized among them "the language of the inhabitants of Galey," situated barely four kilometers away!

Material culture and language were not the only differences among the peasants, for the village communities of the nineteenth century were locked into ancient patterns of dispute. Many rivalries were motivated by competition over the high mountain pastures: the judicial archives of the eighteenth century are filled with reports of the clashes and legal proceedings between, among others, the inhabitants of

Massat and Bellissens, Massat and Ercé, Ercé and Aulus, Erp and
Soulan, Soulan and Riverenet, Vicdessos and Goulier, Esplas and
Boussenac, Suc and Sentenac, Bonpas and Arnac, Argein and Sor,
and Audressein and Sor. In these constant rivalries, communities
would occasionally join forces against each other, for example, Argein and Aucazein against Irazein and Illartein, always about the use-
rights to forests and pastures.

The War of the Demoiselles was structured in direct opposition to
this communal differentiation and rivalry. Indeed, one of the defining
features of the revolt was the participation of peasant men across
valley and village boundaries. When the wealthy landowner Trinqué
proposed in Riverenet in April 1830 to abandon the forests to the
commune with the exception of two-year reserves, he was shouted
down on two accounts: "All or nothing"; and that the offer be extended to include the commune of Massat, with which Riverenet had
long struggled over the same forest. At Esplas, according to the testimony of the guard Pujol, the individuals who pillaged his house were
"from Riverenet, Massat, Esplas, and Castelnau: they were acting in
common, and loudly declared that they would everywhere fight a war
until death against all the forest guards." The Demoiselles made
global, universal claims about their rights, the rights of all the mountain peasants, and, in one of their posted writings of March 1830,
the rights of Demoiselles from all of France to the forests. In this
sense, the disguise did serve, as historians of the revolt have noted,
to express the solidarity of the community, to unify the peasants of
the Ariège, despite their local differences, against a common set of
enemies.

Yet the twofold interpretation of the disguise as a mask of individual identities and a symbol of a united peasantry must remain defi-
cient. First and foremost, it fails to account for the specificity of the
disguise: the Demoiselles were peasant men who caricatured the appearance of women but also of animals, while maintaining and deepening their self-representation as men. The emphasis on the functions
served by the disguise also fails to make sense of the way in which
peasant communities drew on a fund of cultural ideals and practices,
which in fact had little to do with women themselves.

Women in Revolt

The War of the Demoiselles was one of the most dramatic instances
of peasant men "dressing as women" within popular rebellions in

early modern Europe. Such revolts came to the attention of social and cultural historians beginning in the late 1960s, especially Yves-Marie Bercé and Natalie Zemon Davis. Examples from Great Britain include the blackfaced "servants of the fairies," who in 1451 stole the deer of the duke of Buckingham; the bands of men dressed as women calling themselves "Lady Skimmington" in Wiltshire during 1641 who rioted against royal enclosures; the numerous instances of men disguised as women in the early nineteenth century, including the famous "Rebbeca riots" against turnpikes during the late 1830s in western Wales. In France, instances of what are sometimes mis-leadingly called "transvestite" or "crossed-dress" revolts include the 1630 uprising in Dijon, where "Dame Folly" and her infantry took on the tax-collectors; the revolt at Guéret in 1705 and at Montmo-rillon the same year against tax-collectors; the more extensive rural revolt in 1774 in the Beaujolais, when male peasants blackened their faces and dressed as women to attack surveyors working for the local landlord; a revolt in the Vivarais of masked and costumed peasants in 1783; and the other revolt of the Demoiselles: in February 1765 in the Franche-Comté, men "disguised as women" chased guards from the domanial forest of Chaix.

To this list might be added, among other examples still buried in the mountains of documents left by the French state, several cases from throughout the Pyrenees: the peasants of Ossau (Béarn) who rebelled in 1743; those in Sainte-Marie d'Oloron (Pyrénées-Atlan-tiques) in 1767 who appeared "disguised as women"; and more ex-tensively, the peasants of Castelloubon (Hautes-Pyrénées) beginning in May 1819. Among the villages of the Couserans and the pays de Foix, which were to make up the Ariège, I found no mention of the rebellions or disputes during which peasants disguised themselves as women in the seventeenth, eighteenth, or early nineteenth century, but I did uncover one instance of masked peasants involved in a strug-gle between the villages of Ercé and Aulus. On 7 August 1765, twenty men from Aulus attacked their neighbors. According to the judicial report, "they had disguised their faces with charcoal dust, which the people call *fagieu*."

In interpreting such uses of the female persona, the cultural histo-rian Natalie Davis explored how the image of the unruly and disor-derly woman could be used by men to "defend the community's inter-ests and standards, and to tell the truth about unjust rule." Cultural, literary, and scientific traditions, all informed by Christian doctrine and practice, attributed the quality of disorder to women in their

positions of structural inferiority and exclusion. Woman threatened
the social order through her sexuality and through her inclination
toward and her embodiment, after Eve, of evil. The disorder attributed to women worked at the religious, social, and cosmic levels; at
any point, it threatened to disrupt the stable hierarchies of the social
and natural worlds. Davis and other historians of women have noted
how the subjection and exclusion of women "was gradually deepening from the sixteenth to the eighteenth century as the patriarchal
family streamlined itself . . . and as progress in state-building and the
extension of commercial capitalism were achieved at a cost of human
autonomy" (Davis 1975, 126), and as women were more and more
excluded from public roles in the polity and the economy. Within
this exclusion, the perceived unruly nature of the disorderly woman
became available to both men and women to make a wide range of
criticisms about the social and political order.

Twenty years of historical research has clearly documented how
women, despite and by virtue of the discourse which disempowered
them, became central actors in a variety of rebellious activities.
Women took part, and often led, food riots and tax revolts during
the Old Regime, and they were central in the march on Versailles in
October 1789, the most famous female uprising of the French Revolution. During the nineteenth century, women participated in a wide
range of collective actions. Some historians have argued that women,
legally excluded from the public sphere, nonetheless served as provid-
ers and consumers in their communities, which led them to take part
in, and frequently to lead, a wide variety of uprisings in defense of
the livelihood of their families, neighborhoods, or villages. In doing
so, they drew on their symbolic authority as protectors of family and
community. Other historians have pointed out that women were held
legally less responsible for their actions than men, and took conscious
advantage of the fact that they were less likely to be punished. Drawing on this range of associations, ideologies, and symbolism of
women in revolt, male rioters could and did make use of the disguise
as women.

In the villages which made up the Ariège, the image of powerful
and disorderly women might have been especially available and ap-
pealing to male peasants in revolt. For in the peasant culture of the
Ariège, as throughout the central and western Pyrenees, women had
traditionally been authorized to act in certain public contexts. The
peasant communities which came to form the Ariège department had

practiced a strict form of primogeniture that valued the integrity of the household *(casa)* over the specific sex of the household head *(cap de casa)*. The result was that households were not infrequently headed by women, who held that right not simply as widows but as legitimate heirs with public responsibilities and privileges as local citizens or "neighbors" *(bezi)*. Such rights were recognized in the customary law codes of certain Pyrenean regions, such as Barèges, Labourde, Soule, and the Basque country, written down in the sixteenth and seventeenth century. According to Cavaillès, writing about the central Pyrenees, "Women were considered as capable as men in maintaining traditions and defending the integrity of the household" (Cavaillès 1931, 77–78). To date, little is known from painstaking archival research of the actual roles of women household heads in village public life in the Pyrenees under the Old Regime, but it is clear that as a function of customary inheritance laws, women were juridically empowered in the public domain of village life to a much greater extent than in other peasant societies of Europe.

That "traditional" condition began to change in the central Pyrenees well before the Revolution, when the monarchy—imposing the primacy of masculinity over primogeniture—intervened systematically in marriage and family practices at the expense of customary law. Yet it was the state's unifying and centralizing revision of inheritance laws during the Revolution and under Napoleon, culminating in the Civil Code of 1804, that subjected women to patrilineal authority and severely devalued their public status. Although peasant families throughout the Pyrenees evolved a set of marriage and inheritance strategies to subvert the legal order of bourgeois society in the interests of preserving the integrity of the household, they were ultimately forced to comply with a legal order in which women were subordinated in civic and political life.

Like many peasant uprisings of the early modern period, the revolt of the Demoiselles, in its opposition to the twin forces of state-building and capitalism, posited a return to a mythic past, a golden age of autonomy and freedom. The peasants sought to restore a world of liberties and practices "passed on to us from our ancestors which we could not change without altering our existence and making life impossible," as the inhabitants of Prade claimed in a petition of 1841. Part of the male peasants' self-representation as women in 1829 may have involved an invocation of a golden age in which women had held greater power and authority than in the present; after all, the same agency which took away the authority of women (the state) also usurped the peasant community's inherited rights to the forest. Thus a folksong from the late eighteenth century records the resentment in the Lavedanese valleys following the reform of customary inheritance laws in 1769: "All is suffering/in all the houses/especially of the heiresses/The King be damned/who has made the law/Against the heiresses" (in Soulet 1974, 226).

The examples of Pyrenean peasants dressing as women, all drawn from the regions where the practices of primogeniture and the protection of the integrity of the household predominated, suggest how male peasants during the War of the Demoiselles may have disguised themselves as women as part of a broader, mythic story about the Old Regime, when women could rule and peasants retained possession of their forests. Such was no longer the case after the Revolution, the Imperial Forest Reformation, and the Civil Code. The image of women was available to the rebellious male peasants of the Ariège in 1829, then, at a moment when women themselves were increasingly disempowered, both within peasant communities and within the wider French society.

Yet an image of women was also available to rebellious men elsewhere, in regions where partible inheritance customs predominated, and at a time long before the reform of family law in the Civil Code. Such was the case during the other revolt of the Demoiselles, when in Burgundy in February 1765 peasant men "dressed as women" and chased royal officials from their forests. Moreover, to pursue an interpretation that turns on the changing status of women may be taking entirely the wrong path, for it must be remembered that despite the insistence of the authorities that the peasants were "disguised as women," they were only masquerading as women, caricaturing an image of women. Moreover, the "disguise," if it was one at all, was only one element in an elaborate and dramatic enactment of a set of grievances against the state and the rural class of notables. Curiously, the meaning of the War of the Demoiselles cannot be disclosed through a history of women alone. Instead, the significance of the "disguise" and of the "revolt" itself will be sought within a broader account of the symbolic world of peasant culture and society, from the place of the forest in peasant cosmology and ecology to the practices of festive life during the calendar year.

2. DEEP PLAY IN THE FOREST

ho were those strangely masked men, the Demoiselles of the Ariège? It was a fundamental question for the authorities charged with the repression of the uprising during the late spring and early summer of 1829. As the bands of noisy men, "armed and disguised as women," spread through the western districts of the Ariège department and high into the Pyrenees, the authorities were divided over the identity of the rioters, and thus the nature of the rebellion itself. The royal district attorney of the Haute-Garonne was the official most willing to concede from the beginning that "politics" was at stake, that "antimonarchist forces" lay behind the uprisings. The captain of the royal constabulary in the Ariège was convinced that Spanish Carlists were instigating the local peasants to rebel. The commander of the infantry divisions placed in the Ariège thought that mutual recruitment was taking place between the mountain peasantry and groups of Spanish brigands called *malcianos,* active in the civil wars taking shape across the border.

The belief that "foreign" elements were at the heart of the war was linked to the notion that the forest itself was essentially opposed to civilization. "Forest," *forêt,* in French, is derived from the latin *forestare,* meaning that which comes from the exterior, outside, something foreign (Huffel 1910: i, 302–303, 320; ii, 81–82). It was a conjuncture of identity and place: the forest bred foreigners. In legend and in law, throughout the Middle Ages and the early modern period, the forest was the place of refuge for criminals and outlaws. It was beyond the pale of civilization, the site of revolt and subversion by alien and opposed elements of the structured, hierarchical social order.

But it is hard to gauge whether there was not some truth to that claim in the Ariège itself, since the peasants who resisted the forest administration may well have entertained relations with "foreigners"—the Spanish and Andorran peasants of the high mountain valleys. These people were both similar and distinct: the political boundary was acknowledged, and it remained relatively permeable. Moreover, the existence of a unique border culture was reinforced by the institutional links between the French and Spanish peasant communities that held mutual grazing agreements on both sides of the Pyrenees effective during the summer season. The recruitment of Spaniards by the Demoiselles is suggested in the observations that the rioters spoke "Spanish," as witnesses noted in Sentein and Bonac during June 1829, at Buzan on the night of 22 August, and at Illartein in September. But even this is inconclusive. When one leaves aside the question of bilingualism among the mountain peasantry, it is likely that "Spanish" was itself just a word for "different"—or even simply a different local dialect or part of the disguised and ritualized speech of the peasant rioters. The only firm evidence of recruiting by Spanish brigands took place in the eastern valleys of Cabannes and Vicdessos at a time when the Demoiselles had not yet gained that region.

If the forest was a site of the foreigner, it was also the space of convicts and brigands, those outside the law. The authorities, in trying to make sense of the revolt, also saw deserters and criminals at work. "These people at Saint-Lary," wrote the sub-prefect during the early stages of the revolt, "were in part convicts and deserters of the communes of Saint-Lary, Portant, and Coutedax." Deserters were noted at Esplas and Seix as well. "They command and do their service well," testified one witness at the trial of several captured Demoiselles at Boussenac. Such comments suggest that deserters undoubtedly participated in the rioting, and indeed may have helped give to the group its distinctive military symbols and insignia. An example was Joseph Faur, called Patourrat, leader of a group of Demoiselles who burnt the cabins of charcoal-makers in the Ustou forest in July 1829, and in whose house was found "a French [soldier's] hat, a wolf's tale serving as panache for this hat, a net for masking his face, a rifle, a pistol, two sacks of powder, and a pair of blue pants." This was no ordinary Demoiselle, but a leader, an "officer." In fact, the "Lieutenants," "Captains," and "Generals" of the Demoiselles were frequently dressed in these more elaborate military uniforms, some of which may well have been kept by soldiers who had deserted.

But it is difficult to judge the extent of deserters' and convicts' participation in the rioting. Many were those who lived in permanent refuge in the high mountain reaches of the Ariège, and these men probably joined the revolt in the Castillonais. Beyond the hyperbole of the political and military authorities, the judicial records of those captured and tried suggest that most of the active participants were relatively well established members of the village communities.

By the end of the summer, the opinion of the forest inspector of Saint-Girons had prevailed. Writing to the prefect, he explained:

> These assemblies are very real, but I don't think that they are made up, even in part, of outsiders or strangers to the region. In fact, what goal would strangers have in chasing out the charcoal-makers from the areas under exploitation? Why should they bother with the guards? These are local people who revolt, and who wish to scare off the forest guards in order to use and abuse the forests. Such is my opinion.

The other authorities came to see the light. Sr. Jean de Pointis, a rich notable and mayor of Ustou, expressed his conviction, in reference to the recent pillage of his forests, "that these people are inhabitants of the commune." And even the captain of the royal constabulary relented in his theory of Spanish influence when, in September 1829, he agreed that the Demoiselles were entirely made up of "peasants of these parts."

But what kind of peasants? The judicial records of repression produced some evidence of who they were, but it is limited at best. There were five trials resulting from the riots, with a total of twenty-five individuals indicted for such crimes as destruction and pillaging of property, rebellion against forest agents, attempted assassination, and so forth. Nearly all those arrested and indicted—including those arrested in Ustou in August 1829, the seven indicted in Seix after the events of April 1830, and the eight condemned after the Caplong affair in March 1830—were "farmers" *(cultivateurs)*. This, unfortunately, is a vague category which included self-sufficient landowners, peasants who owned land but also rented some from richer members of the community, and those who worked in share-cropping relations with the wealthy bourgeois of the region. True, there were a few Demoiselles who supplemented their income from farming with crafts, and others who were identified as artisans in acts of indictment. In Boussenac, there was a weaver and a wool-spinner, and in Saint-Lary, a tailor. But most, by far, worked the land as peasants, and as the district attorney himself suggested, peasants "rich enough to own several animals; for them, free pasturing, without any surveillance, would be an important source of profits."

A closer study of a dozen arrested rioters from Massat in 1829 confirms this impression. These Demoiselles were on average above the sixtieth percentile of wealth within the landowning class, and many held significant properties of twenty-five to thirty parcels, including some woods or pasture of their own. But this, too, is inconclusive, since economic status within the peasant community was not in itself the primary determinant of those who rioted.

In the first year of the revolt, all the Demoiselles—both those captured and those seen from up close—were men. This alone makes the events of 1829 and 1830 unique, for during the Old Regime, and throughout the nineteenth century, women had been active participants in both forest revolts and other forest transgressions. Before the Demoiselles, women might join with men, and even occasionally lead them, in retrieving herds of sheep confiscated by forest guards, as happened in the commune of Oust in May 1806. And after the Demoiselles, in 1867, women were responsible for one-quarter of the so-called forest crimes—an interesting statistic, given the "traditional" prohibition of women cutting wood in the forest. During the War of the Demoiselles, women could give encouragement or even lend active support to the male rioters. So when the Demoiselles of Saint-Lary attacked thirty charcoal-makers in July, Jean Cointre's sister encouraged him to take action "against those brigands, the charcoal-makers." Yet those who took direct part in the riots were exclusively male.

Moreover, in the court testimony of the forest guards, the only authorities to come consistently close to the Demoiselles, the rioters were frequently designated as "young men." In point of fact, this could refer to a wide range of ages. At Buzan in August 1829, two guards surprised three youths "aged thirteen or fourteen, disguised as Demoiselles." At the Gudannes castle, witnesses noted that one group breaking into the wine cellar were "aged twelve to eighteen." At the other end of the scale, one witness from Boussenac designated a peasant rioter as a "young man" even though he was thirty-five years old. In fact, the average age of the Demoiselles arrested in March 1830 at Massat was thirty-five, and the average age of eight Demoiselles arrested at Boussenac in January 1830 was thirty. Less important than their chronological age, perhaps, was their marital status: nine of twelve Demoiselles arrested at Saint-Lary in 1829 were unmarried; at Buzan, the figure was six of eight.

This, then, is the picture of the peasant rioters derived from the primary sources. The Demoiselles were for the most part younger men, many without their own claims to property, yet those who were landowners were neither wealthy nor by any means the poorest peasants. About three-quarters of them were unmarried, and some were former soldiers, military deserters, and occasionally convicts at large.

Despite the accusations of administrative and military officials, there was a certain ambivalence in the relations of the Demoiselles to their local communities. They were "supported" by the communities, as evidenced by the vast webs of complicity spun during the trials of captured and indicted Demoiselles. At Boussenac, for example, fourteen of eighteen witnesses claimed that they had neither seen nor heard anything of the preparation or execution of the pillage of the Caplong farm on the Peguère mountain in March 1830. In other cases, witnesses provided the accused with ready alibis. At Saint-Lary, during the events of 30 April, one accused peasant was "on the mountain" with the thirteenth witness, a second was in a meadow two hours away with the seventeenth, another was fishing with the twenty-fifth, and so forth. It is true that many villagers refused to testify because they purportedly feared the vengeance of the Demoiselles. Jean-Baptiste Porte, of Onac, claimed at the trial of the rioters at Luzenac that "in the position where I find myself, threatened as I was, troubled as I am, I could not without exposing myself to a certain death answer the questions put to me . . . I will tell the whole truth when peace is reestablished in the region, and when I won't have anything to fear." The Demoiselles did threaten fellow villagers, occasionally forcing them to participate in the riots, and in some instances punishing those who were reluctant. During February 1830, one witness testified, the Demoiselles "entered all the houses of the village [of Esplas] and forced each family to furnish a man to increase their group." Yet many witnesses relied on the arguments of coercion and fear of vengeance to avoid having to testify against the Demoiselles, thus suggesting complicity as well.

For there were as many occasions when the communities worked actively and directly in support of the peasant rioters. On 17 August at Buzan, the "entire population of the commune" rose up against the forest guards. Led by several masked Demoiselles, they reconfiscated the village herd of sheep seized by the guards. At the local feast of Balaguères in 1830, the inhabitants likewise chased off the forest guards. More generally, in the early moments of the rioting, the Demoiselles received the support of the communities, including, as the authorities reluctantly noted, the richer peasantry and the town bourgeoisie, who frequently had interests in preserving communal use-rights to the forests.

Overall, the Demoiselles were supported in the initial phase of the revolt by the village communities and most of the mayors, who maintained an impressive silence about the identity of the rioters. The wealthier proprietors in the villages, who often held municipal posts, revealed nothing to the authorities, nor did the several lawyers, doctors, and notaries of the small towns of Saint-Girons and Foix. These men of the professional classes were hardly the movers behind the War of the Demoiselles, but they were complicitous, at least until the economic repression began in March 1830. Indeed, they had strong and interested links to the peasantry, as many authorities noted, since they often leased herds to the peasants and had a stake in maintaining local use-rights.

By contrast, the wealthy landed proprietors, the noble and wealthy bourgeois owners of forest lands and the iron masters of the Ariège— the class of rural notables of the post-Revolution in the department— shrilly condemned the Demoiselles. In this opposition, they identified themselves with the agents of the forest administration and the state, and their interests were backed by military force. The lines of opposition were clearly drawn: the Demoiselles expressed the anger and defended the rights of the local communities to the forests against the provisions of the 1827 Forest Code, and against the destruction of "their" forests by the ironworks.

The Marriage of Ritual and Revolt

Those who rioted during the War of the Demoiselles drew heavily on a familiar set of cultural practices associated with the village youth group—the loosely organized age-grouping of unmarried men who played important roles in the festive and social life of the village. This observation is a familiar one, frequently made by an earlier genera- tion of social historians. My claim here is different: it is not that the rioters *were* youth groups, even if many of them were young and unmarried, the significant characteristics of youth groups. Rather, I suggest that the rioting peasants *modeled* their activities on those of youth groups, in their relations with the local communities and with outside powers. The Demoiselles used the culture of youth groups as symbolic material out of which to fashion a language of revolt.

In particular, the rioters adapted a set of customs and prerogatives of village youth groups in their enforcement of widely accepted no- tions of popular justice. Borrowing from the rites of youth groups, especially those concerning a jurisdiction over marital relations, the Demoiselles enforced the communities' rights to the forest. This mar- riage of ritual and revolt took place in the forest—literally in the space of the forest, but it was also metaphorically structured, as I shall argue, by the symbolic identity of the forest as a woman.

In nineteenth-century rural France, youth groups were loosely or- ganized gatherings of adolescent men. Each community had its own group; larger villages might have several, organized by hamlets or neighborhoods. Their names, corresponding to distinct patterns of sociability, varied from region to region: in southwestern France, north of Garonne, they were called *bachelleries;* in Languedoc, they were *royaumes,* or "kingdoms"; throughout the Pyrenees, such groupings of young men do not seem to have been named. More informally organized and fluidly constituted, the "village youth" or "parish youth" nonetheless gained an identity evident in their fre- quent appearances in the judicial archives of the eighteenth and nine- teenth century.

Boys became identified as youths generally after their first commu- nion and could remain active in youth groups through the first year of marriage, or until the birth of their first child. In the Ariège, men often married at the relatively late age of twenty-nine at the end of the eighteenth century, a mean which dropped rapidly, by as many as four years by the mid-nineteenth century, in part because of the practice of marrying young to avoid the draft. Thus youth groups might, at their most inclusive, refer to adolescents from the age of thirteen to young men around thirty. Despite the sometimes ambiva- lent boundaries of membership and their informal structure, youth groups gained a visible and coherent identity within the festive and social life of the village.

Although young women, too, might be grouped as an age-cohort, men's activities and prerogatives as youths were more formally marked by a wide range of activities and festive practices. In their totality, these activities suggest how village youths exercised a certain kind of authority and jurisdiction—a special sovereignty—over the village community. In the rural world of nineteenth-century France, this jurisdiction involved a responsibility to enforce the territorial boundaries and social identity of the village. This role as the boundary guards of village life was clearly expressed in the ritualized and violent confrontations between youth groups of neighboring villages or hamlets, frequently when communities were contesting rights to waters, pastures, or forests among themselves.

More generally, young men were authorized to guard the social boundaries of the community by acting as the sexual police of village life. Youth groups were responsible for defining and enforcing a series of norms and expectations of what constituted "proper" sexual behavior in the village, especially concerning marriage. During the month of May, as we shall see, youth groups assessed the morality, and hence marriageability, of young women of the community. Throughout the year, they would ritually initiate "outsiders" who married into the community, forcing them, according to a late-nineteenth-century description of the Ariège, to pay a fee called the *dret de rouminguéro,* the "weed tax." At village weddings, they exacted a payment from the families of the newlyweds, and in the Ariège, they undertook a mock assault on the household of the bride. In Massat, an important center of the rebellion in 1830, one description of a mock battle during a marriage ritual, published some fifteen years after the revolt itself, strongly evokes some of the dramatized violence of the Demoiselles:

> In the district of Massat, the new bride undresses at the urging of her husband, and finds refuge in a house where young girls, armed with swords, take charge of defending her. These young girls take the name of *espaséros,* from the weapon they hold in their hands. The young men, companions of the husband, don't hesitate, of course, to besiege the fortress where the young bride takes refuge, and as they too carry swords, they are called *espassés.* After a long struggle, the *espaséros* concede, and the vic-

torious *espassés* carry out the young bride in triumph. (in Nore 1846, 113–114)

This rite was a local version of a widespread marriage custom, in France and throughout European peasant society, in which male youths symbolically and festively exercised their sovereignty over marriages in the village. Their privilege extended to the policing of marriage partners and, more broadly, to the enforcement of village norms of marital behavior. The distinctive means of such enforcement lay in the noisy rites of what was commonly known as the *charivari*.

Charivari, or "rough music," refers to the shouts and discordant noise made with unmusical instruments: pots and pans, whistles, horns, guns fired in the air, shouts, and so forth. It was a noisy, boisterous ritual intended to publicly humiliate the victim, and it ended only when the intended victim paid a "fine" of money, food, or drink. The time of charivaris, as the privileged time when youth groups ruled, was during the carnival season, as consistently revealed in the police and administrative records of the nineteenth century. During these charivaris, youth groups would adopt sometimes elaborate disguises and masks. Although dressing as bears or wild animals was common throughout the Pyrenees, the practice was surprisingly absent in the districts which made up the Ariège, where instead the masquerade as women was a frequent costume adopted by youth groups undertaking charivaris during Carnival.

The origins of the charivari remain obscure: early descriptions from the fourteenth century suggest that the charivari was a prerogative which seigneurs granted to youth groups. According to Roger Vaultier, such ritual enforcement of marriage standards was considered a "normal event," at least within the Paris region. The best descriptions of the rituals from the early fourteenth century on emerge from ecclesiastical condemnations. Most often, youth groups organized charivaris against either spouse on the occasion of the second marriage of a widow; the public humiliation was performed before or during the actual marriage ceremony, at which point the village youth would exact—"extort," according to the authorities—a compensatory payment. The Catholic Church, which had abandoned Roman law, did not expressly prohibit second marriages, and between 1350 and 1450, almost a dozen synodal decrees condemned the practices of charivari. Yet until the sixteenth century, the church was not consistently supported by royal authority in prohibiting the rites. Indeed, one of the most celebrated charivaris in French history took place during the third marriage of a noble woman during Carnival at the royal court of Charles VI in Paris in 1392, with the young king himself, dressed in bearskins, as the likely instigator. Thus, until the sixteenth century, royal officeholders in the parlements, the royal law courts, and municipal authorities of the great urban centers tended to tolerate the ritual judgments and punishments of charivaris. Only during the course of the sixteenth century did the civil authorities begin to condemn harshly such practices.

Earlier generations of folklorists, social historians, and anthropologists who have commented on charivaris during the early modern period frequently assumed that the charivari was a coherent and identifiable ritual. They variously interpreted the charivari as an attempt to placate the soul of the dead spouse affronted by an improper second marriage, the signifier of a disrupted chain of marriage alliances, or the ritual defense by young men of a pool of marriageable young women. The problem was in trying to account for the range of marital and sexual practices condemned in a variety of charivariesque rituals: marriages of disproportionate ages, adultery, husband-beating, and other transgressions would frequently provoke a charivari. Indeed, from the sixteenth century onward, the charivari was a flexible code, not clearly distinguishable from a variety of ritual punishments, such as the one forcing transgressors to "ride the donkey," ass backward, in a public procession of humiliation. Normally associated with mismarriage, remarriage, or cuckoldry, the charivari was also available to make a range of criticisms about sexual and social practices in the village.

The history of charivaris beginning in the sixteenth century suggests a further disjuncture between theory and practice. In theory, the charivari was harshly condemned. The royal courts which legislated against it considered the charivari under the rubric of a "royal case": it was an "illicit assembly" which fell under the purview of the king's justice, even if the transgressions concerned only marriages, and the jurisdiction in which they took place suggested they were to be dealt with locally. The notoriously harsh views of the Toulouse parlement, which had jurisdiction over the districts that came to make up the Ariège, denounced the practice five times between 1537 and 1551. In the later seventeenth century, the court joined the church in a renewed battle against the rite, and in March 1681, the Toulouse

parlement prohibited charivaris, raising the fine for participation
from 1000 to 10,000 pounds. The court argued that

> these assemblies are always occasions for dissolute behavior and
> debauchery, and they almost always give themselves the freedom
> to destroy the reputation of their neighbors and divulge family
> secrets, which not only produces implacable enmities but also
> favors anger and vengeance, excites feelings, and disturbs the
> public peace; it is these disruptions, as well as the dissolute mores
> that produce them, which it is important to restrain.

Such prohibitions echoed the renewed, second wave of condemnations by the Counter-Reformation church. During the 1660s and
1670s, the priests of Tarascon, Ganac, and Saurat in the county of
Foix complained about young men, "masked and disguised," who
proffered insults against Jesus Christ by undertaking charivaris on
the occasion of second marriages. The bishop of Pamiers, in response,
repeatedly prohibited charivaris in his parishes. Such prohibitions
were included in more general condemnations by the church—there
were at least twelve prohibitions recorded in synodal statutes between 1640 and 1687—and accompanied the civil condemnations of
Carnival by municipalities and royal authorities.

Yet in practice, despite such spectacular counter-examples, charivari was considered a folkloric and customary rite, a popular jurisdiction largely accepted and tolerated by both royal and local officials.
It was only when the victims of charivaris refused to accept judgment
of their marital practices—as when, during Carnival in 1761, a wid-
ower named Daustry in Labastide de Sérou refused to pay a fine imposed by a group of youths for his remarriage—that charivari become the object of repression. For every such case of a charivari gone
awry, how many "ordinary" charivaris took place without the intervention of the courts, and thus the knowledge of the historian?

During the Old Regime, renewed prohibitions and condemnations
of the charivari were more likely under one of two conditions. When
youth groups attempted to extend the sphere of their jurisdiction to
include the marital transgressions of public officials, charivaris became subject to censure. Or when, as seems increasingly to have been
the case, youth groups adapted the codes of charivari to castigate
officials for not carrying out their public functions, the popular rite
was far from tolerated. From the sixteenth century onward, it is pos-

sible to list dozens of incidents when youth groups in towns and villages of France used the rituals of charivari to criticize ecclesiastical
or political authorities whose conduct in some way represented a
transgression of communal codes of justice. Although the principal
objects of charivaris remained second marriages throughout the nineteenth century, as historians and anthropologists have long demonstrated, the practices were flexibly extended to claims about justice,
which had nothing, apparently, to do with marriages.

Such was evidently the case with the War of the Demoiselles. In
chasing off the forest guards and charcoal-makers, the Demoiselles
relied heavily on the cacophony of shouted threats, cries, guns shot
into the air, and the wails of horns and seashells. More generally, the
Demoiselles modeled their activities on those of youth groups during
carnival season, exercising a ritual of popular justice which they knew
well. The peasant rioters enacted a version of this noisy popular judgment, a kind of charivari, in order to take possession of the forests,
which they believed were theirs by right and which had been usurped
by the guards.

But why should the village rioters have enacted a variant of charivari against the forest guards and charcoal-makers? Social historians
have argued, about this and other cases, that the rites of rough music
were used in revolt because they were available. The charivari, in this
argument, was purely instrumental: it was used as a language of protest to defend claims that had nothing to do with mismatched marriages or sexual transgressions. Yet perhaps it is worth taking the
metaphor of marriage seriously in trying to understand how it was
that the peasants could extend the ritual codes of charivari far beyond
their domestic and marital contexts. The uses of charivari in a public
and political sphere might in this scenario have something to do with
the peasantry's sense of a mismatched marriage involving the forest.
To see this, it will first be necessary to reconsider the significance of
the forest in peasant culture.

In the organization of the peasant agro-pastoral mode of production, the forest played, as we have seen, a number of important roles.
Yet to reconstruct the meanings of the forest within the peasant culture of the Ariège Pyrenees, one must look for clues beyond these
practices of the pastoral and subsistence economy. The significance
of the forest lies within a peasant cosmology of the nineteenth century—a body of ideas and metaphors which provided the frame of
reference for both beliefs and practices. The forest was part of a

meaningful system, but not essentially a coherent one, as an earlier generation of structural anthropologists would have it. Still, it was a cosmology that can be glimpsed through interpretations of the ecological practices and mythical representations of the forest in nineteenth-century French peasant culture, while connecting these to other images and etymologies of the forest within learned culture in Europe in the early modern period.

Such a story about the forest, distinct from the narrative told in Chapter 1, leads in two directions: on the one hand, it directs us toward the world of legend and myth, the supernatural world of the forest and its numinous inhabitants. On the other hand, the significance of the forest in peasant cosmology must be sought in a symbolic order which itself structured the practical activities and especially the peasant mode of (forest) production.

Fairies of the Forest

For peasant societies in early modern Europe, forests were not the object of extensive mythical representations or the site of elaborate ritual practices as they were in many Southeast Asian or African cultures. Nineteenth- and early-twentieth-century inquiries into French forest folklore were concerned principally with the extremely specific and local: the origin of forest names, or the magical and religious "survivals" of ancient tree cults of Celtic and pre-Christian origins. Robert Polge Harrison has beautifully captured this sense of place in his meditation on the meaning of the forest in classical Rome:

> The forests were obstacles—to conquest, hegemony, homogenization. They were, in a word, asylums of cultural independence. By virtue of their buffers, they enable communities to develop indigenously; hence they served to localize the spirit of place. This is confirmed by the fact that in their woodlands lived spirits and deities, fauns and nymphs, local to *this* place and no other. Through these local inhabitants the forests preserved the spirit of difference between the here and the there, between this place and that place. (Harrison 1992, 51)

Local beliefs and legends in the Ariège also named and narrated the behaviors of specific supernatural beings, and thus offer important clues to the meaning of the forest within nineteenth-century peasant culture. These supernatural beings—fairies, ghosts, goblins, witches, "masks," and so forth—were anthropomorphized inhabitants of the natural world, the mountains and forests which remained beyond the pale of culture and cultivation. Although these beings were male, female, and without gender, the most widely described and complicated of the supernatural inhabitants of the forest were the feminine fairies.

Indeed, the Demoiselles, by virtue of their disguise, the time and space of their appearances, their volatile relations with the guards, and their unflinching defense of conceptions of justice, parallel legendary and folkloric accounts of forest and mountain fairies, both in the Pyrenees and throughout Europe.

Fairy beliefs have a long and complex history in western European culture. Since the medieval period, these rustic beliefs have been variously identified with the "fates," with the spirits of the ancestral dead, and with non-Christian or pagan ancestors. Literary cultures of medieval and early modern Europe consistently appropriated, while redefining, the significance of fairies. In medieval romances, fairies appear in such aristocratic forms as the Lady of the Lake and Morgana le Fay, half-mortal beings with magical powers of enchantment. In the Ariège, legends identify a "White Lady" as the daughter of an Albigensian leader of Montségur, the last refuge of the Cathars in 1244. Such legends accord with the views of the French folklorist Alfred Maury, who considered the belief in fairies the most persistent "vestige left by paganism . . . the symbol of religions conquered by the cross."

In the late seventeenth and eighteenth century, however, a new genre of fairy tales made its appearance at the court of France. Writers such as Charles Perrault and Madame d'Aulnoy took fairy tales from rural peasant culture and turned them into a set of moral parables addressed to an aristocratic audience. The enchanted world of fairies was toned down: the tales frequently featured a fairy godmother, associated with more classical notions of destiny and prophecy. More important, the aristocratic appropriation of fairy tales stripped them of their rusticity, of everything crude, scatological, and "uncivilized" about peasant culture.

But then, fairy beliefs, written down and conventionalized in a literary culture of the late seventeenth century returned to peasant culture in the form of cheap, popular chapbooks, which by the nineteenth century circulated widely among the popular classes in the countryside. Thus "contaminated" by this recycling between peasant and learned culture, fairy tales and beliefs were widely told and retold throughout rural Europe in the late nineteenth and twentieth century, at the moment when folklorists were able to inscribe them with greater specificity. Remarkably, for the villages of the Ariège where the Demoiselles made their appearance around 1830, a local folklorist, working with ethnographic sophistication in the 1940s and 1950s, recorded a series of legends and fairy tales. These accounts complement more traditional folkloric sources of the late nineteenth and early twentieth century, giving an amazingly complete picture of fairy beliefs in the Pyrenees.

> The *encantadas* were women dressed and crowned in white who disappeared from sight when one got close. Armed with washing boards made of gold, they went down to the Caudo stream [commune of Celles]. Once the owner of the Caudo farm took a small board which they had forgotten. That night, they came knocking on the door, crying, "Give us back our golden washboard." The man refused, and to punish him they made him fold in two, as if his spine was broken. His son (whom our informant knew) was himself struck by the same disability, all because of the stolen board. (Joisten 1962, 19)

In these nineteenth- and twentieth-century descriptions of southern French beliefs, fairies were called *demoiselles* or *dames blanches;* in the Ariège, they were also given names which suggest a strong link to parallel beliefs in northern Spain and Catalonia: *hadas, dragas,* or *encantadas*. These supernatural feminine beings lived in grottos and caves and, more generally, in the forests—they were the permanent inhabitants of the sites where the peasant rioters played out their struggles. In many regions of France, fairies were linked to specific trees. Joan of Arc, for example, revealed much about fifteenth-century peasant rites and beliefs in Lorraine when interrogated about the "fairy tree" in her native Domrémy. When fairies are described in myths and folk tales, they invariably wear white shirts, as did the peasant men in Ariège. The variation in their headdresses was as great as that of the masks of the Demoiselles themselves, although the fairies generally wore only flora. And like most of the rioters, the fairies appeared only at night, frequently around midnight, drawing on the dangerous and mysterious potency of the hour. This singular fact suggests a remarkable identity with the Demoiselles, who most often chose to appear at night, and were consistently reported seen "around midnight."

Much of the fairies' purported power was linked to fertility and reproduction, both natural and human. In many accounts, the fairies were identified with a mythical period of the forests' greatest extension and fertility, and sometimes with great treasures buried deep within the grottos on the mountain. They were further linked to running water and were normally seen from a distance around the streams, rivers, and water sources of the mountain communities. Water sources and fountains were the genesis of life, the center of regenerative purity; as one modern account has it, "The eye of the forest, the source or the fountain is also the attribute of femininity" (Barrier 1991, 44–45). Fountains and waters were the symbolic point for the defense of the forest in the War of the Demoiselles. The Demoiselles had gathered "at the bridge of Hioulat, where several rivers form a junction" in May 1829; in April 1830, they were sighted at the Bacqués fountain in the Andronne forest; and in July 1829, the Demoiselles of Fougaron warned the mayor that "he [would] meet his end at the fountain of Sallen" in the Saleich forest if he continued to accept the complaints of the forest guards lodged against the rioters. Whereas the Demoiselles concerned themselves with the social "fertility" of the village communities, the fairies were literally identified with rain, given certain powers over the natural growth of vegetation, and could claim responsibility for human fertility as well.

In the Pyrenees, the fairies' dwelling places—their grottos and river sources—were sometimes linked to fertility rites, practiced as recently as the 1950s. Deep within the forests, the springs which they inhabited were an unequivocally feminine space, as were the fountains within the villages themselves. In rural Burgundy and other parts of the French countryside, peasants identified the fountains and fairies with a class of women who held social and ritual functions centering around the birth of children and the preparation of the dead for burial. In both their legendary and their social representations, the fairies were closely linked to the ritual of washing.

In legends, they were invariably seen washing their white clothes with golden washboards, while in the traditional villages of Burgundy, the "women who help" *(femmes-qui-aide)* were responsible for washing the newborn and the recently deceased, as well as administering the annual "Great Wash" in the village, "as much a grand material scouring as a generalized and symbolic whitening of spirits, of souls, of seasons, the timing of which within the calendar was not arbitrary" (Verdier 1979, 98). Washing was a powerful feminine activity which recalled the special procreative and destructive strength of women, as in George Sand's "night washerwomen" of the Berry, in *Rustical Legends* (1858). Washing empowered women, such that in the south of France a proverb recalled that "a woman who comes from washing at the stream will eat her husband alive." Washing purified, but it also evoked the dangerous powers of femininity.

With male peasants, the fairies entertained ambivalent relations. For one, like the Demoiselles, they were rarely seen up close: "Here at one point, there at another, such that one can never get near to recognize any of them," wrote the sub-prefect in 1829 about the Demoiselles, anticipating later descriptions by peasants of the fairies' appearance. "I saw something like a white ghost, which quickly disappeared," stated Ambroise Lahille, a weaver at Augirein, in his testimony against the Demoiselles. And like the Demoiselles, fairies acted vindictively, punishing human offenses with a developed sense of justice. In the standard narratives of encounters between men and fairies, men could make an appeal to their beneficent powers, but more often the fairies defended themselves against attacks on their persons and especially their properties—their golden washboards, in the standard account from the villages of the Ariège recorded during the mid-twentieth century. The fairies, when attacked, countered with swift and retributive justice. "Give us back our golden washboards," they would cry as they followed the peasants back to the villages. The peasant rioters disguised as Demoiselles shared a similar sense of justice; they claimed only to be restoring to the peasant communities their own inherited possessions and source of livelihood, the forests.

In many of the tales recorded by Charles Joisten in the 1950s, the peasant men attempted with high levels of success to take the fairies in marriage, attracted by their gold fortunes or great beauty. The peasant men possessed the fairies, domesticating them and turning them into loyal wives. The couples consummated their marriage, and the peasant's lands remained fertile as long as a single condition remained inviolate: the husband could never verbally admit that his wife was a fairy. As soon as the words were spoken, generally in a moment of anger, the fairy disappeared from sight, never to return. This linguistic dimension of the fairy tales recalls the "secret" or "incomprehensible" language that the guards and charcoal-makers reported was used by the rioters. In the tales, the fairies nonetheless remained around the household, leaving their marks in the linen cabinets—like the Demoiselles, who sometimes ransacked these cabinets as part of their nocturnal visits to the cabins of forest guards.

Everything happened as if, to invoke the structuralist incantation, the peasant rioters in 1829 modeled their actions on the notions of retributive justice and supernatural power characteristic of the fairies of the forest. Yet at no point in the vast archival record generated by the repression of the revolt is there any claim made by peasants themselves that the fairies served to legitimate their behavior. The Demoiselles of the Ariège were unlike, for example, the peasant rioters in Burgundy in 1774—when villagers there were questioned about the "white robes" on the mountains, they simply blamed the "fairies." Yet the striking parallel structures of behaviors and activities suggest an identity between peasant rioters and local representations of fairies: the peasants drew on a wealth of village beliefs about fairies in frightening away the guards and workers and destroying their properties, whereas their "enemies," themselves peasants, took fright at the appearance of the white robes.

Previous accounts of the War of the Demoiselles have made the equation between the disguised peasant rioters and the fairies of the forest. Prosper Barousse, for example, offered in 1839 the first reconstruction of the revolt of the Ariège peasants in frequently fictional terms and from collective memory. Although much of the information provided in Barousse's account can be corroborated in the archival sources, he embellished his narrative with lyrical descriptions of the "popular imagination." Thus his reference to the world of the fairies: "Seen from afar, with their undefinable faces, passing in the night like white ghosts, they were taken for mysterious apparitions. But the people, who long recognized these light and brilliant forms running like nymphs along the paths of the forest, called them 'Demoiselles.' This is the lightest, smoothest, and most poetic word in their language; it's what they call today 'the white fairies of the past'" (Barousse 1839, 12). Marcel Dubédat, writing at the turn of the century, also relied on collective memories of the revolt, though he returned to the archival sources for his scholarly reconstruction of the trials. Yet he too equated the Demoiselles with the beliefs in supernatural beings: "The people's imagination was pricked. In these backward districts, the people believed that the Demoiselles, like the fairies or witches of the woods, spoke a mysterious language, went out at night into the beech forests, and vanished in the first light of day. They were given the power to gather clouds and make it hail and rain" (Dubédat 1899–1900, 288).

Both recollections, with their romanticization of the peasant mind, evoke a naive, unreflective, and "superstitious" worldview of the Ariège peasants, who believed, transparently, that the Demoiselles were supernatural inhabitants of the forests. Barousse, Dubédat, and I were all faced with the same silences in our research, even if they could turn to collective memories of the revolt, whereas I could not. Despite our shared sense of some kind of linked identity between Demoiselles and fairies, our interpretations move in opposite directions.

Like these accounts of the Demoiselles, early attempts by social historians to link the worlds of folklore and protest more generally assumed that peasants drew instinctively and unconsciously on their "traditional" beliefs and behaviors in acting as "primitive rebels," and that as they became more rational and political, so too did they become more sophisticated. My reconstruction of the disguise and the symbolism of the Ariège rebels points to a more sophisticated, deliberate, and dramatized adaptation of the beliefs and practices of peasant culture. The fairy world was a model available to the Demoiselles, who drew playfully and dramatically on the characteristics commonly attributed to fairies. The Demoiselles did not believe in fairies so much as they used the belief in fairies to structure their revolt against the forest guards. The use of popular culture in protest was not simply the retrieval, an unself-conscious expression of "folklore" or "tradition," for the protest involved practical reason and dramatic play with the symbolic resources of customary beliefs and practices. This dexterous relation to fairy beliefs was part of the drama which the Demoiselles enacted; the white-robed figures appearing in the forest at night were the actors, while the guards and charcoal-makers—peasants themselves—were the audience and the victims.

The links between fairies and rioters are irretrievable today, given that no oral tradition of the War of the Demoiselles survived into the late twentieth century. Yet perhaps an identity between fairy beliefs and descriptions of the Demoiselles can be found elsewhere. The villages where Charles Joisten recorded the elaborate tales of the fairy

world in the 1940s and 1950s were the same villages where the Demoiselles had been active. Is it possible that the fairy tales Joisten
collected were in some way displaced and submerged memories of
the War of the Demoiselles?

"The Forest Is Like a Woman"

The forest, Philippe Barrier recently noted, was a bit of a fairy herself
(1991, 44). Or, at the very least, there were moments when the peasants could identify the forest as a feminine supernatural being. The
Demoiselles rioters drew on the images of fairies as models for their
own actions, but they also identified themselves with a gendered representation of the forest.

The forest, as we have already seen, was considered a wild and
hostile place, a refuge for outlaws and dangerous criminals, for the
excluded and proscribed members of society who lived, to borrow
the phrase of Robert Polge Harrison, in the shadow of civilization.
But as Harrison so evocatively suggests, the forest was more than the
place of outlaws and of refuge; it was the site of inversion, of the
world upside down, of ruse, irony, deception. That is why, according
to Harrison, the forest was so often the setting for comic inversions
and disguises in the literature of the early modern period, especially
in Elizabethan England. Forests became the scene (quite literally) of
disguise and gender reversals, "the site where conventional reality
loses its persuasion and gets masked or unmasked in a drama of errors and confusion" (Harrison 1992, 80).

Yet literary and dramatic texts used the forest as a backdrop for
the world upside down, symbolic inversion, and comedies of errors
at the moment that scientific communities of discourse abandoned
the notion of a vital, organic universe. Within the animate and organic cosmos conceived by natural philosophers, following Aristotle,
the forest, with its powers of destruction and creation, was a wild
and uncontrolled yet fertile and beneficent entity. Only the Scientific
Revolution of the seventeenth century, announced by such prophets
as Francis Bacon and René Descartes, managed to turn the vitalistic,
organic notions of forest and of matter more generally into a natural
world composed of neutral matter subject to immutable natural laws.
Nature, and within that, the forest itself, was stripped of its vital
characteristics; although it remained an irrational space, full of darkness and danger, it could also be managed. Descartes, and the state

forest administration after him, could take a straight line out of (and around and within) the forests.

But prior to this domestication of the forest and of the natural world, the forest had certain disorderly and savage characteristics associated with women; or at least it replicated the procreative and destructive powers of women. Classical precedents of European civilization reveal some of these feminine characteristics, although they might also be linked, in a structural rather than a genealogical mode, to the feminine forest deities and earth goddesses of the ancient Sumerians or Egyptians. In ancient Greece and classical Rome, the goddesses of the forest, Artemis or Diana, were the sexual but virginal goddesses who reigned, ferociously and seductively, in the uncivilized reaches of the forest wilderness. The legend of Rome's foundation was of a city born in the forest, a founding father (Romulus) born *of* the forest in a feminine incarnation (Rhea Silvia) and *in* the forest itself (Harrison 1992, 46–49). The early, "armchair" anthropologist Sir James Frazer was himself inspired by the "strange and recurring tragedy" at the sacred grove and sanctuary of Diana Nemorensis, or Diana of the Wood, where the candidate for the priesthood was required to slay his predecessor in order to succeed him. Frazer collected for his multivolume study, *The Golden Bough,* a series of myths, beliefs, customs, and rituals which all somehow related to the cult of Diana of the Wood. Among many other examples, he cited the folkloric rituals and myths about feminized trees found among the peasantries of his native nineteenth-century England and Europe.

The philological evidence for a description of certain feminine characteristics of the forest goes back to the notion of matter itself in the classical tradition. Aristotle's conception of matter *(hyle)* contains the idea of embryonic genesis; it is elaborated, by Aristotle, through the analogy of motherhood, giving birth to what Neumann calls the "childbearing maternal significance of the tree" (1955, 243). *Hyle,* maternal matter, means "forest" in Greek. The Latin cognate is *silva,* which means much the same thing. Marcel Mauss, writing about the anthropological notions that preceded modern ideas about matter, described it as follows: "*Silva* is the germinative power conceived as feminine, it is the forest. In this idea of forest there is . . . something undisciplined, savage, and dangerous, but also animative and receptive" (1968, 163). It was this wild and disorderly, feminine quality of the forest that eventually disappeared from the cosmology of nature in the seventeenth century, including in the work of Descartes. Colbert's Forest Code of 1669, as we shall see shortly, partook of this de-gendered universe. The idea of nature was further disenchanted in the eighteenth century: the forest became considered a rationally organizable, coherent, and unified space, part of the larger natural world moved according to physical laws of attraction and impulsion, although it was not before the nineteenth century that the management of forest space, founded on such a vision, was put into practice in the Pyrenees.

In fact, the etymology of the forest in the classical world and notions of the forest in western civilization during the Scientific Revolution can only with great difficulty be linked to the cosmos of the nineteenth-century peasantry in the Pyrenees. Certainly there are linguistic filiations: *sylva,* for example, was the term used in the eastern Pyrenees and Languedoc, as in medieval Europe, to designate the totality of forest lands, including brush and pastures. But there is little explicit evidence to make claims about the symbolic meanings of the forest in local peasant culture, especially the identity of the forest as feminine. After all, the forest could be considered a male space, insofar as it was primarily men's responsibility to gather firewood and building materials from the forest. Moreover, many of the supernatural creatures who inhabited the forest had masculine characteristics, not to mention the phallic possibilities of trees.

Yet the peasantry's modes of exploiting the forests, their material techniques adapted to the harsh mountain environment, were clearly identified with a female space and as women's work, for the male peasants "gardened" the forest. To the forest administration, this gave the appearance of disorder and chaos. But to the peasantry, the forest was exploited in a mode that matched its material and symbolic characteristics: vitalistic, disorderly, and feminine. It is possible to reconstruct this mode of production using archival sources to reassemble the prosaic techniques and adaptive strategies of the mountain peasantry to its environment. It is in this context that the metaphor of a feminine forest gains its meaning.

The ambivalent place of the forest in the Ariège mountain peasant economy has already been described. The forests provided the food, firewood, and timber essential to a peasant's livelihood; they protected villages from rockslides and floods; they provided a source of cash income; and they gave protection, sites of refuge from the law. But for all these benefits, the forests were also inherently destructive, the enemy of both arable lands below and pasture above. Periodically, in the interests of livestock-raising, the creation of meadows, and the cultivation of lands (linked by the importance of manure as the unique fertilizer used in agriculture), the forest had to be burnt back. This was the practice of clearing *(défrichage)* by fire.

Mauss noted the homologous qualities of fire and forest: both were at once dangerous and destructive, but germinative and fertilizing. To maintain livestock, the peasants needed pastures, produced by burning back the promiscuous forest. But the forest also needed fire in order to reproduce itself. In the Ariège Pyrenees, where low-altitude clouds and fog gave to the medium elevations a generally fertile character, in and around the forest grew a great quantity of underbrush. Every spring, the peasants burnt the forests to thin the trees and extend the pastures; the ashes of burnt wood fertilized the forests themselves, returning nutrients to the soil, as well as the arable land, since ashes were gathered for use as fertilizer. The forest was thus an "obstacle to their well-being," as a forest inspector remarked in 1859, but it was also a necessary condition of productive life itself.

Preserving the forests' ambivalent status within the local political economy, peasants exploited them according to a logic of production identifiable with the disorderly (feminine) qualities of the forest—one at odds with the ordered (masculine) rationality of state forest management. The local technique was known as "gardening" *(jardinage)*. Gardening was a term and technique derived from the exclusively feminine work in the household garden. In the peasant communities of the Pyrenees, women traditionally did not cut trees in the forest, although they sometimes gathered wood. The forest was primarily a male space, yet there men gardened. Peasant men exploited the forest by extending, spatially and metaphorically, a specifically feminine mode of production, proclaiming in the process the feminine identity of the forest it/herself.

Gardening in the forest was an adaptive technique linked to a profound knowledge of the environment and the generative cycles of the trees. It was also tied to a specified system of needs, especially the need to keep livestock. In the largely beech forests—a slow-maturing hardwood that reproduced by shoots—gardening was a technique of letting forest growths reach their productive maturity, a relatively long cycle (sixty years). As the beech matured, shoots of the largest diameter from each trunk would be gardened by male peasants for use as firewood, building materials, and agricultural tools. The eco-logic to the system lay in the fact that the shoots would be thinned, and the larger of the uncut shoots would protect the newest growths from the deadening weight of the mountain snows and, in theory, the teeth of pasturing animals.

For in addition to allowing the forest to reproduce, the techniques of gardening provided the necessary resources for livestock and thus the fertility of arable land. In the largely infertile lands on the mountainside, with yields of less than three to one, dung was an essential fertilizer. By gardening in the forests, peasants were able to maintain a large number of livestock, which they pastured in the forest in spring, before the summer pastures were clear, and for which the forests provided essential protection and sanctuary during summer storms. In the fall, the peasants again led their herds into the forest, to "eat the leaves." Hence the importance of local pasturing rights in the forest, rights which the forest administration consistently opposed.

From the earliest attempts at state forest management in the fifteenth century, through to the creation of the modern forest administration in the late nineteenth century, the state considered *jardinage* fatal to the forest: to garden in the forest was to recognize the forest as a chaotic, disorderly being. From the thirteenth century onward, the king had attempted to regulate, not just the extent and quality of forest lands, but their mode of exploitation as well. In England, the underlying cultural order of this management lies in the idea that the Latin etymology of forest *(foresta)* means not only "outside," as we have seen, but also "to keep out, to place off limits, to exclude." The forest became in England a space outside the public domain, protected by the king, "for his delight and pleasure; which territory of ground so privileged is meered and bounded with unremovable marks, meers, and boundaries" (Manwood, 1592, in Harrison 1992, 72). In France, forest law was more likely to be conceived of as the king's administration of a public good, excluded from private use, first and foremost, in favor of the "public" needs of war.

Colbert's Forest Reformation Ordinance of 1669 was a general attempt to impose "order and discipline" through the "management" *(aménagement)* of forest lands. The idea of management was teleological: it had a particular end in mind, the rational exploitation of forest lands for a purpose, such as firewood, lumber, or tree sales. In the eighteenth century, the idea of the royal management of forests became identified with the state's obligation to conserve a public trust. As the game warden of the park of Versailles, Monsieur Le Roy had written in that monument of the Enlightenment, Diderot's *Encyclopédie*:

> It seems that in all ages one has sensed the importance of preserving forests; they have always been regarded as the property of the state and administered in its name: Religion itself had consecrated forests, doubtlessly to protect, through veneration, which had to be conserved for the public interest. Our oaks no longer offer oracles, and we no longer ask of them the sacred mistletoe; we must replace this cult by care; and whatever advantage one may previously have found in the respect that one had for forests, one can expect even more success from vigilance and economy. (in Harrison 1992, 115–116)

Evoking a pre-modern, enchanted universe, this Enlightened vision heralded the birth of modern forest management; yet it was more than a century later when reforestation became a state policy.

In the early nineteenth century, management was a mode of policing in the Old Regime (and Foucauldian) sense—as much a means of administering as an attempt to "prevent disorder and confusion," as a printed instruction claimed in 1828. In practice, according to Dralet, it was "the art of establishing the parts [of the forest] which must be cut each year"; laying boundary markers and carving up rationally, geometrically, in a pure Cartesian logic, the space of the forest.

It is no surprise, then, that the state should have condemned the peasant practices of gardening on the basis that this method gave the *appearance* of disorder. In the 1670s, Louis de Froidour decried this mode of exploitation, which made the forests look as if they had been ravaged and pillaged; a century and a half later, Etienne Dralet, the dominant legislator and ideologue of the modern French forest administration, repeated his claims, with greater rhetorical force and political efficacy. Dralet, in text after text, denounced "this disastrous *jardinage*" and vehemently sought its prohibition.

> [The peasants] undertook no regular exploitation [of the forest]; each inhabitant took from wherever he wanted, all year round, the wood necessary for his heating, and in some places, to make ashes for fertilizing the fields. He cut and left on the ground five

or six lateral branches of a beautiful trunk of oak or beech in order to take the stronger one, which he carried away. And he continued this disastrous *jardinage* until he achieved his provision. The growth contained trees of all ages; as for the mature growths, everyone took the best trees he found, leaving the ones without hope of maturing aside. They cut six young pines to make six blocks which a single mature tree would have provided if sawed; a pine tree barely reached fifteen centimeters diameter before it was cut to make sandals; two pines were thus necessary for one man's shoes, six for the year, two thousand for a village of one hundred families. (Dralet 1813, 78–79)

A forest gardened represented the essence of disorder, not simply because of such excesses, but also because it was an undifferentiated space. No areas were put off limits, and because trees were cut at all ages and at different heights from the ground, the forest looked "ravaged," at least according to a certain aesthetic sensibility. Dralet placed blame for the forest's condition squarely on the shoulders of the peasantry: in doing so he anthropomorphized the forest, identifying its "disorder" with that of the peasants who exploited it.

In place of this disordered garden, Dralet and the forest administration, as they had since the sixteenth-century, called for the clear-cutting of areas, a technique called *tire-aire* (with its sixteenth century meaning of "arranged areas"). The 1669 Ordinance, drawing on earlier practices, specified that the forests were to be divided into multiple areas of exploitation *(coupes),* to be subjected in rotation to felling, with a certain number of trees left standing to reseed and renew the growth. The areas of exploitation were marked by boundary stones, a symbolic act of taking control and possession of the forest space.

Such Cartesian practices were thus modes of control and domination. The forest administration marked out specific areas of the forest and then permitted local inhabitants to take firewood and building material (they rarely permitted pasturing). The 1669 Ordinance came under attack in the eighteenth century, as informed observers noted that the law failed, for technical reasons, to provide adequate means to replenish forests after exploitations; at the same time, after Colbert's death, forests tended to be administered as a source of revenue for the state, although not in the inaccessible mountains which were to make up the Ariège.

Yet despite its failures, Colbert's system of management formed the basis of the early-nineteenth-century forest legislation as applied to state and communal forests. "Forest lands must be exploited by 'arranged areas,'" wrote Dralet, "so that the growth is regular, easy to guard, and so that the new growth has an equal rate of growth." Dralet and the Imperial Forest Administration sought to observe and police local uses of the forest, to abolish the "disorderly" practices of the peasants, and to pursue rationally the straight lines out of the forest.

Despite the state's condemnation of forest gardening in the early nineteenth century, many sympathetic observers, including some personnel of the forest administration, recognized that in areas of abundant snowfall and steep slopes, the practice made more sense than exploitation by *tire-aire*. As the mayor of Cabannes, experimenting with both methods, explained:

> In the coldest areas with abundant snows . . . the vegetation begins to grow very late [in the spring], and the growing season lasts but three months; because of this, during the first year, when the seedlings are very small, the considerable snows destroy them if they are exploited by *tire-aire*. A second growth follows, but with the same consequences, and so on until the entire root is destroyed. I myself have tried the experiment in the Arcon forest, where a growth was planted [by *tire-aire*] in 1811 but died after four years. Another one, exploited by the technique of *jardinage,* has matured with success . . . It so happens that the smaller branches which remain in place when you "garden" serve as a shelter for the smaller plants, protecting them against the weight of the snow and the animals' teeth.

Even more important, the techniques of gardening would permit the peasants to pasture their herds in the forests. According to the forest conservator, reporting to the forest commission in 1830, the peasant communities

> are not complaining, nor have they ever complained about not having enough wood; there would be much less contention if we simply let them garden because then there would be . . . no more prohibited areas . . . The inhabitants of the Castillonnais wish only to return to this pernicious practice of gardening, and that

is the goal of the revolts which they have periodically undertaken. They would complain neither of the sales of forest land
for the state's profit, nor of the concessions distributed, if only
they could exploit the forests by gardening.

The peasants were particularly opposed to the management of forests
by private owners, since the latter would randomly restrict use-rights
by designating the smallest growth of trees in the middle of the pastures a "protected" area, restricting all pasturing, and thus forcing
the peasants into a state of delinquency.

Even the forest administration could not remain blind forever to
the logic of gardening the forests of the Pyrenees. In his later writings,
Dralet came to recognize the value and efficacy of gardening as a
mode of exploiting beech forests in the steeper mountains and valleys
of the Pyrenees, and within a century, French forest management
sanctioned a modified version of the peasant technique. Jean Salvador, the conservator of forests in 1930, described his "discovery"
that gardening could work, despite its aesthetic limitations.

A forest growth which has been gardened seems to offer the character of complete devastation; and yet this way of exploiting the
forests has been practiced for centuries throughout the Pyrenees;
it has guaranteed the conservation of beech forests. The mature
growth which has been gardened has the advantage of never
leaving the soil uncovered; it stops erosions; and it leaves the
pastures less damaged. Further, it doesn't require the limitations of being put "in defense" for any length of time. (Salvador
1930, 69)

But in 1829, the peasants had to fight to preserve their mode of production founded on a conception of an animate, feminine forest
whose danger and source of fertility lay precisely in its disorderly
attributes.

There was, of course, an important disjuncture between the "theory" of the peasant mode of production—with its "reservoir of rules
organized with a profound knowledge, acquired at the cost of historical essays of the possibilities of the environment" (Chevalier 1956,
381)—and the practices. The techniques of gardening had clearly de-
generated by the late eighteenth century, as evidenced by the decreasing ability of village councils to enforce their authority over commu-

nal management of the forests. In November 1786, the village council of Alzen complained of its inability to enforce restrictions on forest usage against abuses by both its own inhabitants and those of neighboring villages. Such complaints were echoed by the municipal councils in Alos in 1756 and in Vicdessos in 1789. The communities occasionally tried to protect the forests; in 1771, in Orgibet, the community created a communal forest with a guard to prevent degradation.

The experience of the Revolution further limited the municipality's attempts to police the forest, although many communes, such as Moulis, did try, generally without success, to regulate the exploitation of the forests despite the breakdown of municipal authority. There is no doubt that the rules and regulations governing the practices of gardening collapsed during the revolutionary moment, strained already by serious demographic pressure. Yet even the prefect Brun admitted in 1804 that the claims of Dralet and others were suspect, and that "despite the revolutionary destruction, one still finds in the district of Saint-Girons some fairly well conserved communal forests."

Yet more important than the abuses of the peasantry in the ravage and devastation of the forests of the Ariège was the activity of the ironworks. Such was the conclusion of the prefectoral commission, made up of forest inspectors, civil administrators, and judges, which reported its findings in December 1830. The commission unanimously agreed that the privately owned forests had greatly deteriorated: their proprietors, usually men who acquired the domains during the Revolution, cut down their old-growth trees and multiplied the number of new growths in order to sell wood to the forge owners. They restricted all use-rights in the process, and had welcomed the new Forest Code, which "served them marvelously." As for the royal and communal forests, the commission was divided, but some agreed that when in the hands of the communities before 1807, they were in a much better state.

Here was no "tragedy of the commons," the greater ecological destruction of a natural resource in communal as opposed to private hands, which sociologists since 1968 have expected. Comparisons of woodland surfaces in the Castillonnais in 1668 and 1813—based on surveys done by the forest administration, which are necessarily suspect—suggest that where ironworks did not exist before the nineteenth century, the forest lands actually increased, from 7000 to more than 12,000 hectares. But after the Imperial Reformation, the state had been greedy in selling concessions in order to pay the expenses of the forest administration, and it had sought to administer the forests as a source of revenue. According to the commission, "The conservation of this kind of property interests public order, and the government should not shrink from an expense which could be raised on other revenues without recourse to useless and destructive concessions."

Other voices suggest that the communal forests were less ravaged than royal or private ones. In Massat, to the surprise of a forest commissioner writing in 1844, the communal forest had almost quintupled in surface in less than thirty years, "despite the tooth [of animals] and the hatchet," confirming Dralet's much-quoted observation that "the trees grow despite men's efforts."

"Trees are like women who become sterile in old age," argued some French forest officers during the eighteenth century, urging that seeding trees should be cut at younger ages before they became sterile (in Huffel 1910, iii, 162). In sixteenth-century England, a fruitful cross-fertilization of a tree was called a "wife," one without result, a "maiden" or a "widow" (Thomas 1983, 219). These isolated similes and metaphors were as close as forest administrators came to approximating a feminine character of the forest. The peasants of the Ariège never explicitly identified the forest as feminine, but in "disguising" themselves as women during the War of the Demoiselles, they identified themselves with an unruly and disorderly feminized forest. For the mountain peasantry, the forest was partly feminized in the mythical and narrative tales of the forest's numinous inhabitants. As fairies of the forest, the Demoiselles protected their habitat against the thefts and assaults by the forest guards and charcoal-makers. More generally, in their struggle to define and use the forest, the peasant men took on an abbreviated feminine identity as a sign of the feminine and disorderly forest itself.

But if the rioters represented themselves as feminine, caricaturing the appearance of women, they also retained their identity as young men, as evidenced in the elaborate military symbolism which formed part of their "disguise." Acting as young men, defending their possession of the forest as if it were a living feminine being, they exercised a kind of charivari, a ritual act of sexual policing, over the forests. Indeed, we might consider the War of the Demoiselles a gigantic charivari against the arranged but mismatched marriage of "outsider" forest guards and the forest. The forest belonged to the peasants; they claimed to "master" and to "possess" it. When the state forest guards "usurped" the peasant communities' possession of the forest, the peasants acted as if they opposed a mismatched marriage. The Demoiselles claimed to replace the guards, fulfilling an obligation to protect the forests, and thus restoring a proper marital relation, with themselves as "husbands." Toward that end, the Demoiselles subjected the guards and charcoal-makers to the fear and public humiliation of a huge charivari. When the guards and the administration frustrated the Demoiselles' efforts to repossess the forest, the peasants, in "an act of impossible love" (Baby 1972, 137), burnt the forests rather than seeing them possessed by another.

If the peasants maintained an ambivalent relation to the forest, so too did they remain only ambivalently disguised: the costume worn by the male peasants during the War of the Demoiselles included both masculine and feminine symbols. This conjuncture—or perhaps disjuncture—of both gender identities represents the ambivalence of the male peasantry's simultaneous identification with the forest and their "marital" possession of it. The male peasants who undertook to defend their inherited rights to the forest were only partially "disguised as women." The costume, which evoked the image of women but did not entirely mask the peasants' manliness, was purposely ambivalent. The peasant community's dramatization of their design to exclude the forest guards and charcoal-makers from the forest was undertaken with several audiences in mind—themselves, their enemies, and the political and military authorities—and its form was conceived not from a logic of utilitarian calculation but as part of a deeper play with the image of the forest in local peasant culture.

The notion of "deep play" is borrowed for the title of this chapter from Clifford Geertz, who took it from Jeremy Bentham's understanding of apparently irrational acts such as high-stakes gambling. Geertz used the idea in his interpretation of the betting patterns at a Balinese cock-fight, suggesting the symbolic pursuits of status and honor which underlay apparently irrational bets—irrational from the (western) utilitarian perspective of cost-maximization. The War of the Demoiselles was a kind of deep play in the forest, with its own logic and its own moves, incomprehensible within the bourgeois culture of the mid-nineteenth century. The play of revolt took place within a specific cultural frame of the Ariège peasantry's relation to the forest; and it was this culture which informed the peasants' choice of tactics in defense of their inherited rights. The War of the Demoiselles was a dramatic revolt in which the stakes and strategies were defined in terms of cultural values (possession and mastery of a feminine forest) which themselves structured issues of marginal utility (defense of pasturing rights). Such an explanation can begin to appreciate the trees "from the natives' point of view" while not losing sight of the forest from the perspective of bourgeois political economy. The War of the Demoiselles was, of course, a revolt undertaken against the perspective and practices of a bourgeois political economy, but it was also a dramatic enactment of the culturally specific relation between the peasant communities of the Ariège and their forests.

3. FESTIVE REVOLT

The Revolt in Time: May 1829–June 1830

eginning in May 1829, the War of the Demoiselles spread quickly through the forests of the eastern part of the Couserans. By mid-July, even as agricultural work reached a peak period, appearances of the disguised rioters continued apace. On Sunday, 12 July, the Demoiselles were again at Ustou, scaring off the charcoal-makers of Sr. Trinqué; they appeared as well at Galey, where they came at night to pay a visit to the houses of the royal forest guards. The Demoiselles showed themselves briefly beyond the boundaries of the Ariège, in the communes of Fougaron and Saleich in the Haute-Garonne, spending a Sunday afternoon drinking at an inn, where witnesses noted their particularly elaborate costumes. Yet by the end of July, the costumed rebels had virtually disappeared from the forests. "No new troubles have erupted," reported the sub-prefect of Saint-Girons. "Everything seems quiet in the district—I have no news to the contrary." The month of August, however, brought a rash of new incidents. On 17 August a royal forest guard seized a herd of sheep grazing near Buzan on a restricted area of the mountain. Unfortunately for him, it was the day of the local patron saint festival. Led by several youthful Demoiselles firing guns into the air and screaming threats, and backed by the community gathered for the feast, the peasants seized the herd back. On Saturday night, 22 August, the Demoiselles appeared in full garb in Augirein, chasing off new charcoal-makers assigned to work in the Engomer forest.

Yet by September 1829, the sub-prefect's wishful remark had come true: the Demoiselles had disappeared from the forests. Peasants were seen cutting wood illegally, not bothering with the areas set aside for them by the forest administration, and new forest guards or charcoal-makers whose predecessors refused to work were subjected to harassment and occasional incidents of "rebellion." The forest administration actively prosecuted, as best it could, crimes against the new Forest Code, but with a single exception, the masked rioters had vanished. The exception was the sighting of two Demoiselles at "around midnight" in the Aucassein forest on Sunday, 31 October, the night of All Saints. According to a witness, they "did nothing to anyone but refused to allow themselves to be approached."

For the authorities, it was too good to be true; and, indeed, by mid-December 1829, new reports of Demoiselles alarmed both local and national officials. For not only did they appear with great frequency, but their gatherings became much larger, public demonstrations of strength. On 15 December, more than 80 masked rioters confronted royal forest guards in Balaguères; a week later, 50 or 60 chased out private forest guards at Villeneuve. By January 1830, the revolt had entered a new phase, with its center shifting noticeably eastward to the valley of Massat. On 26 January more than 120 Demoiselles threatened the farmhouses of Sr. Lafont; the next day, between 400 and 500 men, "masked or with blackened faces, almost all wearing shirts or white skirts, and all armed with guns, hatchets, or hoes," marched in formation onto the town square at Massat. There they confronted the local authorities and demanded the removal of Sr. Fournier, the head forest guard employed by the Roquemaurel family, which owned much of the forest land near Massat. Over the next month, the incidents multiplied. On 17 February more than 800 peasants again marched into Massat, and later that day many were seen in the hamlets of Bernède and Guioulat, where they pillaged the houses of the forest guards Loubet and Rivière. The festive rebellion continued from February through May, spreading through the department, despite the military and economic repression instituted by the departmental and central authorities. Then, in early June, the rioting slowed noticeably, and it once again appeared that the War of the Demoiselles had run its course.

How to explain the timing of the rioting, and within it, the shifting character of the protest—from small guerrilla-like bands to large public displays of authority? Judicial and administrative officials whose concern was to repress the revolt asked themselves at least the first part of the question, and their correspondence offers a number of plausible explanations. The prefect and his subordinates, for example, were sensitive to the price of grain and the food supply, and they attempted to link high prices and food shortages directly to collective actions on the part of the mountain peasantry. But most officials did not believe that peasants revolted because of empty stomachs, and they sought instead to correlate the appearance of the Demoiselles with the environmental conditions of the mountain communes.

The cold temperatures and heavy snowfall of the long Ariège winters seemed to present an insurmountable obstacle for the peasant rioters, as they had for the forces of order which sought them out. In November 1830, the minister of the interior wrote to the prefect that "the winter will, in any case, place a natural obstacle on these reprehensible actions, and these circumstances should help us formulate a more efficacious system of repression." In January and early February 1830, the minister of justice wrote from Paris that "the rigor of the season and the snows covering these parts make access to the mountains and forests nearly impossible in the Castillonnais." However, he continued, there was reason to fear that the melting snows, "in reestablishing communications, will awaken the spirit of insubordination."

Yet this correlation between the meteorological conditions and the riotous actions of the peasantry is contradicted by the events themselves, and for this reason alone it remains an insufficient account of the timing of the rioting. In December 1829, the royal district attorney noted the "increased number of incidents committed even in the most rigorous season." And the same official who had informed the minister of justice about the inaccessible mountains and forests noted that "these obstacles have not stopped the undertakings of these evildoers."

More important, the model of rioting that rests on anticipated reactions to climate and environment fails to grasp the cultural logic which could and did condition the appearance of the Demoiselles. The authorities' focus on weather conditions and the environmental determinants of behavior implicated their own notions of what was practically and instrumentally possible: the utilitarian logic which they offered as explanation rationalized the meaning of the disguise and its appearance in time according to common sense—a logic they understood. But from such a perspective, the officials could not take note of a cultural frame of reference which helped to structure the timing of the revolt. For if the War of the Demoiselles, as I have already suggested, drew its meaning from the beliefs and practices of local peasant culture, the timing of the events was at least as much shaped by the peasantry's conceptions of time, and in particular, the experience of time constituted within the festive calendar. Although the events of the revolt were not limited to festive moments of the calendar year, the Demoiselles put to use the symbolic practices of the festive calendar, and the languages of festive culture in nineteenth-century France.

Rites of Spring

Why did the War of the Demoiselles break out during the month of May in 1829? Or better put, when the peasants appeared in the forests of the Castillonnais in early May to chase out the guards, why should they have decided to go about "disguised as women"? The most evident explanation of the timing of the revolt itself can be found within the calendar of agro-pastoral activities that the forest administration, determined to enforce the provisions of the 1827 Forest Code, severely disrupted. Only in early May, beginning the summer transhumant cycle, would the peasants take their herds of sheep into the forests on the way to the upper-mountain pastures—only at that time had enough snow melted for the charcoal-makers, in the employ of forge owners, to begin to make fuel for the ironworks. And it was only then that the guards began to make seizures and impose fines, as they had in the years before the application of the 1827 Code. Prior to 1829, clashes between guards and peasants were more frequent in May than in preceding months; and in 1829, the second year of the Code's implementation and the first moment of the new regime, when the communities found themselves without legal recourse to their titles and claims of use-rights, a serious confrontation was inevitable.

Yet why should the peasants have appeared "armed and disguised as women" as a sign of their resistance to the forest administration during the month of May? In fact, as early as February 1829, the prefect, the baron of Mortarieu, reported in the district of Saint-Girons "a spirit of resistance against the execution of the new code." Throughout the month of April, peasants from the commune of Moulis had gathered periodically, and once, while "armed with hatchets, sticks, and guns," they had even demolished the workers' cabins put up by M. Marrot and burnt the forest. Only in May did they actually don the "disguise." The explanation for this timing must be sought, in part, in the ritual expressions of the calendar year. The Demoiselles appeared initially during the month of May, for May was first and foremost the month of demoiselles.

Nineteenth-century peasant culture marked the passage of time both in the regular performance of the tasks and activities of the agricultural year and in the festive life of the community. A succession of distinct feast days punctuated the year, festivals in which specific ritual acts and kinds of celebrations took place. From Carnival through Easter, from the rites of May through the patron saint festivals of the summer and fall, the festive calendar was a complete system of symbolic reproduction. Among European peasants as elsewhere, the calendar gave shape to a vision of the world founded on a recurrent cycle, a drama in several acts in which the village community narrated a story about its identity and social existence, about the reproductive cycles of the natural world, and about the institutional and political order. As a sequence of festive rites and practices, the calendar should be understood as a story the peasant community told itself, a drama about creative and destructive forces of birth and death; about sexual procreation and marriage and the reproduction of the social order; and about hierarchy and authority both within the community and between the community and the wider worlds of the state and the church.

I shall reconstruct, shortly, the structure of these dramas in the calendar year. For now, it is important to see how the month of May stood at a critical juncture in this calendrical narrative. In the agrarian cycle around which both festive and economic activities were organized, May marked the return of spring, when vegetation was at its most fertile and vulnerable. In the Ariège mountain communities, as throughout the high Pyrenees, the peasants began to burn back the forest, to prepare the fields for planting, and to lead their herds from the granges through the fields and forests toward the summer pastures. In the festive calendar cycle, the rites of May made explicit reference to agrarian and vegetative fertility, while incorporating statements about female sexuality and reproduction. The rites of May thus served to express the logical and metaphoric connections of the human and natural cycles of fertility and reproduction in peasant culture.

Catholic and Protestant reformers saw evidence of pagan rites; the "survivalist" theories of early anthropology in the nineteenth century continued to interpret the peasant's May as shadowy evidence of an ancient religious cult of a female vegetation spirit. Folklorists, such as Van Gennep, were less willing to see in customs and beliefs a survival of earlier practices, being more concerned with their contemporary significance. But they, too, pointed to the essentially feminine characteristics of beliefs, practices, and festive celebrations during the month of May. May was the month of a certain kind of Demoiselle.

Early in the eighteenth century, the French church had designated May the month of the Virgin, but in ancient Europe, May had been the period when the powers of feminine sexuality and reproduction were expressed symbolically. May was believed, in traditional peasant culture, to be an inauspicious month, a period when feminine sorcery was especially potent. Certain days of the month, particularly the first of May, were also identified with supernatural feminine beings—the fairies—and their distinctive activities of washing. In the province of Lorraine, the May tree, a giant, extensively decorated beech, was actually called the "Fairy Tree" or "Ladies' Tree." Throughout France, the month of May was considered the time to clean the wells and fountains in the villages, an activity at once practically motivated and symbolically structured, yet in many regions, women were prohibited from washing clothes during the month of May, suggesting perhaps the dangers of excessive fertility.

Throughout France, folklorists have inscribed beliefs and practices that might seem to identify the month of May as a time of relative liberation for women. In the Franche-Comté, accounts suggest that wives could take revenge on their husbands for beating them, a nineteenth-century custom that derived from an ancient practice of female justice, administered formally by the wives of mayors and magistrates in the fifteenth century. May was still considered a time when women were powerful and sexually dominant: throughout France, it was a moment relatively favorable to free sexual choice, outside the institution of marriage. Ancient and proverbial warnings of May marriages—"May marriages, deadly marriages" went the proverb in the Ariège—had some practical impact in southern France during the nineteenth century, as marriages greatly declined during May.

Marking a period of temporary feminine powers, the rites of May also borrowed directly from the languages of power and sovereignty: central in this idiom was the figure of the May Queen. According to most folkloric accounts, the chosen or "elected" queen was generally a young girl, a virgin still removed from the dangerous and disorderly powers of femininity. (Young women of marriageable age—demoiselles—by contrast, sometimes assembled during May in youth groups which paralleled those of young men, although these groups and their festive roles were much less clearly defined.) From Saint Genevieve to Joan of Arc, virgins occupied a special place as symbolic embodiments of community, and the May Queen played this role in village culture. The anthropologist Victor Turner has noted that the categories of marginal and inferior social groups, and especially women in patriarchal and patrilineal societies, were used to symbolize "the wider community and its ethical system." Such was the case in the May rites of nineteenth-century rural French society, as the figure of young women symbolized the totality of the community.

Yet the centrality of young children and virgins, as opposed to the sexual disorder of marriageable young women, suggests that the "liberation" of women and of femininity during May was only relative: the power and temporary authority of women remained constrained within a set of institutions and practices dominated by men, and during May, young men. May was equally a time when young women were subjected to male jurisdiction and judgment, to the inherited misogyny of village life. The rites of May, in this context, tended less to "liberate" women than to articulate statements about village communities using an imagery of women and the dangerous powers of femininity. May rites described a gendered ordering of power and authority within the peasant community in which femininity was domesticated and disciplined.

The erection of May trees gave dramatic expression to these cultural and social constructions. Within the village, male youth groups exercised the prerogative during May—but especially on the first of May—to evaluate the moral and physical qualities of potentially marriageable women in the community, limiting the temporary female domination associated with the month itself. In the ritual planting of May trees, youth groups erected freshly cut trees in front of the woman's house and topped them with those species of plants and flowers that best designated the woman's character. The forest served as a kind of language system in which differentially valued plants and flowers were signs used to affirm a young woman's relative worth. The specific language of trees and flowers varied from region to region, and often between neighboring communities, but everywhere French village culture stated the linkage between human and natural fertility, while affirming the social control of young men and ordering the relations of men and women within peasant communities.

Another kind of May tree used a similar language, linking the natural and social worlds, to make statements about the village community in relation to others and to outside authorities. In many regions of France, including the Pyrenees, male youth groups cut tall trees from the forest—generally on the night of 1 May, but sometimes on the first Sunday of May—which were either erected in the collective, public space of the village or placed in front of the houses of seigneurs or rural notables. In southwestern France, it appears that seigneurs actually required the erection of May trees in front of their houses as an expression of honor and respect beginning in the sixteenth century, as they sought to strengthen their hold on village communities. By the nineteenth century, village youth groups saw their ability to cut down and plant the May tree as a fundamental privilege, one which the forest administration was to dispute in the course of the nineteenth century. Each community would have its own May tree, and youth groups of neighboring communes would often try to steal each other's tree, or simply attempt to erect the tallest and most elaborately decorated one. The planting of May trees thus made reference to the separate identity and independence of the village, and could easily be turned into a statement about the rights and interests of community members against their seigneur, about their liberties (in the Old Regime sense of privileges) challenged by the lords. It was this ritual of planting May trees that the French revolutionaries transformed into the planting of "liberty trees," and which has since become part of the revolutionary tradition in France.

The male peasants who, "armed and disguised as women," chased guards and charcoal-makers from the forests, were drawing on the symbolic identifications of women with the regenerative powers of spring, the creative but dangerous feminine sexuality ritually articulated in the month of May; they were also linking their feminine personae to the identity of the village community. But the rioters did not disguise their identity as men; as we have seen, in the elaboration of military symbols the rioters affirmed their masculinity. In this sense, there was a logical fit between the identity of the rioters—men appearing as women without disappearing as men—and the month of May, when female sexuality and power was expressed but controlled by young men.

The barely disguised peasants, then, used the symbols and rituals

of the month of May as part of their language of revolt. This instrumental relation to folk culture—the uses of the festive calendar—
presupposed a set of symbolic meanings already in place. The Demoiselles used the festive expressions of bridled feminine disorder as a
resource in their revolt, itself a dramatized enactment of their claims
to the forest. The *uses* of May, then, like the uses of the disguise itself,
were possible because May rites were part of an already constituted
set of meanings.

In this light it is possible to make sense of how the Demoiselles
used the rites of May beyond the traditional May cycle of festivities.
Rioters enacted a version of May rites on 29 November 1829, in a
kind of inversion of the festive calendar year itself. That day, forest
guards reported a "decorated" tree in the forest of Buzan with an
inscription pompously addressed to "The Gentleman Charcoal-Makers," warning them to stay away from the forests. At Saint-Lary in
July 1830, a piece of wood placed against the house of the village
constable with an "abusive message" was perhaps derived from the
same custom, although like the Buzan May tree, it was used outside
the May cycle and with a derisory intent. Such adoptions of May tree
rituals were complemented by other acts that recall the peasant
ethno-botanical beliefs in the magical and prophylactic powers of certain plant species during the month of May. The third of May, the
feast of Saint Croix, for example, represented a Christian overlay of
preexisting ritual practices that was common in rural festive life. On
this liturgical feast day, peasants made small wooden crosses and
planted them in cultivated fields. The Demoiselles of Montagagne
derisively transformed such a rite when they placed in the forests "a
cross made of freshly cut beech wood, planted and crowned with
green juniper, and a little piece of paper at each end, one of which
said 'commune de Montagagne.' " "This cross," reported the chief
forest guard in Foix, "signified death to the forest guards."

This carnivalization of May rites demonstrates how the Demoiselles used elements of the festive calendar outside of the temporal
structure dictated by the calendar itself. And indeed, as we shall see,
the languages of festive practices, most notably that of Carnival, informed the entire War of the Demoiselles. Yet the Demoiselles' appearance in time remained linked to their calendar year, determined
roughly by the cycles of popular festivity in the villages of the Pyrenees. The fit between the appearance of masked rioters and the traditional cycles of holiday feasts was only proximate, yet it was signifi-

cant. Because as the Ariège peasants appropriated the festive calendar for their own purposes, they redefined the character and timing of festive life itself.

The Drama of Peasant Time

The festive calendar year was divided into two halves, which stood opposed in almost every respect. The first, and more highly marked, consisted of the cycles of festivals which ran from December through June, framed by two moments: Christmas (25 December) on the one hand, and Saint John the Baptist (24 June) and Saint Peter (29 June) on the other. Encompassed by these two moments, often considered Christian transpositions of celebrations of the solstice, the winter and spring cycles of feast days included Carnival, Lent, Easter, and the rites of May. This first half of the calendar year was the time of intensive festive life within the Christian liturgical calendar, consisting of the moveable feasts of Mardi Gras, Ash Wednesday, Easter Sunday, Ascension, Pentecost, and Corpus Christi, as well as those celebrations fixed at certain dates.

These festivals can of course be distinguished among themselves. Thus Christmas and Saint John were opposed but complementary feasts: Christmas was a familial and domestic celebration; Saint John was municipal and collective. At Christmas, families celebrated among themselves, and the protective supernatural powers of fairies were invoked at the level of the domestic group. At Saint John, every family brought firewood for a collective bonfire, which held purificatory and generative powers and was linked to a series of courting rituals among young men and women. Indeed, the festivities that ran from Christmas to Saint John or Saint Peter were unified by the fact that youth—principally male youth groups, but also, as we shall see, young women and children—were the privileged actors and celebrants. This sociological primacy of youth groups, their special privileges and jurisdictions founded on inversion, laughter, and a mockery of the social order, marked the first and more dramatic half of the festive calendar year.

The second half of the calendar year was defined essentially as the season of patron saint festivals, when each village or parish celebrated its corporate identity on the date of its adopted patron saint. Here was an evocation of age and experience, of the established social order. The patron saint celebrations were collective, municipal state-

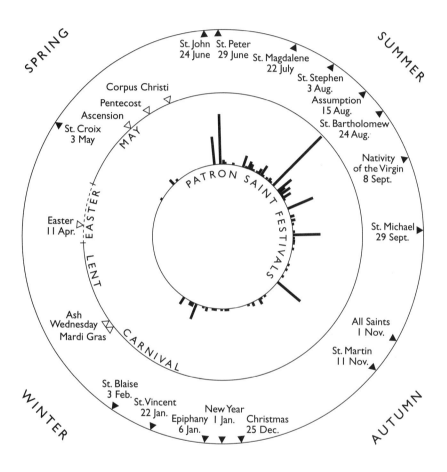

SPRING

SUMMER

St. John
24 June
St. Peter
29 June
St. Magdalene
22 July
St. Stephen
3 Aug.
Assumption
15 Aug.
St. Bartholomew
24 Aug.

Corpus Christi
Pentecost
Ascension
St. Croix
3 May

MAY

PATRON SAINT FESTIVALS

Nativity
of the Virgin
8 Sept.

St. Michael
29 Sept.

EASTER

Easter
11 Apr.

LENT

Ash
Wednesday
Mardi Gras

CARNIVAL

All Saints
1 Nov.

St. Martin
11 Nov.

St. Blaise
3 Feb.
St. Vincent
22 Jan.
Epiphany
6 Jan.
New Year
1 Jan.
Christmas
25 Dec.

WINTER

AUTUMN

▲ Fixed feast days

△ Moveable feast days, depending on the calculation
    of Easter. In 1830, Easter Sunday fell on 11 April.

Incidence of patron saint festivals
(districts of Foix and Saint-Girons)

Model of the Ariège Peasant Calendar

ments about local identity. They frequently combined a formal ceremony, under the official direction of the municipal councils and local
clergy, with collective meals and public dances.

Of course, youth groups actively participated in these celebrations,
and sometimes used them as the occasion in which to elaborate their
ritual functions as boundary-keepers of the village community. As
the royal district attorney at Saint-Girons noted, "It is unfortunately
the custom in this district that on the days of the patron saint festivals,
the young people from neighboring communes get together to quarrel
and fight. Thus, made hot-headed by wine, these unfortunate souls
undertake all kinds of excesses." Yet youth groups were not the organizers or premier celebrants of the patron saint festivals. Rather, such
festivals tended to be the domain of village elders and household
heads, as well as of the priests and mayors who constituted the official
and institutional representatives of the village community.

In the Ariège, as more generally in France, the season of patron
saint festivals ran from Saint John (24 June) to December, a season
of festivity that complemented, while it stood opposed to, the winter
and spring festivals. In general, this second half of the year was a
much less marked or festive season, since each village celebrated only
its own patron saint festival, while all villages partook of the festivities from Carnival to Saint John. A list of 172 feast days in the two
mountain districts of Foix and Saint-Girons in 1877 reveals that only
25 parishes held their feast days between Christmas and Saint John,
less than 15 percent. Most communes celebrated their patron saint
festivals in the period from June to September. One hundred and fifty-
nine parishes, 92 percent of the sample, held their village feasts during
these four months; half of those were celebrated in the month of August, with 28 of 172 celebrating theirs as the Feast of the Assumption,
15 August. There appears to be some correlation between the months
of most intensive agricultural work and a smaller number of festivals
celebrated (for example, July, with only 19 of 172), but this correlation is far from determinate. After September (32 of 172 festivals),
the rest were spread out from October to January, a period of moderate work. There was some concentration of patron saint feasts in
November, since a large number of villages (14) celebrated the feast
of Saint Martin (11 November). In contrast to the summer and fall
months, the period from February to May saw only 8 of 172 villages
celebrating their festivals.

During the first season of rioting in 1829, the Demoiselles of the

Ariège modified, by their appearance, the distinctiveness of these two seasons of festivity. In making use of the symbolic order of the calendar, they changed it. For after their debut in May, the masked rioters continued to appear during June (there were seven incidents reported, including three surrounding the feast days of Saint John and Saint Peter, which fully 20 percent of the mountain communes celebrated as their patron saint day). In July, the rioting slowed (there were only five incidents), but August witnessed an estimated three hundred more Demoiselles in the Castillonnais. July and August were, of course, months of hard agricultural work in the fields, but they were also within the season of patron saint festivals. The rioting continued, then, into the summer, coinciding with the first half of the season of patron saint festivals.

More generally, during the first two years of the revolt, patron saint festivals were inevitably occasions—or excuses—for revolt. Thus in 1829, incidents were plentiful in the communes of Castillon, Saint-Lary, and Illartein during the period between the feast of Saint John on 24 June and the feast of Saint Peter on 29 June.

In August, patron saint festivals were times when people gathered to express their notions of community. The authorities were well aware of how dangerous this could be. As the prefect wrote to the minister of the interior in 1830: "Movements noticed in the communes of Lorcat and Aston, several words overheard . . . suggest that on 10 June, day of the Fête Dieu, and a feast day for the inhabitants of these communes, some project against the properties of Sr. Astrié is being planned." The prefect ordered military forces to protect his chateau, and, as expected, on 10 June local peasants burned and pillaged his woods.

The Demoiselles' initial appearance in May was inspired by the cultural ordering of the calendar, but the continued presence of disguised rioters during the season of patron saint festivals followed a different logic. For one, the rioting developed a momentum of its own, a historical trajectory structured by the largely ineffective attempts to repress it. More important, the coincidence of rioting with patron saint festivals makes sense insofar as those festivals *could* function as occasions of and excuses for revolt. Their function in the revolt was contingent and historically determined, while their meaning was established as part of a narrative drama of the festive year. Yet once engaged in the logic of revolt, the meaning of the patron saint festivals could itself be transformed. Increasingly, both during the War of the Demoiselles and in the course of the nineteenth century, the summer patron saint festivals became more and more like Carnival.

But even this temporal extension of the festive rioting was limited, for the momentum of the rioting died by September, at the heart of the season of patron saint festivals. The Demoiselles quite simply disappeared for three months in the fall of 1829. It was not as if the issues which motivated them had been resolved; in fact, in the season of gathering firewood, the number of disputes with the forest administration increased, as a report of September 1829 suggested:

> Infractions were committed, indictments were drawn up, judgments applying all the articles [of the Forest Code] were pronounced, and delinquents were condemned to enormous fines. Some paid, but a great many without money went to prison, as per article 213 of the Forest Code. There were many unhappy people, and since we prosecute almost 600 incidents each year it is easy to see how many malcontents are in the district [of Saint-Girons].

But as the sub-prefect of Saint-Girons noted at the end of October, "It has been some time since we've seen disguised groups in the Castillonais because they are useless. Freed from the forest administration, absolute masters of the forest, why should the inhabitants have recourse to these armed and disguised assemblies?" The language of the forest administration stressed the *functions* of the "disguised assemblies" in achieving their goal of reclaiming the forest. Yet the functions of the disguise remained secondary: the chronological appearance of the Demoiselles and the logic of their revolt were inspired by the festive calendar. That is why in 1829 the Demoiselles disappeared during the fall months—at the heart of the season of official, established hierarchies the War of the Demoiselles made no sense.

Winter of Discontent

On 10 December 1829, a group of some fifty Demoiselles, in full masquerade and led by several rioters playing drums and horns, chased the royal guards from the forest of Argein. That night, in nearby Audressein, a grange belonging to the forest guard Ribet a few kilometers outside the village was burnt, and the next day, near

Buzan, a group of Demoiselles threatened the guards with certain death as they ran them out of the royal forests. Over the next two weeks, larger groups of rioters, "armed and disguised as women," appeared throughout the villages of the Castillonnais, warning the guards and charcoal-makers to stay away from the forests. By January, the Demoiselles were widely seen throughout the western districts of the Ariège, and they shifted their center to Massat. At Saint-Lary, where the revolt first broke out, the "Captain of the Demoiselles" posted a placard on the church door declaring, with only slight exaggeration, that "the entire department of the Ariège is ours."

The return of the partially disguised peasants, this time in larger and more public gatherings in January and February 1830, and the extensive rioting between February and June 1830 coincided with the winter and spring festivities. In the dualism of the festive calendar, this was the moment of youth and youthful sexuality, which appeared as a disruptive and destabilizing force in the carnival festivities, but which was domesticated and incorporated into the social order at the end of Carnival, during Easter, and in course of the May cycle of feast days. This narrative of disruption and stabilization, of inversion and incorporation during the first half of the festive year, is a story of how the community domesticated the violent, creative, but dangerous forces which lay at the center of its own social and natural reproduction. It is thus a story about the disciplining and domestication not only of violence but also of sexuality and femininity acted out in a village community. The peasant rioters of the Ariège used this calendrical narrative to tell a story about popular justice in a revolt.

But what was the narrative of Carnival about? Carnival stood at the beginning of the winter and spring festivities, forming a cosmological rupture with the staid and official ceremonies of the patron saint festival season. It was "about" many things in nineteenth-century rural society. It was a festival within the Catholic liturgical year, a celebration of "fat days" before the privations of Lent. It was a seasonal festival situated at the juncture of winter and spring, expressing the symbolic and cyclical relations of human fecundity and agricultural renewal. And Carnival was a dramatic and theatrical enactment of the social and political order, pitting disorderly and boisterous youth against the mayor, the priest, and the state. These three dimensions of Carnival were potentially available in the historical enactment of any given carnival celebration.

The Demoiselles first reappeared during the winter of 1829–1830 in early December, long before the climax of Carnival during Mardi Gras ("Fat Tuesday"), which was calculated as forty days before Easter Sunday. (Easter itself was a moveable feast celebrated on the first Sunday following the first full moon after the spring equinox; in 1830 it fell on 11 April.) But Carnival, in its extended calendrical meaning, could be considered the period between December and Easter, the winter celebrations of the end of the year. (Until 1564, the calendar year still began at Easter; in nineteenth-century rural culture, the drama of death and rebirth reproduced this earlier archeological layer of meaning.)

December festivities in rural France during the nineteenth century were in some sense echoes of the ecclesiastically sanctioned Feast of Fools that was celebrated in early December in medieval urban culture. In these rituals of inversion, young clerics undertook many of the festive practices associated with the nineteenth-century rural Carnival: an inversion of official hierarchies, a parody of secular and ecclesiastical rituals and sermons, a period of feasting, dancing, and games. At Easter itself, the "Easter Laughter"—the parodying of the official liturgical rites by young men—was an important ritual of inversion at the heart of the solemn ecclesiastical ceremony. Although the Feast of Fools and Easter Laughter had disappeared by the end of the sixteenth century, the victims of long and persistent condemnations by the church, the period from December to March within rural and urban calendars was the time when the festive languages of the world upside down predominated. Indeed, through the middle of the nineteenth century, every year from December through Easter, an entire group of festive rites can be identified with Carnival and its symbolic, alimentary, sexual, and social expressions and excesses.

Strictly speaking, by definition and timing Carnival was a Christian feast. It represented a period of alimentary abundance before the privations of Lent. Hence its most popularized but probably false etymology: *carne vale* ("farewell to meat"). Carnival *was* a feast. Central to its celebration was an excess of food and drink. In this, and in many other ways, Carnival represented a break with daily life, a festive moment lived differently. In the Ariège, as elsewhere, youth groups made ritual rounds to the houses of the village, collecting "fat" foodstuffs (eggs, lard, pork sausages); on the village squares, they might make gigantic crepes for public consumption.

But the good food of Carnival—the "fat days" opposed to the "thin days" of Lent—was only one manifestation of the excess represented in carnival festivities; indeed, it may well have been the Christian gloss of a more general and unbridled authorization of sexual and social excess. (In a similar fashion, the English word "feast" narrows the French connotations of *fête*, derived from its Latin root *dies festus*, originally designating days consecrated by Numa to the Gods.) Carnival was the moment in which the villagers transgressed the normal rules of social intercourse with sexual and scatological games, songs, and dances. This celebration of violated taboos was common to Carnivals wherever they were held. In Languedoc, carnival games such as "blowing the ass" included young men slinging feces and mud on unwilling villagers. It is important to remember that such carnivalesque forms of sexuality and scatology referred not, as the Russian literary critic Mikhail Bakhtin put it, to the "narrowly sexual, isolated individual" of bourgeois thought, but to the "collective body of the people." The phallic and scatological imagery signified the positive, regenerative, and creative dimensions of bodily functions, dramatizing the movements of death, birth, and resurrection. In this way, carnival rites linked the symbolism of the human body to the seasonal renewal of agricultural fertility.

Carnival, then, as its many commentators have underscored, had a universalizing and cosmic significance; it corresponded to a vision of the world founded on cyclical, recurrent time, in which the community annually reaffirmed its identity and social existence at a critical moment of the calendar year. Carnival offered a disruptive and opposing vision of the social order, the structured, hierarchical vision of society which dominated during the rest of the year. But the time of Carnival was not merely one of "excess" or "disorder," for Carnival represented the momentary replacement of one order by another— the unofficial, egalitarian, "kingdom" of youth.

During Carnival, youth reigned supreme. Frequently masked as wild animals or dressed as women to symbolize the violent and destructive forces of the natural and social orders, youth groups disrupted the official world with their laughter. Village communities tacitly authorized young men in their unruly forms of behavior to perform their songs, dances, and practical jokes. Above all, Carnival, as folklorists and historians consistently stress, was the period of charivaris, of the popular judgments of village youth groups against the past year's infractions of "normal" marital behaviors and alliances.

The world upside down, the symbolic inversions of Carnival, thus parodied the institutions and figures of official culture, the political and ecclesiastical establishments. Festive laughter transformed the language of sovereignty and rule into its own image. In Languedoc, the leader of the village youth group was called "the king of play," consonant with the widespread and longstanding tradition which borrowed the imagery of kingship. In medieval villages, "kingships" were commonly sold or won in sporting competitions; and throughout early modern France, the youthful "king" and his constituted "court" exercised a special kind of authority during the festivities. Whereas their medieval predecessors had satirized and parodied ecclesiastical practices in the Feast of Fools, young men in the villages and towns of the nineteenth-century Ariège, as elsewhere, enacted parodies of civil institutions. Widespread were the "mock courts," trials replete with prosecutors, witnesses, bailiffs, and executioners. These courts sat during Carnival and passed noisy judgments on members of the community who had transgressed accepted forms of behavior. In the Ariège, the primary victims of this popular justice were married couples who had failed to live up to publicly sanctioned codes of conduct during the previous year. As recalled in one account dating from the 1840s:

> The court sat each year in January to judge domestic affairs of the year, and the judgments were executed during the last three days of Carnival . . . Each year it met in order to punish and ridicule through caricature and charivari marriages which diverged from the expected norm. There was a prosecutor, called the "horned attorney," charged with calling witnesses; if these did not come when assigned, they were condemned to be jeered at and made the subjects of little songs, which the people sang in front of their houses. The court sat with the greatest seriousness and dignity. The judge was dressed in a red robe; the bailiff, armed with a pole on top of which were hung two bulls' horns, kept order in the court . . . The members of the *cour corneulo* went in a wagon to the house of the guilty party. They were escorted by individuals who dressed as the unhappily married couple. In front of the house, they undertook a series of highly displeasing ceremonies, with noise and satirical songs improvised for the occasion. (Jalby 1971, 145)

According to other nineteenth-century accounts, the court did not restrict its judgments to domestic (mal)practices. One verse survives from a court in the town of Saint-Girons from the 1820s: in addition to attacking cuckolds, it offers satirical treatments of the parish priest, the "arrogant butcher," and other public figures. Folklorists in the twentieth century, among them Van Gennep, have also noted how easily such carnival practices slipped into "political" attacks on representatives of the wider society. In this sense, Carnival, borrowing heavily from the language of sovereignty and rule, authorized young men to give voice and identity to village communities, to make claims about normative behaviors within the communities against disruptions both from within (mismatched marriages) and occasionally from without (political authorities who failed to meet community standards).

The climax of carnival festivities during the nineteenth-century was the village youths' mock trial and execution of a mannequin, generally made of straw, who in the Ariège was simply called "Carnival" or "Goodman Carnival," and in neighboring Languedoc, "King Carnival." Burned, drowned, sawed in half, or torn apart, Carnival was commonly tried and sentenced first. Sir James Frazer saw the Carnival as the survival of an agrarian cult that marked the end of the year: the mannequin represented a winter god (death) and its execution was realized for the benefit of the next year's crops. The god was put to death by fire, with its symbolic properties of destruction and regeneration, in order to ensure its resurrection with renewed youth and vigor. Others have focused on the role of the mannequin as scapegoat. In any case, the trial and execution of the "Carnival" marked the end of the period of social license and symbolic inversion and the beginning of a phase of disciplining and domestication of the unbridled sexuality and excess of Carnival itself.

In 1829 and 1830, the Demoiselles of the Ariège made explicit and deliberate references to the festivities of Carnival. For example, the traditional right of bands of young men to enter households during the carnival season and demand foodstuffs was universally recognized in rural society during the nineteenth century, and Demoiselles made use of the custom during Carnival in 1830. The Friday before Mardi Gras saw nine disguised men undertake a ritual quest in the town of Massat, stopping at some houses asking for cooked potatoes, and at the house of Marie Icart demanding an egg ("as is the custom here during Carnival," she testified). During March of that year, groups of youthful rioters in Seix continued the practices of Carnival,

demanding sausages, bread, and lard from the villagers. The borrowing of such rites from Carnival was even more apparent in the
case of the Demoiselle who wore a mask "left over from Carnival."

The youthful rioters who demanded "fat" foodstuffs during March
1830 had extended their riotous Carnival far beyond Mardi Gras,
which fell on 23 February. The extension of carnival rites past the
date of Mardi Gras may have been unwittingly sanctioned by the
bishop of Pamiers, who on 6 February had issued a directive which
permitted the consumption of "fat" foodstuffs during Lent. Heavy
rains in September and October and early frosts in November had
destroyed most of the potato crop.

> The rigors of winter that we have experienced destroyed most
> of the edibles with which one is nourished during Lent, and has
> caused those saved to become prohibitively expensive. This has
> led us to decree that for this year alone there will be an indul-
> gence permitting the use of meat during three days of the week:
> Sunday, Tuesday, and Thursday . . . We permit the consumption
> of milk, of butter, and of cheese during the whole of Lent, and
> the consumption of eggs until Ash Wednesday . . . We shall allow
> the use of lard, especially by the poor, to supplement their mea-
> ger foodstuffs.

In taking such an action, the bishop implicitly extended, beyond the
traditional termination of Mardi Gras, not only the alimentary excesses of Carnival, but also its social ones.

Yet the adoption and use of the festive language of Carnival was
not restricted to the carnival season, even in its extended version of
1830; throughout the course of the revolt, the peasants deliberately
put to use the rites of Carnival. On Sunday, 19 July 1829, for example, eight men from the town of Saint-Girons were arrested in Aspet,
in the neighboring department of the Haute-Garonne. They had spent
the day in elaborate disguise, running through the forests of the commune. They returned in the late afternoon to the village inn, where
they spent a quantity of money on drink. According to the arrest
record, they were led by Jean-Baptiste Lafforgue-Vidalou, who called
himself "Captain" and was wearing a military uniform. "He com-
mands the troop of Demoiselles and seems to have a certain authority. He is, in fact, only a peasant who affects to speak French, but
who barely knows the language," reported the royal district attorney.
A second peasant, Jacques Detouilbe, "is known among the Demoi-

selles under the title of 'Executioner' and wears a sort of Harlequin suit." A third, "known by the name of 'Priest,' wears clerical garb, with a square hat on his head. He is the treasurer who paid the expenses of the Demoiselles at the inn. It was his costume that gave strength to the rumor that these Demoiselles were nothing but Jesuits and that these groupings had Jesuits at their head. But the people of Saint Gaudens don't believe in these absurdities."

Such explicit adoption of carnivalesque masquerades and popular judgments was, however, rare; more frequently, the linkage can be seen in the Demoiselles' ritualized and dramatized judgments and punishments of their enemies, the forest guards, modeled on Carnival. Effigies and mannequins themselves were not part of the repertoire of dramatic and symbolic acts during the War of the Demoiselles. Yet the ritual violence and symbolic executions of Carnival became the punishment and "execution" of the forest guards. While not itself a ritual, the violence of the Demoiselles against the guards and workers was ritualized, in the sense that it was at once limited and symbolically constituted. The Demoiselles themselves, or at least their leaders, worked to keep the violence within limits. As the charcoal-maker in Saint-Lary described the attack during April 1830, the band of Demoiselles "would surely have killed me" had not their leader, Jean Tougne, turned on the Demoiselles and, taking aim, shouted, "Don't come any closer or I'll shoot."

But more than simply limited, the violence of the Demoiselles was self-consciously dramatic and symbolic; it was founded on metaphor. In fact, the "victims" and the higher authorities consistently and successfully misinterpreted the language of the peasants. For despite the adamant claims of guards and workers in their court testimonies and verbal reports, the intention of the rioting peasants was not to "commit murder," to "kill," or to "assassinate." Threats themselves were a principal weapon of the revolt as the rioters abused their victims verbally. They claimed to want to "slaughter," "to kill," and, in a carnivalesque inversion, to "turn the guards' eyes inside out" or to turn the stones of their houses "upside down." The proffered written threats and warnings ranged from the taunt "Your hours are numbered" (to the charcoal-makers of Saint-Lary) to the gruesome threat "The limbs [of those who preach against the rioters] will be sent to all the parishes, to better set an example" (to the bishop of Pamiers).

But the peasant rioters sought only a symbolic death: the ritual execution and expulsion of the forest guards and charcoal-makers. The guards and workers were scapegoats, displaced carnival mannequins. Their execution was most often realized in absentia: once the guards had fled, the Demoiselles pillaged, burned, or drowned their wooden furnishings or the wooden fixtures and trim of their houses and shelters in the forests. In June 1829, the Demoiselles near Engomer broke into pieces the furniture and cutlery of a forest shelter; and at Belesta in 1830, the magazines of building wood and wood storage bins were broken up. These wooden objects were variously treated. At the Chateau d'Allens in 1830, they were thrown into the nearby river. The same treatment was reserved for a guard at Prayols, who was threatened by twelve rioters that he would be "hung by his shoulder band and drowned in the water"; at Boussenac, the Demoiselles actually did throw a guard into a nearby river. But more commonly, the wooden objects were taken into the forests and burned, and the cabins themselves were burnt to the ground.

But the revolt itself was not an ordinary "Carnival," even if carnival rituals were an important source of inspiration. In their protest against the forest administration, in their revolt against the forest guards, the rioters adopted many of the practices of Carnival, from the boisterous and laughing rule of youth groups to the disguise as women, albeit in somewhat reduced representations. The War of the Demoiselles was a concrete historical and interested realization of the structure of Carnival. Of course, the rioters held their Carnival outside its customary timing during the festive calendar year. In Fougaron, the rioters enacted their popular tribunal in July 1829; in Seix, they undertook their ritual quests for foodstuffs in late April; and the wooden crosses derived from the May cycle were found in July, November, and March in the various communes of the Ariège. The calendrical rites were practices which the Demoiselles detached from their traditional position within the calendar year and used in the revolt.

Yet the overall patterns of the timing of the revolt still remained connected to the festive calendar year. From September to December 1829, no Demoiselles appeared in the forests. From December 1829 to late June 1830—a period of time which coincided exactly with the festive cycles of Carnival and May—the peasants, "armed and disguised as women," appeared continually in the forests.

Subversive Rite or Safety Valve?

During the carnival season of 1830, the political, judicial, and military authorities, alarmed by the reappearance of the Demoiselles and the increase in rioting during the winter of 1830, were not insensitive to the immediate linkages between Carnival and revolt. Indeed, in January 1830, at the beginning of the carnival season, the mayor of Massat had issued a decree "pertaining to charivaris, songs, and masks," following such "theatrics" directed against "the ministers of religion, people attached to the government"—and especially the mayor himself! Meanwhile, the Ariège prefect issued a general decree "against the wearing of masks" during Carnival. Of course, their efforts were in vain. On 17 February the Demoiselles appeared in Massat, some eight hundred strong, threatening to come back with as many as two thousand "during Carnival." Ten days later, taking advantage of the seasonal festivities, hundreds of peasant rioters in Massat dressed up as Demoiselles and undertook a gigantic charivari in demanding that the forest guards be removed. Marching in formation and following the orders of their "superiors," the Demoiselles adopted in their placards and their actions the language of official rule. As the batalion commander at Foix solemnly reported, "This was not a farce, since I can assure you that concerning February I never joke."

Such attitudes raise questions about the ways in which Carnival was perceived as a subversive practice, both in nineteenth-century peasant culture and more generally as it found expression in rural and urban communities in early modern Europe. On the one hand, historians, following Natalie Davis, like to cite the sixteenth-century French lawyer Claude de Rubys, who offered an early and enduring version, in the metaphors of a preindustrial age, of what modern social scientists call the "safety-valve theory" of festivity: "It is sometimes expedient to allow the people to play the fool and make merry, lest by holding them in with too great a rigor, we put them in despair ... These gay sports abolished, the people go instead to taverns, drink up, and begin to cackle, their feet dancing under the table, to decipher King, princes ... the state and Justice and draft scandalous defamatory pamphlets" (in Davis 1976, 97). Such a view has been well represented among members of the upper classes in western culture, including churchmen, aristocrats, magistrates, and scholars. A version of it—"wine barrels burst if from time to time we do not open them and let in some air"—already appeared in a letter circulated in 1444 by the Paris Theology Faculty permitting the Feast of Fools to be celebrated (in Bakhtin 1968, 75). In one version or another, the "safety-valve" theory of Carnival entered scholarly discourse and found its fullest elaboration in the structural-functionalism of the English

anthropologist Max Gluckman. Gluckman, describing the Swazi Incwala, or "first fruits" ceremony at the end of the calendar year,
underscored how such "rituals of rebellion," during which men
dressed as women and commoners criticized the king, functioned to
shore up a social structure and to reinforce official hierarchies and
the institutional order.

On the other hand, historians and social scientists have been attentive to the ways in which carnival festivities could be truly subversive—indeed, in which they could and did lead directly to protest
and revolt against the social and political order. This particular perception has a long history in western Europe. Denounced by religious
reformers of the Middle Ages, the subversiveness of Carnival was
celebrated within the rediscovery of popular voices by social historians in the 1970s and 1980s. Perhaps the most famous event of a
subversive Carnival in France, a Carnival gone awry, was the annual
festival celebrated in the town of Romans in the Dauphiné during
1580. As described by Leroy Ladurie, the different factions of the
town, artisans and leading citizens, manipulated the language of Carnival and the social organization of the festival. In a context of socioeconomic antagonism and religious war, both sides used the institutions of Carnival at once as the pretext and the constituting language
of their revolt. Unlike the War of the Demoiselles, this insurrection
involved two Carnivals colliding, each with its own festive institutions and symbols; and unlike the Ariège revolt, the social and political conflict had a tragic and bloody outcome, as the town magistrates,
fearing for their lives, arranged the murder of the artisans and their
leaders.

Yet historians and others who claim that the Carnival was by its
nature an oppositional practice, that it was inherently subversive of
the social and political order, simply turn the functional model of
Carnival upside down: in this view, instead of strengthening hierarchies, Carnival worked to subvert them. Even more limiting, in this
perspective, is that although many Carnivals did turn into revolts in
early modern France, an infinitely larger number did not. In fact, the
vast majority of Carnivals, repeated annually in villages and towns
across France, never became the vehicles of revolt or protest, yet revolt and protest were common features of rural life in early modern
France. Of course it is possible, following Yves Bercé and others, to
rediscover elements of the carnivalesque within peasant revolts
throughout early modern France, and to see how the languages of

Carnival actually structured the language and experiences of uprisings. Yet it would be misleading to universalize the argument that the Carnival was a subversive practice, or the contrary—that it was, by its nature, a "safety valve." Clearly, Carnival could and did play both roles in peasant society. Yet once again, these functions cannot exhaust the meanings of the rural Carnival. Instead of looking at the functions of Carnival, one should consider how its instrumentality was in each case presupposed by its symbolic structure and language. The early modern Carnival, with its narrative of disruption and domestication, was available within peasant society to make a range of claims about the social and political order.

The rites of Carnival belong to a category of calendrical festivals outside of Europe, which the disciplines of comparative ethnography and classical philology have usefully illuminated. Accounts by travelers, missionaries, and observers of non-Western cultures since the early modern period describe a range of ceremonies and festivals whose formal features clearly parallel the rural Carnival of early modern and nineteenth-century Europe. The Swazi Incwala ceremony in southeastern Africa, the Apo festival of Northern Ghana, the Milamila rites among the Trobriand Islanders in the South Pacific, and the Makahiki ceremony in traditional Hawaiian culture all shared, with others, certain essential, structural characteristics. So too did the Roman Lupercales—which can thus be added to the list in the spirit of comparative ethnography, and not, as it has in the past, in the antiquarian search for the pagan origins of the European Carnival.

All these festive celebrations took place at the end of the agrarian cycle and marked off a period before the beginning of the new year. Like the rural French Carnival, all symbolically demonstrated a series of links between human and agricultural fertility. At the same time, these festivals described in ritual dramas the social and political order: they constituted festive expressions of the principles of rule and authority. These were communicated in rituals of symbolic inversion, boisterous enactments of the world upside down. In these moments marked by feasting, song, and dance, different forms of social and sexual license gained precedence, as did the ability to criticize and satirize the formal institutions of kingship or chieftainship. The parody of official rule, borrowing the language of sovereignty and relocating it among women or young men or among certain structurally inferior clans, tribes, or social groups, was accompanied by a wealth of rituals of social and sexual reversal—men dressing as women, women dressing as men, social inferiors taking on the trappings of their superiors, and so forth. In all these cases, official hierarchies, institutions, and modes of rule were initially subverted, sociologically and symbolically: these festivals represented the momentary precedence of joyful, boisterous, satirical, laughing rule over the rule of everyday life, located in the persons and institutions of the official hierarchy, which remained judicious, staid, and oppressive.

In this way, the peasant Carnival and its analogues beyond Europe embody what Georges Dumézil called, in his philological account of the language and myths of Indo-European cultures, the "dual representation of sovereignty." Early anthropologists, from Sir James Frazer to A. M. Hocart, have seen the problem of dualism as an even more universal model of the origins and exercise of sovereignty. The rituals describe a model of kingship and rule that appears from outside the community, as an alien and violent usurpation of authority. This usurpation is dramatized by a moment of ritual disorder and chaos, when the world is turned upside down. But this inversion of the world takes its meaning from the fact that it is followed by the symbolic death of the king as he is absorbed and domesticated by the "people." Sovereignty is stabilized; it is returned to its structured, hierarchical principles.

Georges Dumézil calls the two principles of rule enacted in these ritual dramas, following their Roman names, *celeritas* and *gravitas:* they stood opposed as night to day, youthful to mature, creative to conservative, chaotic to ordered. Each was the opposed but necessary condition of the other, and their complementary relationship was played out in the rituals of symbolic inversion at a critical point in the festive calendar year.

Among early modern and nineteenth-century European peasantries, Carnival was the moment during the calendar year when communities articulated the principles of the cosmological order; and within this order, Carnival narrated a story about political authority and rule. The narrative was not as developed as it was, for example, in Hawaii or among the Swazi; it did not involve the explicit act of violent usurpation by an outside power. But during Carnival, male youth groups acted out the disruptive, creative principle; and by executing the carnival king, they domesticated their own violence and stabilized the social and political hierarchies of the established order. It is significant, in this sense, that the festivities following the "world upside down" of Carnival restored the ecclesiastical and municipal

authorities to the top of the social order. During the calendrical celebrations of Easter, it was these established powerholders, and not the
disruptive kingdom of youth, who dominated. True, as commentators, including Sir James Frazer, have long pointed out, this central
moment in the Christian liturgical year contained carnivalesque elements, among them the trial and destruction of the carnival king,
Jesus Christ. Yet such transpositions remained pallid approximations
of Carnival itself: the sovereignty of youth was replaced with the centrality of prepubescent children. More generally, Easter celebrations
describe a community whose identity was defined by the hierarchies
of patriarchy and officialdom.

But after Easter, that official order was again disrupted, only this
time partially and incompletely, during the rites associated with the
month of May, the rites of spring. May represented, in one sense, the
world upside down, insofar as it was identified as the month of the
woman, in opposition to the patriarchal order which dominated during the rest of the year. Yet May represented a new, contained order,
in which the sexuality of young women was consistently checked and
disciplined by the authority of young men.

The festivities and celebrations linked to the feasts of Saint John
and Saint Peter (24 and 29 June) marked a certain resolution of the
drama of the calendar year. In the course of these celebrations, the
principles of boisterous laughter were reincorporated into an established order. Both were transitional feasts. Saint John in particular
marked the culmination of the youthful celebrations of the winter
and spring cycles. At Saint John, youth groups again were central,
but they played a less disruptive and parodic role. Saint John was,
in fact, a festival of courtship, in which pairs of young men and
women would jump over the collective bonfire in a fertility rite assur-
ing the reproduction of the community. Saint John was the logical
and temporal end of the process of domesticating the disruptive and
creative forces dramatized in the first half of the festive year; and with
the feasts of Saint John and Saint Peter, the stable hierarchies of village life were affirmed ritually and socially in the patron saint festivals
that dominated the second half of the festive year.

The Domestication of Carnival

Carnival was the first moment in a festive and dramatic articulation
of different kinds of rule and authority, both within local communities and between local communities and the official institutions of the

church and state. As a story about the village community, Carnival told the tale of the creative and disruptive forces embodied in the boisterous, disorderly, disguised, and laughing group of village youth, who both domesticated and were domesticated by the stable and enduring hierarchies of village life. As a story about the community in relation to the outside world, Carnival narrated the disruption of the staid, judicious, sober, masculine order of the state and church by a youthful, boisterous, disorderly, feminine community; but it was a temporary disruption. Beginning with Mardi Gras, the remainder of the spring festivals dramatized the domestication and disciplining of the creative forces of community, symbolized by the world upside down, and returned that community to its everyday order.

But if this drama of domestication occurred within the cyclical time of the festive calendar, to be repeated year in and year out, it was also revealed in the historical time of rural communities in early modern France. Beginning in the sixteenth century in the context of a greatly expanding state apparatus and the transformations wrought by commercial capitalism, the twinned and contrasting notions of youthful, boisterous sovereignty and staid, judicious sovereignty evolved into a distinctive hierarchical relationship. In apparent contrast to the experiences of parallel rites of sovereignty in African, Polynesian, and Roman societies, Carnival was continually, if unsuccessfully, prohibited in Europe from the sixteenth century. What has been called, since at least Peter Burke, the "reform of popular culture" began with the Protestant and Catholic religious reformers of the sixteenth century and continued with urban magistrates, royal law courts, and the councils of the kings of France. As such, the domestication of Carnival and folk festivities closely parallels the disciplining of charivari, discussed in Chapter 2.

The character of this reform varied widely across religious and cultural boundaries, as well as across time, but it seems clear that around the mid-sixteenth century, both civil and ecclesiastical authorities developed a strict intolerance for the festive practices of popular culture. Before this time, the authorities tolerated and even sanctioned a wide variety of carnivalesque practices; indeed, parodies of court justice, popular judgments, and a range of symbolic inversions were legitimately enacted within the calendar year. As Natalie Davis points out:

In Paris the king might be attacked under his very nose, as in 1516 when the Basoche put on a farce demonstrating that the

Mère Sotte reigned at court and that she was taxing, pillaging, and stealing everything. At Dijon, the 1576 anérie of Mère Folle and her children ridiculed the king's Grand Master of Streams and Forests in Burgundy not only for beating his wife but for devastating for his own profit the forests he was supposed to protect. In Lyon, the Lord of Misprint and his band used their carnival license in the 1580s to protest the folly of religious war, the high costs of bread, and the empty stalls of merchants. (Davis 1975, 118–119)

Yet from the mid-sixteenth century onward, the purveyors of a domi-nant, elite culture were increasingly concerned with disciplining Car-nival and related festivities, and they frequently prohibited the festive "abbeys" in the towns for going too far in their attacks on urban magistrates, officeholders, or the king himself.

Thus in sixteenth-century cities, municipal authorities took in-creasing care to police the festive program, laying claim to the respon-sibility of organizing and shaping such festive organizations to serve their municipal ideals. By the beginning of the seventeenth century, most of the "popular" organizations of confraternities and "abbeys of misrule" had been prohibited, and the role of youth groups and the pervasive feminine imagery which had been central to the enact-ment of Carnival became increasingly muted. In the countryside, where Carnival had never achieved the same kind of institutionalized character, it was nonetheless periodically disciplined and subjugated by the law courts and state officials. Like the charivari, it was sub-jected to fines and punishments which in their severity and frequency suggest the nature of Carnival's threat: the celebration represented a transgression against the organizing principles of the official model of monarchical sovereignty. For as political theorists from the late sixteenth century came to insist on the absolute indivisibility of sover-eignty in the person of the king, so royal officers and urban magis-trates increasingly refused to tolerate and acknowledge the manifesta-tions of a different kind of sovereignty as it found expression in Carnival.

In practice, the prohibitions of Carnivals and charivaris emerged from a wide variety of motives between the sixteenth and the eigh-teenth century. Thus the religious reformers of the early seventeenth century, such as Claude Noiret, Jean Saveron, or Jean-Baptiste Thiers, complained especially about the superstition and disrespect of theological doctrine and practice involved in carnival activities, notably the practice of dressing as women, which was formally prohibited in Biblical texts. For such reformers, Carnival was at once a morally reprehensible practice and an intolerable evidence of the survival of "pagan" rituals in a Christian society. Municipal and royal officeholders and royal councillors, for their part, were more likely to make arguments about public morality and the need to preserve the social order, using the same language against Carnival as they did against its associated practices of charivari. More generally, learned and elite culture developed an ethic, a mode of life, which stood opposed to the "vulgar" and boisterous expressions of festivity found within Carnival. As described by Peter Burke:

> We find in [the sixteenth and seventeenth century] two rival ethics or ways of life in open conflict. The ethic of the reformers was one of decency, diligence, gravity, modesty, orderliness, prudence, reason, self-control, sobriety and thrift, or what Weber called "this worldly asceticism." The traditional ethic is harder to define because it was less articulate, but it involved more stress on the values of generosity, spontaneity, and a greater tolerance of disorder. (Burke 1978, 213)

Burke may have been overly influenced by the German sociologist Max Weber, if not by the moralization of bourgeois consumption patterns put forth by Adam Smith, an eighteenth-century Scot. Yet Burke's claim describes well the opposition, not simply between two "ways of life," but between two languages of authority and two kinds of rule.

The reform of popular culture, in this sense, appeared in conjunction with a notion of "civilization" which began to find expression, first in Christian moralists of the early sixteenth century, and later in the court culture of absolutism during the seventeenth century. As described in different ways by Norbert Elias and Mikhail Bakhtin, the "civilizing process" involved a disciplining and domestication of bodily functions and imagery, and of riotous laughter itself, which increasingly became identified as the uncivilized behaviors of the "people."

This expulsion of Carnival and the carnivalesque from court and aristocratic culture, its transformation into the civilized laughter and festive life of masked balls and spectacles, coincides with the elimination of carnivalesque acts of sovereignty by the king himself.

I have already mentioned the infamous charivari of Charles VI in 1392; as late as 1584, it was still possible for a king of France to exercise, in public, the kind of festive license permitted during Carnival. As the Parisian diarist Pierre de l'Estoile noted, disapprovingly, in February of that year, Henri III and the duke of Anjou

> went together through the streets of Paris, followed by all their favorites and *mignons,* mounted and masked, disguised as merchants, priests, lawyers, etc., tearing about with loose rein, knocking down the people, or beating them with sticks, especially those who were masked. This was because on this day the King wished it to be a royal privilege to go about masked. They went to the fair in Saint Germain, and committed infinite insolences, riotings and disturbing the good people. (Estoile 1958, 99)

But after that, as the ritual regulation of "licensed" behavior developed during the seventeenth century, it would become more and more unthinkable for a king of France to act like a carnival king. As the political theory and practice of absolutism took shape, it refashioned the monarch as the unique source of sovereign authority. Indeed, apologists of the absolute monarchy among the political and religious elite in France stressed, following the later sixteenth-century humanist Jean Bodin, the indivisibility of sovereignty. The result was an increasing intolerance of the dual, alternating, and complementary model of political authority and rule expressed in the annual festive rites of Carnival.

The domestication of Carnival from the early sixteenth to the late eighteenth century followed cycles of alternating repression and toleration. Such cycles were complicated by the different groups—church officials, municipal councillors, royal officeholders—engaged in sometimes contradictory actions within this collective project. Nonetheless, there were two distinct moments during the Old Regime when they came together, moments which also coincided with renewed attempts to police and manage the royal forests of France.

The first was in the middle decades of the seventeenth century, at the height of the Catholic Reformation's offensive against the licentious and superstitious practices of popular culture. Joining the church in its condemnation of Carnivals, the French provincial parlements and the royal council itself renewed their attack on the "disorderly" practice of Carnival and charivari. Early in the reign of Louis XIV (1661–1715), the royal government was engaged in strengthening and deepening the ideal of absolute monarchy. The condemnation of Carnivals and charivaris formed part of this project, as did the attempts to legislate the management of French forests in the 1669 Ordinance. In the course of the seventeenth century, magistrates, clerics, and royal officers refused to sanction the dramatic enactments of the political order as they found expression in local communities during Carnival, just as the king and his ministers in Versailles refused to permit disorderly modes of forest production that ran counter to the ordered rationality of forest management.

The parallel between these two projects of "reform" continued into the eighteenth century; yet during the first part of the century, after the death of Louis XIV, the monarchy seemed to show itself more tolerant of the "disorders" and "superstitions" of Carnival and related festivities as long as these produced no victims of note or any open attacks on the authorities. So too were local peasant practices in royal forests tolerated, at least until the last decades of the ancien régime.

The second moment when church, state, and local officials coincided in their repression of Carnivals and charivaris was during the last decades of the Old Regime. In the 1770s and 1780s, as the French monarchy found its sovereignty increasingly under attack, both Carnival and the forests became the objects of governmental repression and "management." In the years before 1789, the French monarchy and its apologists, assisted by the royal officeholders and clerics, renewed their attack on popular festivals, charivaris, and Carnivals, seeking once again to be the monopoly of indivisible sovereignty. At the same time, and perhaps with even less success, the monarchy renewed its efforts to apply certain provisions of the 1669 Forest Ordinance in France.

The long history of Carnival and charivaris during the early modern period amounted to occasional repression—with justifications shifting away from religion—coupled with a general toleration of disorderly practices if they were not too disorderly. Carnival, as commonly practiced year in and year out in rural culture, remained a narrative of a different and complementary kind of rule on the periphery of the everyday institutions of authority. As a tale of power and authority, Carnival was in its essence neither subversive nor conservative; rather, it was a drama enacted by the peasants themselves that symbolically ordered relations within communities and between communities and the wider society. In any given instance, Carnival could become either a language used to subvert the political order or a "safety valve" to help shore up that order.

At the two moments of relative intolerance during the mid-seventeenth and late eighteenth century, when more actively repressed by the church and state, Carnival took on the status of an oppositional language, which allowed communities to put forth claims of their own against the established authorities. More often, however, Carnival served to reaffirm social and political hierarchies, within the village as well as between the village and the state. Both functions were implicit in the rural Carnival, and both were realized in sometimes unexpected ways in concrete, historical situations.

Spring 1830: Carnival and Class Struggle in the Ariège

What is striking about the uses of carnival customs within the War of the Demoiselles is the extent to which the most explicit borrowings of Carnival coincide with a deepening of the social and political conflict, both within the communities and between the communities and the notables who owned the forests and ironworks. For it was precisely during the much-extended carnival season of 1830 that the first open signs of class struggle became apparent in the mountain communes of the Ariège. In this case, Carnival, far from masking and sublimating social tensions, actually functioned to bring them into the open.

The dramatic intersection of Carnival and revolt in the early spring of 1830 forced the national government to take more drastic measures of repression: in addition to the extra troops brought in, the prefect, acting on orders from Paris, attempted at once an economic and judicial repression of the insurrectionary communes. Truth be told, the judicial repression, originally launched during the summer of 1829, was surprisingly lenient. There were five trials before August 1830, resulting in the indictment of twenty-five men. Of those, only five were caught and one condemned. The courts were remarkably indulgent toward the rioters. At Saint-Lary in March 1830, the district attorney justified himself by claiming that "the facts themselves are well established, but since the royal law court did not have a sufficient case for the accusations against the accused, deceived perhaps by the great number of false witnesses who slipped their testimony into the trial, it was forced to free those individuals indicted."

The only trial that produced a conviction was held at the beginning of March 1830. Widely reported in the national press, the trial centered on a certain Bertrand Cointre, called Falot, of Boussenac. The only one of nine Demoiselles caught in the royal forest of Augirein on 19 August 1829, he was accused of violent theft, setting a fire, and participation in "an association of evildoers." Cointre was eventually sentenced to ten years in prison. But the other trials failed to produce sentences. The band of Demoiselles who had been caught in full masquerade in the woods of Saleich and Fougeron were released on 11 March, again because of the absence of corroborating evidence and witnesses willing to talk. If the Demoiselles and the village communities who supported them did not turn the courtrooms into theaters of carnival celebrations—as several fictional reconstructions of the revolt suggest—they nonetheless rendered them ineffective.

It was at this point, in early March 1830, that the departmental authorities, acting on orders from Paris, attempted to institute an economic repression. On 15 March, the prefect announced that the municipal councils were legally responsible for damage done to private property within their territory. The fines—as high as 20,000 francs in the commune of Boussenac, 24,000 francs for Ustou, and 41,600 francs for Massat—were to be paid by the twenty wealthiest proprietors, who were then to be reimbursed.

What resulted was the division of the village communities and the small towns more deeply along class lines: as many officials were to note, those responsible for putting up the fines were the doctors, notaries, shopkeepers, and larger proprietors. These were the men who had originally backed the uprising because, in part, it protected their interests in stockraising. After March 1830, they publicly opposed the Demoiselles.

The economic repression, far from calming the village communities, seemed only to escalate the intensity and gravity of the rioting. More repression brought on more serious actions by the rioters, especially as the Demoiselles spread eastward from the Castillonnais, shifting their center to Massat and the upper Ariège river valley in the pays de Foix. The character of the conflict began to change from the more playful and dramatized encounters between masked rioters and forest guards and charcoal-makers that had characterized the War of the Demoiselles since 1829. No longer content to chase forest guards and charcoal-makers from the forests, the peasants began to focus their opposition on the local notable owners of forests and ironworks, proprietors whose rapacious greed in exploiting the forests and restricting usufruct rights was recognized even by the authorities.

Already in mid-February 1830, the sub-prefect of Saint-Girons reported rumors that the peasants were going to rise up and "assassinate the rich." For the authorities, such fears evoked the memory of the experience of the French Revolution. "All this seems to resemble that which took place in 1790 and 1793, and one should fear the same results if we don't take measures that such a state requires," commented the sub-prefect. Such fears were clearly exaggerated, but on 13 March, in an event that had been talked about publicly for some weeks, sixty to eighty armed and disguised Demoiselles assaulted the Caplong farm belonging to the Lafont family in Boussenac. Lafont had bought the mountain of Peguère, where the farm was situated, during the Revolution, and he was involved in litigation with the surrounding villages over their pasturing rights there. During the attack, the sharecroppers were allowed to leave with their possessions, after which the Demoiselles pillaged the buildings, beehives, fruit trees, and properties. Economic repression was applied, with the result that for two consecutive nights after 3 April the Demoiselles returned to complete the destruction.

At the same time, there were signs that the "disguise" as Demoiselles was becoming, to some rioters, more of a liability than an asset. The description of the disguise and the definition of the Demoiselles as an "association" within the published and posted decree of February 1830 tended to reify the costume as a sign of rioting. According to the sub-inspector of forests in March 1830, the publication of the prefect's decree naming the rioters an "association" made the local inhabitants "no longer want to disguise themselves," but instead to hide in the forest and "shoot us dead," according to a forest guard. Or, as the sub-prefect reported in a letter to the mayor of Castelnau-Durban, "Those of my commune have unmasked their feelings and intentions: they breathe only, for the most part, revolt and pillage with all the accompanying horrors."

Of course, such statements reveal as much about the mentality of local and political officials as they do of the Demoiselles' intentions. In fact, the Demoiselles clearly raised the level of anxiety of the officials and of the rural forest owners, both in their threats and in their actions. Yet they did so within the language of Carnival; as the elements of Carnival became more explicit within the War of the Demoiselles in February and March 1830, so too did the class dimensions of the conflict. The result was a politicization of the revolt in a new and unexpected way: officials and administrators in Paris began to see the forces of politics at work. During April and May, the Demoiselles of the eastern Couserans and the pays de Foix continued their actions in the forest, directing their anger more often toward the charcoal-makers than the guards. Yet by early June, the frequency of their attacks slowed significantly, even as officials in Paris began to demonstrate greater concern for the events in the Ariège. For the growing political crisis in Paris during the summer of 1830 inevitably colored the perception of the War of the Demoiselles, just as the outbreak of the Revolution in Paris at the end of July transformed the language of revolt and opposition to the government, both in the Ariège and throughout France.

4. REVOLUTION UNMASKED

n 15 April 1830, a two-act melodrama entitled *Les Demoiselles* opened at the Théâtre de la Gaité, a boulevard theater in Paris. The playwrights described its backdrop as "that veritable plague of society . . . a rather large band of thieves who, under the name and costume of the most amiable and gentle sex, undertook all the horrors of banditry." The drama took place in an unspecified site somewhere "around Carcasonne," although theater directors were authorized by the playwrights "to locate the play in the departments where the Demoiselles are known." This geographic slippage was intended to reinforce the perceived threat that, in the context of a growing political crisis, "banditry" similar to that in the Ariège was spreading throughout France, occasioned in part by the economic downturn of the years after 1827.

Les Demoiselles, however, told the less threatening story of domestic morals in the household of a bourgeois tax-collector and his wife. It was, in fact, a standard melodrama about mistaken and manipulated sexual identities. In the course of the play, the tax-collector mistook the young milkmaid for a disguised criminal, while a "young [male] Spaniard, without family, home, or hearth," disguised himself as a woman to fleece the tax-collector, who was all too willing to stray from the path of domestic virtue. As it turned out, both the tax-collector and the criminal saw through the disguise, the thief was unmasked, the moral order restored, and the melodrama ended happily—although it did not run for long. The critical reception was far from enthusiastic: not only was the execution deemed "weak," but the "mysterious figures" on which the play was based were said to be "less faithfully portrayed than they were in the judicial trial" of Bernard Cointre, about which a literate Parisian public had just been informed. The play closed after two weeks.

Les Demoiselles was the first literary rendering of the peasant revolt in the Ariège, a revolt which has since inspired almost a dozen dramatic works. Yet as close in time as it was to the events themselves, it was also the furthest in space—geographic space, of course, but also social, political, and cultural distance. In 1830, the bourgeois milieu in Paris out of which the play emerged and the peasant culture of the Ariège where the riots took place were distinct; the differences between them appeared in the way that the same play on sexual inversion was used in different media toward widely divergent ends. Whereas the playwrights (unsuccessfully) used the imagery of sexual inversion in a melodrama which preached submission to the social order and conformity to bourgeois morality, the peasant men (more successfully) partially represented themselves as women in defense of notions of peasant and communal justice and in disobedience to and subversion of that same bourgeois order.

But less than six months later, these two settings and cultures revealed more in common than either peasants or Parisians might have expected. In the revolutionary moment of July 1830—a Parisian event with profound provincial consequences—peasant and middle-class Parisians borrowed from each other the languages of revolution and of folk culture. The July Revolution of 1830 established the liberal monarchy of Louis Philippe. Although historians often dismiss its slight political impact, the 1830 Revolution was a critical event in redefining the relations between bourgeois and popular culture in France. For just as it forced the Ariège peasantry into a world of national political developments, so too did it provide the occasion for the political classes of France—and especially a nascent republican middle class—to draw its political language and imagery from popular cultural practices, a movement which culminated in 1832 when the journalist Charles Philipon and the lithographer Honoré Daumier reworked this grammar of folk culture into lithographic satire in the daily newspaper *Le Charivari*.

This chapter differs from previous ones, in that it takes a more or less Cartesian path, a straighter line out of the forests of the Ariège, moving back and forth between Paris and the Pyrenees. Here, I leave the worlds of the forest and of the cyclical festive time of peasant culture to consider the War of the Demoiselles in historical time, as a local version of the 1830 Revolution. Unlike previous chapters, this one looks directly at the notion of "politics" and political discourse and reconsiders their relation to "popular culture," symbolized by the already familiar, noisy, ritual judgments of charivari. I am concerned here with the ways in which these separate languages, of politics and popular culture, were symbolically linked in the aftermath of a revolutionary moment.

Between 1829 and 1832, the language of charivari moved back and forth from Paris to the provinces, across class lines, through different media, and along the shifting boundaries of the political. The practices and representations of charivari from the War of the Demoiselles to the founding of *Le Charivari* thus evoke a long-standing concern of French historians of the early modern period: the appropriations between "learned" and "popular," between high and low cultures. I have already suggested one such example in my brief account of fairy beliefs as they circulated across cultural boundaries. So too in the nineteenth century did folk beliefs and practices move back and forth across social strata. They did so, however, in an independent and unacknowledged way. As I shall show, the exchanges of bourgeois notions of liberty and popular practices of charivari took place without an awareness of the parallel and symmetrical character of the exchange.

The exchanges of charivaris took place across a set of intersecting boundaries: between peasant and bourgeois culture, rural and urban society, the provinces and Paris, oral traditions and the commercial production of texts. Moreover, these exchanges occurred in a post–early modern world, at a moment of revolution, in a new political setting. The 1830 Revolution in France and the consolidation of the bourgeois monarchy produced a collapse and reconstitution of high and low cultural gestures and performances while it redefined in enduring ways the languages—verbal, textual, gestural, and visual—of politics. In particular, peasants and urban middle classes used the practices and representations of charivari in a variety of media, helping to give shape to the language of republicanism and the republican tradition in France.

The Politics of Charivari

The status of rural popular culture in early-nineteenth-century France can be traced briefly by following the fate of post-revolutionary urban and educated elite perceptions of charivari. The politicians of the French Revolution and their successors adopted a decidedly ambivalent stance toward folk culture as exemplified in charivari and the symbolic expressions of Carnival more generally. While the Old Regime monarchy had shown itself intensely concerned, in its dying decades, with policing and punishing popular festivities, the new revolutionary governments—founded on the indivisible sovereignty of the people united as a nation—concerned themselves with such otherwise trivial matters only when they became the explicit vehicles of popular opposition. Both urban and rural popular revolutionary movements drew on a wealth of practices involving popular judgments and justice, many of which were inspired by charivari and Carnival, although this feature of the popular revolution has yet to find its historians. Thus there was much in the French Revolution that was "charivariesque," as a nineteenth-century opponent of both charivari and the Revolution was to argue. Yet at the height of the Revolution, the Jacobin leadership's explicit condemnations of carnivalesque practices were relatively rare. In August 1793, the commander of the Rhine army informed the National Convention that in July some men, dressed as women, had joined a largely female gathering demanding bread in front of the bakers' shops, an incident which recalls certain men disguising themselves among the market women of Paris who marched to Versailles in October 1789. Four years later, however, the Convention decreed the death sentence for "any men found in gatherings disguised as women." Then, beginning in late November 1793 and lasting two months, the "Masquerades of year II," as the events became known, gave shape to the dechristianizing projects of the popular revolutionary sections. In a revolutionary refashioning of the medieval Feast of Fools, the popular activists of Paris parodied in burlesque processions the ecclesiastical hierarchy and the church liturgy. Although Robespierre and the Jacobins were strongly anticlerical, they condemned the atheism, destruction of religious objects, and disorder of the popular "masquerades."

In the post-revolutionary political and legal order, however, masquerades and charivaris lost their ability to draw the attention, much less the wrath and fear, of the ruling classes. In legal terms, the charivari was far from subversive. Unlike the Old Regime, which prosecuted and prohibited charivaris as "royal cases," the governments that emerged from the French Revolution would only treat the rural rites as instances of "nocturnal noise," prohibited by several statutes of the Civil Code of 1804. The Code thus trivialized the charivari, all but dismissing the male youth groups' customary rites of judging mismatched marriages.

Of course, in the eyes and ears of prefects and ministers, the charivari was considered a "disorder worthy of times of ignorance and barbarism." The "disorder" mentioned, however, was less a repetition of the Old Regime monarchy's fear of disorder, last voiced in the 1770s and 1780s, than a newer defense of privacy within a bourgeois code of morality. A man's (and even perhaps a woman's) choice of marital partner, a couple's domestic life, were private, not public matters. And the charivari was not a practice that belonged in the public sphere. That is why the charivari contained nothing specifically political, in the narrow bourgeois sense of politics.

For the authorities, the "political" concerned anything pertaining to electoral politics—committees, associations, journals—implicating directly the persons of kings, ministers, and deputies. It was the domain of educated men in the towns, not illiterate peasants in the countryside. According to the worldview of those in power, charivari could not be political because of its origins: it belonged to the realm of the vulgar, popular classes. As the prefect of Finistère wrote, concerning a charivari in Brest during May 1827, "These sorts of events provoked by local customs are never very serious . . . since politics is foreign to them, and by consequence they are not led by instigators, they usually end in the circumstances in which they were born." Politics, in this construction, came from Paris and concerned the parties which divided elite opinion: it was imposed from the center, not generated from below. Charivari came from the provinces, or from the urban lower classes, and concerned only rural, illiterate, peasant communities, or the rabble of the cities.

Yet by the early 1820s, and increasingly during the years preceding the 1830 Revolution, administrative authorities became more conscious of a linkage between charivari and a certain kind of political subversion. Evidence of this shifting concern may be found in a dossier constituted in 1830 by the interior ministry entitled "Charivaris." It consisted of administrative correspondence referring to some twenty-two separate incidents from villages and small towns all over France, including the Ariège, between 1824 and 1830. Most of these events took place during the carnival season. All the charivaris involved the customary victims: men who remarried too soon after having lost their wives, widows who married younger men, widowers who married younger women. In these cases, the "injurious songs," "tumultuous assemblies," and "profane insults" of the instigators— generally masked young men—had gotten out of hand, and complaints were filed by the victims, who were usually wealthier and more powerful members of the communities.

If the local judicial and administrative authorities tended to dismiss the cases, considering them local practices which would eventually disappear, they nonetheless denounced these "old customs" of village culture as "reprehensible," if not outright dangerous. Charivaris might even, as a decree in January 1826 by the Aude prefecture suggested, lead to popular revolts. It was not simply, as the *Gazette des tribuneaux* had reported in March 1829, that "charivaris are becoming more than ever à la mode; it is a growing taste. Until now these scandalous scenes had been relegated to the countryside; and one wouldn't have expected that such disorders could introduce themselves into the town." Rather, as Rolande Bonnain-Moerdyx and Daniel Moerdyx suggest, far from being a mere folkloric rite, the charivari should instead be understood

> in the context of the struggle between communities of customary right and the new class of individuals reclaiming written law . . .; as a struggle between villages ruled by customs, and towns which incorporate them into their networks; as a struggle between the local and the national, and in the last resort, between the community and capitalism. The charivari, far from the ideal figure that ethnologists and folklorists have constructed, is crossed and constituted by the conflict of two spaces and two times, two ways of organizing the land, work, and festivals, two powers. (Bonnain-Moerdyx and Moerdyx 1977, 382)

The subversive character which official culture attributed to the popular practices of charivari in the 1820s constituted an initial politicization of the rite. The fear of charivari, and its definition as a practice opposed to the bourgeois order, formed the backdrop of the Ariège peasantry's use of the rituals of popular justice in challenging the authority of the state and, increasingly, of the local representatives of the dominant classes.

Yet before the 1830 Revolution the Demoiselles of the Ariège— like the practitioners of domestic charivaris—posed no specifically political threat to the government of Charles X. The judicial, administrative, and military officials concerned with repressing the peasant revolt insisted on seeing the events as "completely alien to political affairs," having nothing to do with the "spirit of party" that belonged exclusively to the educated, "civilized" classes of the towns. Thus the prefect reported to the interior minister in September 1829 that the youth of well-to-do classes in the towns of the Ariège (Pamiers, Foix, and Saint-Girons) were generally imbued with the principles propagated in liberal newspapers; the revolt of the peasants, however, was "foreign to all aspects of party politics." It was true that in Massat, on 27 January 1830, nearly four hundred disguised peasants armed with guns and hatchets, their faces blackened, had gathered in the town square, where they chanted, "Long live the king, down with the forest administration." And in a letter to the mayor of Augirein in March 1830, the Demoiselles wrote: "You have been warned, *méssieurs du gouvernment,* that if you do not destroy the forest guards you will see a great war in France before too long. Long live the emperor, long live the Demoiselles. Death to the government of France." But to officials—as to historians who have interpreted these events—such utterances reflect only a lack of political sophistication, a distance and disengagement from the contemporary political sphere. Only one official during the revolt, the royal district attorney of the neighboring Haute-Garonne department, where the Demoiselles had been cited in the spring of 1829 during the first days of the revolt, became convinced otherwise. In early July 1830 he wrote that "the enemies of the king now take part in these events," instigating "sinister and inconceivable noises concerning the intentions of the king's government." "Sinister looking men from Paris, armed with knives, have come to foment disorder, and are running around the department of the Ariège, instigating the most seditious peasants." The political content of the revolt, as that of charivari, would have to come from above, from the middle classes, or from Paris; only popular, "barbaric," and "disrespectful" gestures originated from below, from peasants, and from the provinces. The July Revolution was to redefine these terms and their relationship.

Unmasking Revolution

Strictly speaking, the French Revolution of July 1830 was a Parisian affair. The 221 deputies who in March opposed Charles X and his minister, the prince de Polignac, in defense of the Charter and what

they believed to be their fundamental political liberties; the dissolution of the Chamber of Deputies in May; and the Four Ordinances
reducing the electorate and imposing new press restrictions in July
were not debates that mobilized the peasants of the Ariège, or of
France more generally. And although the crowd that acted to over-
throw the monarchy included many working-class people, inspired
by their own interpretation of revolutionary liberty and legitimate
authority, the *Trois Glorieuses*—the "Three Glorious Days"—nonetheless presented themselves as a fait accompli in provincial life.

The traditional view of the 1830 Revolution was that, like the category of politics itself, it came from Paris and was imposed on the
provinces. Provincial France, in this interpretation, generally welcomed and accepted the change of regime and the terms of the Revolution established by Paris, such that by December 1830, the Revolution was over. In recent years, historians of French provincial life
have suggested the ways in which the July Days initiated a new period
of political protest and economic grievances. Yet little has been said
about the ways in which the Revolution transformed the language
of provincial protests, and how it restructured the character of oppositional politics in Paris itself.

The arrival of the news from Paris in the Ariège during the first
week in August produced "no troubles, and much confidence"—if
we are to believe the frequently self-serving reports sent by the mayors of the communes of the three districts to the departmental administration. "Never have the cliffs next to the commune so resounded
with the celebratory shouts which were the echoes of this immutable
achievement: the shouts, a thousand times repeated, of 'Long live the
duke of Orléans,' 'Long live the nation,' and 'Long live liberty,' were
heard in all the hamlets of the commune," wrote the mayor of Mer-
cus. But if the political news was initially received "with the calm
and submission which suits the peaceful inhabitants of the countryside," as the mayor of Augirein claimed, in the weeks after the Revolution more troubling events took place.

The July Revolution had the effect of accelerating the shifts, first
evident in February 1830, in the character of the festive rebellion.
The Demoiselles were now more likely than ever to attack the properties of rural notables—the forest and forge owners—and the peasant
community to confront more explicitly its class enemies. When the
news of the Revolution arrived in early August, a group of peasants
attacked the chateau of Jerome Stanislas d'Astrié of Gudanes, a forge

owner and mayor of the commune, who had recently taken the commune to court in an attempt to restrict their use-rights in the forest. On 20 August, the mayor of the town of Ax reported that four to five hundred peasants had gathered at the Luzenac ironworks "to do what they call 'justice' [*faire justice*]" against its owners. On 22 August, the mayor of Ax reported to the provisional administration that "a large gathering invaded the town hall and demanded in the name of liberty that M. le marquis d'Orgeix give them their use-rights in the forests that they had fifty years ago; that M. Astrié of Costellet give up his project to delimit the royal forests to the detriment of their use-rights; that they have no more forest guards; and that the excise tax on drink no longer be levied, all under penalty of death and pillage."

The peasants expanded the goals of their rioting beyond the elimination of forest guards and charcoal-makers, as they had already begun to do before the revolutionary moment of 1830. They confronted directly the forge owners and, beyond the forest guards, other agents of the state. At Sein, a band of disguised men attacked the offices of the state mine tax bureau, ransacking them and taking registers out into the street on 23 and 24 August. At Massat, a billboard threatening tax-collectors was affixed to their offices on 12 August. At Vicdessos, on Sunday, 22 August, a band of peasants, apparently instigated by the town innkeepers concerned with the excise tax on drink, invaded the office of indirect taxes and burnt the registers.

Yet the most dramatic undertakings were reserved for the wealthy notables—noble families from the Old Regime and bourgeois heirs of their estates—in the eastern valleys of the department, where the feudal system had been more entrenched than in the west. In the middle of August, under the aegis of the new municipal administration, the commune of Miglos "invaded" the forest lands belonging to Jean Louis Hayacinthe de Vendemois, who had been involved in litigation with the inhabitants over their use-rights to the forest, which they exploited as "communal lands." According to de Verdemois' account, the inhabitants then took him hostage on 15 August, holding him for four days while they demanded the titles to the land. They released him only when the prefect held the new mayor responsible for their actions.

Elsewhere in the eastern districts of the Ariège, under the shadow of the July Revolution, the peasants openly attacked the properties and houses of wealthy landowners. On 27 August, the mayor of Lavelanet wrote to the commander of the gendarmérie at Foix about the events of Belesta, describing the "pillage" of the properties of the richest proprietors. Meanwhile, in the commune of Luzenac, the mayor feared the worst, because Sunday, 20 August was the local patron saint festival. His instincts were correct, for in broad daylight, some four hundred peasants from the communes of Lordat, Appy, Axiat, and Canac—all apparently unmasked, led by drums, horns, fifes, and armed with hatchets, clubs, and guns—went to the chateau of the count of Lordat-Bram at Luzenac to ask for their use-rights to the woods and mountains of Lourdans. Unsatisfied, they turned to his ironworks and trashed his chateau, committing seventy-one thousand francs in damages. The next day, a dozen peasants from Saint Concac went to the house of Lordat's administrator and ransacked his library, from which they took books, family archives, titles, and other papers, reclaiming their rights to the woods of Sr. Lordat.

The events struck terror in the hearts of the rich forest and ironworks owners, for they went far beyond the assaults on forest guards and charcoal-makers that had characterized the War of the Demoiselles in its earlier stages. According to the mayor of Lavelanet, writing to the provisional administration on 28 August, the richer proprietors within the villages distanced themselves from the revolts out of fear for their interests and fortunes. Yet the most original feature of the riot in the aftermath of the July Revolution was the disappearance of the disguise as women. As General Lafitte wrote to the war minister on 22 August 1830, "The Demoiselles are now completely unmasked and show themselves entirely uncovered."

It was not a completely accurate assessment, since there were occasional appearances of masked bands, such as the "masked and armed gathering" which took place in Ganac on Sunday, 18 September, and a few of the rioters who attacked Sr. Vendomois' chateau at Miglos were, according to witnesses, "armed and disguised as women." But generally speaking, the military commander was correct: the riotous actions of fall 1830 were undertaken largely by armed but undisguised peasants.

Why should this have been so? John Merriman has argued that the disappearance of the disguise occurred as the Demoiselles sought legitimacy for their riotous actions in the events of the July Revolution. There is some truth, as we shall see, to this proposition. Yet the disappearance of the mask was structured by two logics and two experiences of time: the cyclical festive time of nineteenth-century popular culture and the linear historical time of political revolution. After all, from September to December 1829, virtually no peasants, masked or otherwise, undertook collective actions against the forest guards. When the disguise disappeared again in the late summer and fall of 1830, then, it was according to a logic structured in part by the festive dualism of the peasant calendar year. Indeed, when the Demoiselles reappeared in the forests between January and March 1831, they were once again masked, and nearly every one of the sporadic reappearances of Demoiselles until 1900 took place between February and May.

But the disappearance of the masks between August and December 1830 also made reference to the historical time, and the political memory, of revolution. For the revolutionary moment of July and August 1830 provided an exceptional occasion during which the peasants sought to legitimate their actions, in reference not to the popular rites of Carnival and charivari, but to their collective experience and memories of the French Revolution of 1789 and after.

For the peasants of the Ariège, as for all social groups in France, the July Revolution took on meaning as part of the revolutionary tradition: it instantly evoked memories of the first revolution, which destroyed the Old Regime. The peasants focused their collective memory of the French Revolution on the radical moment of 1792, the revolutionary Republic. For them, that memory included two distinct dimensions. First, the experience of the Revolution had meant a return to communal possession of the forests, the removal of the forest guards and other obstacles to their free enjoyment of the forest itself. The memory of the Revolution recalled a moment of freedom, both from monarchy and in the struggle against their seigneurs.

Second, during the radical, republican phase of the French Revolution, the peasants of the Ariège attacked and pillaged the chateaux of aristocrats. In September 1792, crowds of several hundred peasants pillaged the properties of seigneurs in Brassac, Benac, and Ganac, in the old pays de Foix. In August and September 1830, it was the class heirs of these noble families, the notable owners of the ironworks and forests, whose properties and persons were singled out. When the riotous peasants modeled their actions on the earlier revolutionary moment, they had no need to disguise themselves as women: instead, they could claim to be acting in the name of revolutionary liberty. Thus the letter received in October 1830 by one such bourgeois descendant of the Old Regime lords, M. Ferreras, owner of the Esque-ranne ironworks at Saurat, read: "The head of the regiment of De-moiselles has the honor of informing you that the ironworks which are close to the forest shall be entirely destroyed, and yours is one of them. *Vive la liberté*."

Clearly, liberty meant different things to different social classes. In the artistic and literary expressions of French political culture, the figure of liberty was represented as a woman: thus Delacroix's fa-mous painting of the July Revolution, *Liberty on the Barricades*. It was a similar (en)gendering of liberty that led General Lafitte to de-clare, in a published plea for order addressed to his fellow citizens in the Ariège: "Oh Liberty! Our brave mountain-dwellers, while adoring you, could well tarnish your snow-white robe." For the peas-ants, however, the idea of liberty within the revolutionary tradition was masculine, in the sense that it was a notion fought over by (undis-guised) men. The idea of liberty evoked a condition and a memory which rendered the "disguise as women" quite literally meaningless. The Ariège peasants thus tucked in their white shirts and employed a different language of resistance.

"The latest events," wrote the minister of the interior to the war minister on 16 September 1830, "have made [the Ariège peasants] believe easily that liberty was the liberation from the laws." To the peasants, liberty did mean a liberation from the oppressive regime of the state as well as the freedom to enjoy, unrestricted, their customary rights to the forest. To the authorities, this looked like anarchy and disorder. The mayor of Prayoles wrote to the prefect that "the liberty which His Majesty Philip I has just given to the French nation has been misinterpreted by our mountain peasants, because they believe themselves to be authorized to violate the laws, and undertake inces-santly all the disorders one could possibly imagine committing against the forest administration." But to the peasants, *liberté* had a historically constituted meaning: it meant the *libertés* (plural) of the Old Regime, a set of traditional rights and privileges to the forest which the post-revolutionary world increasingly threatened.

Paradoxically, then, for the Ariège peasantry in 1830, the idea of liberty made simultaneous reference to the world of the Old Regime and to that of the First French Republic, when the peasants had re-taken possession of "their" forests. An official thus described just a few years later the republican tradition among the peasantry. "The word 'republic' has deep resonance in the spirit of the population because it is immediately translated into a capacity to do *everything* with impunity, to render themselves masters of the public or private forests and to break the yoke of laws protecting property." To the Ariège peasants, the memory of the First Republic signified popular rule, even if it blurred with a memory of the more distant seigneurial and royal authority of the Old Regime itself. The result was an image of a revolutionary Golden Age, a moment when the peasants had been able to "render themselves masters," to claim their sovereign control of the forest, and to attack the properties of the members of the upper classes who sought to restrict their rights. It was this popular republicanism that the peasants sought to revive in the 1830 Revolution, abandoning the language of charivari in the process.

At the same time, more educated and electorally minded inhabitants of the Ariège found it useful, in a moment of revolution, to don the "mask" of the Demoiselles as a threatening weapon within the political arena. In a letter to the new provisional administration of the department at the end of August 1830, the "Captain of the Demoiselles" announced their support of three candidates for the municipal elections in Saint-Girons:

To the Honorable Counselors of the Foix Prefecture:

The revolutionary colors [are the] unique hope for our liberties. Our beautiful dreams have been shattered. If Géraud, Descolns, Souquet are elected, the Demoiselles of Soulan will rise up following the example of Paris and Ustou to destroy the party of the absolutists, and Soulan will liberate itself from its irons . . . Avoid such disasters. We would like as mayor and adjunct people of wise liberal views. Not having the time to attach four to five hundred signatures from liberals and Demoiselles, [signed] the Captain of the Demoiselles.

In its style, language, and substance, the letter is unlike any of those previously sent by the Demoiselles. It reflects a set of interests and concerns explicitly identified with the political liberalism of the educated electorate; yet the strength of the letter's threat draws on the identification of its author with the past activities of the masked rioters.

The letter is a modest example of how, in the aftermath of 1830, middle-class opposition to the new regime drew its language and claims from representations of the popular classes. As the next section suggests, this borrowing was widespread throughout France. With the news of the July Revolution, the peasants of the Ariège temporarily dropped the gestures of charivari and the caricatured disguise as women and adopted, according to their own needs and concerns, the language of republican liberty. Conversely, in the years after the 1830 Revolution, in Paris and in provincial towns across France, the middle-class republican opposition to the new regime turned its attention to the caricatured images and practices of folk culture and charivari.

The Charivari of Politics, 1830–1834

On 1 December 1832, Charles Philipon launched the satirical and illustrated daily *Le Charivari*. The newspaper featured the lithographs of Honoré Daumier and drew on the work of other young artists and writers in Paris, including Grandville, Traviès, and (anonymously) Balzac. *Le Charivari* was intended as a commercial venture to sustain its immediate predecessor, *La Caricature,* which was founded in the aftermath of the July Revolution and then floundered under the weight of heavy fines and prohibitive newspaper taxes. For as the promise of the July Days faded quickly, the electorate remained, after the 1831 law, tiny (less than .5 percent of the population), and demonstrations, if allowed, could be violently repressed. Slowly but surely, the government reimposed censorship of the press, culminating in the September laws of 1835. The government of Louis-Philippe and the National Assembly quickly became synonymous with the rule of "order" and the Juste-Milieu. In these conditions, as historians of the cultural politics of the early July Monarchy have shown, commercial lithography was part of the politics of opposition, as Daumier, Philipon, and others fought their "war of disrespect" against the successive governments of the July Monarchy.

But why should Philipon have named his journal *Le Charivari* in December 1832? And what was the content of Daumier's politics expressed in his lithographic satire? The representations and practices of the codes of charivari and other tropes of French popular culture— carnivalesque laughter, symbolic inversion, and so forth—were central to the constitution of a certain kind of republican politics between 1830 and 1832. In fact, the case of *Le Charivari* appears to be a mirror image of what happened to the Demoiselles: just as the peasants of the Ariège in the fall of 1830 temporarily abandoned the practices of charivari and the mask in favor of a revolutionary language of liberty, so did middle-class opponents of the regime invent their republican politics of liberty in the years after 1830 through borrowing the representations of folk cultural practices, and especially charivari.

La Caricature, using the relatively novel techniques of lithography, was hardly itself an organ of a democratic and popular politics. The journal was begun with the intention, as Philipon later wrote, of publishing a lighthearted satirical review caricaturing contemporary social habits. It was produced by the utterly respectable Maison Aubert, owned by Philipon's brother-in-law, and located on the Parisian right bank among the most fashionable bookshops, cafés, theaters, and spectacles. The original intent of *La Caricature* was to sell prints to a growing middle-class market; the journal was available only by subscription, and it cost fifty-two francs a year, at a time when a worker averaged three francs a day. Caricature became unambiguously oppositional in the spring of 1831, when the government raided the editorial offices of *La Caricature,* confiscated the printed journals, and brought Philipon to trial in June for crimes against the person of the king. But the politics of *La Caricature* remained those of the middle-class critics of the regime.

The criticisms of *La Caricature,* then, were first of all directed toward the conditions of its publication: the publishers and artists sought to uphold the ideal of a free and uncensored press, a right guaranteed by the Charter of 1830, which decreed that "censure should never be established." The ideal was far from the reality, for between August 1830 and October 1834, there were 520 separate press trials, resulting in 188 convictions. In their claims to defend the political liberties of a free press, Philipon and Daumier's politics coincided broadly with the other organs of the nascent republican press, including *La Tribune* and *Le National.* The latter was founded in January 1830, financed by the banker Lafitte, and supported by liberal and opportunist peers, including the baron de Talleyrand. After the July Revolution, *Le National* gave voice to a moderate electoral opposition, and only under the ministry of Casimir Périer, in early 1832, did it begin to use the word "republic." The republican press of the early July Monarchy had its counterpart in political associations, the secret societies which incorporated much of the republican opposition to the Juste-Milieu. The most moderate of these was *Aide-toi et le ciel t'aidera* ("Help Yourself and Heaven Will Help

You"), founded before the July Revolution, with local committees in thirty-five departments by November 1832. Its membership was made up for the most part of middle-class supporters of more progressive electors and deputies, and its politics remained centered around the legal opposition to the government's budgets and electoral issues. The association *Aide-toi,* like the opposition newspapers *Le National* and *La Caricature,* expressed a more moderate and middle-class republicanism than the radical republican associations, including *Amis du peuple* and especially *Société des droits de l'homme.* The latter, during the ministry of Marshall Soult, enrolled many wage earners and artisans into its sections or cells and concerned itself with improving the working conditions of wage earners and questioning the basis of wealth distribution.

La Caricature, as part of the moderate, constitutional opposition, expressed the views of a republican middle-class audience. In the aftermath of 1830, Philipon and Daumier became extremely critical of the government's alliances with the conservative business and professional interests, and Daumier's lithographs satirized these links much as Marx did in his description of Louis-Philippe as the director of "a stock company for the exploitation of France's wealth, whose dividends were divided among ministers, Chambers, 240 electors (from a population of 28 million), and their followers." But Philipon, Daumier, and the artists and writers working on the satirical weekly, though critical of the narrow interests served by the Juste-Milieu, did not promote a politics founded on the social question. Beyond their "negative propaganda" against the government, they championed the issues of free speech and free press, criticized the government for the business interests it supported, and demanded a foreign policy which would assist the Belgian and Polish revolutionaries.

But if *La Caricature* did not address substantively the interests of the laboring people, it nonetheless relied heavily on the languages of popular culture in order to attack the government obliquely. "The people" was the discursive referent of lithographic satire: attacks on the government's policies and its personnel took up the cause of "the people" as well as the practices and representations of popular culture. As Gabriel Perreux long ago pointed out: "If one wanted to determine that which characterized and unified the republican party between 1832 and 1834, one should look . . . at the enthusiasm which directed it toward the people. All was written, spoken, done for [the people]. All is *popular,* journals, writings, balls, banquets, reunions" (Perreux 1931, 271). Middle-class republicans, including Daumier and his friends, were without doubt influenced by Romantic discourse about a "people" that embodied wisdom, justice, liberty, national character, and the essence of the revolutionary tradition. And so it is no surprise that in the years after the 1830 Revolution they borrowed heavily from the tropes and images of popular culture.

Jean-Ignace Grandville's intricate and elaborate lithographs published in *La Caricature* in 1831 frequently drew on the symbols and subjects of popular culture, including his "Carnaval politique," representing Louis-Philippe as a carnival king called "Le citoyen," and published during Carnival, on 17 February 1831. Such a direct borrowing from a repertoire of folk festivity was not isolated: the images and languages of Carnival, including puns, scatological references, and grotesque imagery of the body, were central to the work of other lithographers at *La Caricature,* especially Traviès. Honoré Daumier's most important early satirical lithographs also borrowed directly from folk culture. His "Gargantua," submitted for registration in December 1831, was a scatological and savage attack on the new budget being prepared by the National Assembly, and on Louis-Philippe's abuses in awarding its members honors and titles. About 1830, L'Imagerie Epinal, publisher of popular woodcuts, had issued a large plate of "The Celebrated Gargantua," which Daumier had probably seen. "Gargantua," a carnival king, was tried on 23 February 1832, on charges of "exciting the hatred and the disrespect of the king's government." Nor was such borrowing isolated: two weeks after Daumier's trial for having produced the lithographic print "Gargantua," Philipon published Daumier's "Masks of 1831" (*La Caricature,* no. 71, 8 March 1832), whose subject was fourteen of Louis-Philippe's ministers and deputies at a moment, as Philipon explained, "when they have just been awakened from political inertia by the *charivariesque* noises." At about this time, Daumier began to mold the thirty-six busts of clay which he used for the drawing of the famous portraitures The Legislative Belly, which completed Daumier's attack on the National Assembly. It, too, drew on the visual imagery of bodily functions, to which Philipon gave the verbal elaboration in his claim that "the *belly* is the container of all the intestines into which the digested budget precipitates."

To early modern historians, the scatology and grotesque bodily imagery alongside the use of "popular" folk forms such as Gargantua recalls the Russian critic Mikhail Bakhtin's reading of the sixteenth-century humanist François Rabelais. Bakhtin argued that Rabelais' oeuvre marked an ephemeral moment when a festive folk tradition occupied a central place within high literature. In Rabelais, the "language of the marketplace," with its images celebrating the grotesque body and its regenerative laughter expressing universal popular and utopian truths about "community, freedom, equality, and abundance" found open expression. After Rabelais, scatological imagery of the "lower material bodily stratum" and the accompanying laughter were narrowed down, "reduced" to "the genres of humor, irony, and sarcasm, which were to develop as stylistic components of serious literature" (Bakhtin 1968, 120). In this way, the literary history of Carnival runs parallel to what I have described as its "domestication" in the seventeenth and eighteenth century.

Recent critics have been uneasy with Bakhtin's lyrical and utopian understanding of Carnival and grotesque realism, along with his overly simplified dualism of "official" and "popular" culture in early modern Europe. And even if Bakhtin is convincing about the eventual expulsion of folk humor from the canon of high literature, he severely underestimates the importance of the languages of Carnival in constituting an oppositional discourse within literary culture. Indeed, exactly three hundred years after Rabelais first told the story of Gargantua's son Pantagruel and his boon companions, artists and writers surrounding Philipon and Daumier assisted in the (grotesque) birth of the satirical daily Le Charivari. A close examination of that moment, in December 1832, may help illuminate the ways in which middle-class artists borrowed the codes of folk culture; it may also shed some light on ambivalent boundaries of both print culture and festive tradition, and of representations and practices.

Le Charivari was born in prison: it was conceived and produced while Daumier and Philipon were serving time in the prison-hospital of St. Pélagie, where, according to their associate Charles Gilbert Martin, "we enjoyed considerable freedom of movement; we were only deprived of our liberty." Le Charivari was produced as a business enterprise, one of several undertaken by Philipon to help subsidize La Caricature. According to Philipon, who spelled out in La Caricature the complementary relationship of the two journals, the production values of Le Charivari would be of lesser quality, making it available to public establishments and those amateurs who "prefer variety to biting political sarcasm." If the content of Le Charivari was to be less politically aggressive than that of its predecessor, the journal was also to be more popular: a daily journal with subscriptions at sixty francs a year. By April 1834 it had a circulation of fourteen hundred, jumping to seventeen hundred in September 1835, respectable numbers for an opposition daily.

Yet the "popular" audience of *Le Charivari* was extremely limited. Daumier once claimed that caricatures "are good for those who cannot read," but in fact, the lithographic satire of *Le Charivari* was almost entirely for middle-class consumption. In this sense, it was not a popular journal but a bourgeois journal that borrowed the name of a popular practice to criticize the government, using charivari to signify an opposition and disturbance of "order."

In fact, the bourgeois republican use, in print, of a set of popular practices was mediated: *Le Charivari* referred less to the rural rough music directed against mismatched marriages, or even the uses of ritualized judgments by peasants in revolt, than to a set of codes and practices which by December 1832 had become highly charged and politicized by middle-class opponents of the regime. The political charivaris that inspired the journal originated in the city of Grenoble on Palm Sunday, 11 March 1832. At that moment, during the festivities marking the end of Carnival, according to *Le National,* a group of "young men, following the annual custom, had organized a masquerade. This time, the costumes were taken from *La Caricature*. They represented a procession of the Juste-Milieu" (18 March 1832). Philipon and Daumier's journal had inspired an actual charivari during the Grenoble Carnival, one which satirized the deputies and ministers of Louis Philippe's government. In other words, the lithographic images of *La Caricature,* drawing on the schemes of festive folk culture, inspired the youthful middle-class opponents of the Juste-Milieu to further adapt the practices of charivari, and it was this last appropriation that resulted in the naming of Philipon and Daumier's journal *Le Charivari.*

Between March and December 1832, a rash of similar political charivaris took place throughout the cities of provincial France. Organized mock serenades were enacted in Metz, Bordeaux, and against Adolph Thiers at Aix during the month of April. Indeed, by 24 April, *Le National* had introduced a regular column called "Charivaris et sérénades" to publicize the many noisy greetings directed against deputies returning to the departments as well as other supporters of the Juste-Milieu: against prefects, sub-prefects, aristocrats, and clerics. "The epidemic of charivaris seems to have extended and multiplied its conquests in different towns with the same speed as its compatriot, cholera," wrote an opponent. The linkage was more than metaphorical: the epidemic of cholera that broke out in Paris at the end of March had sent many deputies back to their districts early, even if the session did not formally end until 21 April. Throughout provincial France, "serenades" and "symphonies" of disapprobation were organized against the representatives of the Juste-Milieu upon their return.

In 1833, Gabriel Peignot (under the pseudonym Docteur Calybriat) published a vicious little book entitled *Histoire morale, civile, politique, et littéraire du charivari, depuis son origine vers le IVe siècle.* It was a sustained polemic against the "plague" of charivaris that conveniently listed its victims, among them four prefects, eleven deputies, thirteen other officials, nine nobles, and a dozen other clerics and notables, including several appointees to the Legion of Honor. Wrote Peignot:

> The charivari, like the weeds which infest our gardens and which we pull out every day and which every day grow new shoots . . . has continued to germinate in many provinces. Yet it began to languish, and the Revolution of '89 had almost destroyed it, when politics removed it from the conjugal domain where it withered, took it, and God knows with what an explosion this plant, more alive than ever, grows green under the influence of passions in the burning atmosphere which envelops us now. (1833, 58–59)

By the time Peignot penned these words, the press was muzzled and demonstrations were strictly forbidden: in the south, a pro-Bourbon revolt had failed, while in Paris, a republican-inspired uprising in June 1832 on the occasion of General Lamarque's funeral had been violently repressed. After June, the republican press and associations came increasingly under attack, and with them, the charivari itself.

The legal, political, and epistemological status of charivari became the object of debate between defenders of the government and those of the republican opposition. This debate took place in the courts, in a series of highly publicized trials described in local and national newspapers, some of which were reprinted in pamphlet form. Perhaps the most discussed was the trial resulting from a charivari undertaken against the baron of Talleyrand, prefect of the Pas-de-Calais, in March 1832. Talleyrand had been a member of the association *Aide-toi* before the July Revolution, but on 26 February 1832 he attended a dinner party hosted by the ex-mayor of Arras, a legitimist under Charles X and a firm supporter of his minister, Polignac. To express the disapproval of the "liberal public," two traveling salesmen from Arras organized a ten-minute charivari at night outside Talleyrand's house, consisting of a noisy symphony of casseroles, fire-irons, whistles, and an immense washing pot.

At the trial, the prosecution confronted the question of whether it had been a "political charivari" or simply a "nocturnal disturbance" *(tapage injurieux)*. The defense lawyer, taking the offensive, argued that the "serenade" had indeed been political, and further, that it fell under the right of publication *(droit de publication)* guaranteed by article 8 of the Charter: the charivari was a "mode of publication" which belonged to the "people," and it was just as legal as caricature, brochures, or pamphlets. But the prosecuting attorney refused to countenance it as such, judging it a nocturnal disturbance contravening article 479 of the penal code, and ordering its practitioners to pay fines of eleven and twelve francs.

On appeal, the Parisian defense lawyer tried another approach. He argued for overturning the lower court's claim with an elaborate tongue-in-cheek dissertation on the musical character of charivari. The instigators of the charivari were, in fact, artists who wanted to give a serenade to Talleyrand, but they turned out to be artists "at the primitive state of the musical art," and thus they could not be judged for the mediocrity of their performance. The prosecuting attorney, after elaborating his own, learned account of the history of charivari, citing respected authorities who gave evidence of the long history of its condemnation and repression, argued differently:

> Truly inexcusable abuses have denatured the ceremony. From a kind of Carnival, a foolish thing authorized in a way by the folly of a mismatched union, artists without conscience, illegitimate *charivaristes* have turned it into a fiscal enterprise and gastronomic speculation . . . The present-day charivari, the one authorized by our customs, is essentially political . . . its political uses prove nothing else than that, in the end, the charivari is the great political question of the day. (*Gazette des tribuneaux*, no. 2124, 4 June 1832)

The political interpretation, originally offered by the defense attorney, prevailed in the end. The charivari against Talleyrand, and further charivaris performed during the next year throughout French cities, were judged to be political demonstrations against the government—and thus not guaranteed by the Charter.

The political charivari was a creation of both its middle-class practitioners and its critics in the spring and summer of 1832. Yet such a politicization was possible only because the popular ritual, long before the July Revolution, had become suspect and subversive in the eyes of governmental authorities. Precisely because the middle classes already perceived charivari as an "act of popular justice," however reprehensible the morality which it defended, the charivari became available to the political opponents of the July Monarchy as a statement of "popular" opposition. Most, though not all, of the instigators of political charivaris at this time were members of the middle classes. In Paris, in November 1831, a charivari against the commander of the national guard, Sédillot, was led by a merchant, M. Barry, quite possibly a reader of *La Caricature*. At Dijon in September 1832, a dozen men, "almost all belonging to the well-off class, and among whom one saw several officers of the national guard," organized a charivari.

Le National insisted that the mock serenade was "an act of popular justice," but one undertaken not by "the rabble but by citizens paying the personal tax." The editorial staff of this moderate republican journal quoted approvingly *Journal du Havre,* which admitted that there was nothing legal about the charivari, that it was to be "hated," and that the editors wished to have "fewer charivaris and more electors." In short, respectable people were forced by the Juste-Milieu to use "vulgar" and "trivial" forms of contestation, invoking the "popular" elements of society excluded in the politics of the regime.

The towns of the Ariège, notably Saint-Girons and Pamiers, were the theaters of extensive political charivaris in these years. During the carnival season in 1832, a handful of "partisans de la république" could be found, young men of the middle class who gave voice in slogan and song to support the republic. They organized charivaris and serenades against political officials and deputies, much to the dismay of the prefect and administrators, who had feared their political views and activities since before the July Days. As the prefect wrote to Paris in September 1829, "The youth of the well-to-do classes are generally imbued with the principles of independence that the liberal papers propagate, and these papers are found in much larger numbers in public places than those which defend the religious and monarchical principles." After the publication of Philipon and Daumier's journal, *Le Charivari,* in December 1832, there were fears at the highest level of government that political charivaris, "outrages to our civilization," would continue unabated. The weekly newspaper *Mémorial des Pyrénées* noted in January 1833 that "ever since the charivari has had its official journal, everyone is getting involved: imperceptibly, this popular vaudeville has succeeded in penetrating all social classes" (in Desplat 1982, 134). In June 1833, the minister of the interior warned in a printed circular that more charivaris should be expected as deputies to the National Assembly returned to their districts; in Pamiers, a section of the republican secret society *Aide-toi* did manage to organize a small serenade to welcome, with disapprobation, its returning deputy in July.

But in the Ariège as throughout provincial France, nearly all the political charivaris in the spring and summer of 1832 were already the work of middle-class young men with liberal and republican sympathies. In this context, it is worth remembering that the republican leadership in both Paris and the provinces was extremely young: the "Generation of 1830" and republican opposition to the Juste-Milieu took on the form of a generational revolt. This itself was an implied critique of the age requirements for suffrage (twenty-five) and elected office (thirty), which had been lowered by the July Monarchy, but not enough. Young activists were the force behind the political clubs of the early July Monarchy, and they were the writers and publishers in the republican press, including the collaborators, artists, and staff of *Le Charivari.* Philipon, aged thirty in 1830, was the oldest of the group; Daumier was the youngest, at twenty-two. Traviès and Raffet were twenty-six, and Granville was twenty-seven.

The male peasants of the Ariège mountain communes in 1829 played the role of young men in their charivari against the forest guards, whereas the middle-class republicans in 1832 were young men who in their project of political opposition turned to the codes of charivari. The male peasants' uses of charivari and the urban and bourgeois deployment in practice and print of the codes of charivari were linked by the structural identity of an age-group across class lines. (It is worth noting, in this context, the parallel between the metaphor of childhood consistently employed by official culture to describe the charivari and Philipon's own description of caricature as "our cherished infant, [who] grows and develops in our sight: the

climate of France is that which nourishes it best, we are happy to
have led its development in our country. That child, well directed,
will make its way and will some day be the pride of its family" [in
Goldstein 1989, 34].) They were also linked by war: while the Demoiselles fought their "war," Philipon announced when founding *Le
Charivari* that "in between what we call the great battles of *La Caricature,* there is a small war to fight, a daily war of daily ridicules, a
guerrilla and avant-garde war, a joyous war where next to the usual
caricaturists could sit all those who sense indignation in their hearts
and verve at the end of their pencils."

The politicization of charivari after 1830 within middle-class culture was a recognition on the part of its detractors and defenders that
"rough music" was a form of "political thinking" (as the republican
lawyer Ledru Rollin argued at a trial in Paris). Incorporating the previously conceived "apolitical" charivari into a bourgeois definition
of politics meant subjecting it to the same repressive treatment that
other forms of political expression endured in the years after 1832.
Le Charivari and *La Caricature* thus suffered extensive harassment
and fines for what Philipon had called their "charivariesque" attacks
on the political regime. Between March 1833 and July 1835, *Le Charivari* was prosecuted in 6 different instances, leading to 5 convictions
and sentences totaling 17 months in jail and fines of 18,500 francs.
The September 1835 laws on the press greatly restricted the oppositional practices of political caricature: *Le Charivari* was required to
submit its daily full-page lithograph in advance to the censors. To
justify such measures, the government had to sidestep the problem
of the 1830 Charter by arguing that "article 7 of the Charter says
the French have the right to publish and have printed their opinions.
But when these opinions are changed into acts by the exhibition of
drawings, one speaks to the eyes. This is more than showing an opinion: there is a fact, an action, a life which does not concern article
7." In short, the government argued that caricature was not a representation but a practice, not an image but an act. It was a fitting
conclusion to the long-drawn-out battle over charivari, since the
codes of "rough music" had shifted back and forth from practices
to representations in the years after the July Monarchy. After the
September laws of 1835, *La Caricature* was discontinued, while *Le
Charivari* was saved by a reduction of its explicit political referents.

Between 1829 and 1834, there was much that linked the peasants'
use of a language of revolutionary liberty in their struggles over the

forests in the Ariège and the middle-class republican use of the codes of popular culture in opposition to the July Monarchy. The youthful rioters in the Ariège adopted an abbreviated, caricatured appearance as women while acting out a new kind of charivari in 1829; in 1830, they abandoned the charivari for an understanding of republican liberty. In the years after the 1830 Revolution, Philipon, Daumier, and other young artists used caricature and the language of charivari to define their moderate, middle-class republicanism. This parallel and complementary set of processes was further linked symbolically by the metaphor of war. The Ariège peasants fought a carnivalesque "war" that, in 1830, became a moment of revolutionary politics, while middle-class republicans turned their revolutionary politics into a "war of disrespect" waged by *La Caricature.*

The two sets of events were not dependent on each other: both were new uses of the codes of a popular, domestic ritual regulating marriages. Daumier, Philipon, and their associates may or may not have been aware of the War of the Demoiselles via the official journal *Gazette des tribunaux,* or possibly the melodrama *Les Demoiselles.* But it is unlikely that the peasants of the Ariège were subscribers to or consumers of the not inexpensive journal *Le Charivari.*

The parallel use by peasants and middle-class republicans of their respective languages of protest was thus neither causal nor casual. The immediate circumstances of the exchange lay in the dissolution and reconstitution of the political order during and after the July Revolution. But the conditions which made such an exchange possible lay at once in a long history of exchanges between high and low cultural practices, and in a revolutionary tradition of which peasant and bourgeois classes had different experiences and memories. The July Revolution opened up a space and a time in which the language and practice of the political underwent an important and enduring transformation. Once politicized by the middle classes and the government, rural charivaris would never be quite the same; and once constituted in local terms as a struggle for the possession of the forests, popular republicanism would remain a viable option within peasant culture. The popular republicanism born of the French Revolution, and reaffirmed in the peasantry's experience of the July Days, took on an electoral dimension when peasants got the vote. In the first elections based on universal suffrage—the elections of deputies to the National Assembly during the Second Republic in 1849—the mountain communes of the Ariège voted almost exclusively republican.

The End of the War and the Return of the Demoiselles

"Messieurs," proclaimed the defense attorney Crémieux on 23 February 1834 at the trial of a young *charivariseurs* against the deputy Jaubert, "charivaris seem no longer to be fashionable." The fad had lasted approximately five years, reaching its peak in the spring and summer of 1832, when dozens of political charivaris had been addressed to deputies and governmental supporters throughout provincial France. After that, the political charivari experienced a certain decline, although charivaris directed against mismatched marriages in village communities continued well into the twentieth century.

In part, the political charivari declined because it was recouped by the Juste-Milieu: in October 1832, the government attempted, surreptitiously, to sponsor a competitor to *Le Charivari* that defended the political line of the regime; that venture remained largely unsuccessful, and it folded, ironically, during the carnival season in 1834, on 9 February. The political charivari declined in part because the impact of the cacophonous mock serenade was diffused as critics of the regime turned the political charivari back into a noisy rite of acclaim, a "serenade" of approval honoring deputies returning to the provinces. Finally, the decline of political charivaris was a direct function of the middle-class politicization of the rite and its repression. That politicization had direct and immediate repercussions in the political and judicial authorities' intolerance of "ordinary" charivaris of village life after 1830.

By 1835, under the repressive gaze of the government, *Le Charivari* had turned to satirizing the domestic morals of the bourgeoisie, no longer attacking directly the policies of the government. By 1835, the peasants of the Ariège had long abandoned the elaborate gestures and noisy behaviors derived from charivari in their war against the forest administration and rural notables. Whereas the middle-class republicans had lost their "war of disrespect" against the governments of Louis-Philippe, the Demoiselles had won a brief and pyrrhic victory.

In the aftermath of the July Revolution as it was played out in the Ariège, the new administration pursued a different tack: in addition to the repressive measures already in place—which included, in the fall of 1830, the positioning of six hundred troops in the Ariège under the direction of General Lafitte—the government tried conciliation. In October, the new prefect organized a special commission, composed of six owners of forests and mountains, five mayors of villages with claims of use-rights, and eleven landowners "having no interest other than that of justice and of the law." Their conclusions were reported in December. The commission recommended some modification of the 1827 Forest Code, notably the reestablishment of the right to pasture sheep in designated areas of the forest. The commission also recommended leniency in the future application of the Code; the result was a series of further concessions. In February, March, and April 1831, the peasants secured a series of royal ordinances which met the recommendation of the commission and, in addition, gave amnesty for all past "crimes and transgressions." The April Ordinance permitted pasturing of sheep in royal forests for a period of five years. According to the prefect, clemency would succeed where judicial pursuits and military repression had failed; and with the amnesty, it was highly unlikely that the melting snows would produce "the annual return of the disorders which for several years have preoccupied the administration."

He was wrong. In March 1831, a troop of some eighty masked men, armed with hatchets and guns, attacked the ironworks of Arnave, where they destroyed tools and took away the iron. They then went to the chateau at Allens, taking ham, sausage, and meat from the kitchen and pillaging the house. Yet the prefect was not entirely wrong, since the War of the Demoiselles never did regain the intensity or the popularity it had enjoyed in 1829 and 1830. Isolated appearances of the "white robes" were reported from 1831 to 1871, and there were even rebellious peasants who called themselves Demoiselles as late as 1900, but after 1831 use of the disguise had quickly declined, as had the structure and coherence of the revolt itself. Already in 1831 at the chateau at Allens there were several rioters dressed in black, and others who were not masked at all. In May 1832, fifty to sixty individuals armed with guns chased out charcoal-makers placed in the forest of Ustou and pillaged their cabins: some were masked and some were not. Later that year, on 1 August in the commune of Esplas, seven to eight hundred peasants "dressed mostly as Demoiselles" undertook an open rebellion against the guards and gendarmes who had seized a herd of cows pasturing in the forest. In the skirmish, fifteen peasants were injured, and one was killed—a kind of violence which had not been part of the original "War of the Demoiselles."

After 1831, the battles of the Demoiselles became part of a collective memory, events which could be invoked in other struggles over the forests and mountains of the Ariège. Indeed, the name of the Demoiselles became a threat in the region, one element of a shifting repertoire of tactics used within the newer kinds of struggles over the forest taking shape in the later nineteenth century. The symbolic forms which had given the War of the Demoiselles its distinctive identity became less consistently visible—the ritualized violence against the forest guards, the charivari and mockery of the guards, and the predominance of younger, unmarried men as the active participants were no longer the rule. Perhaps most revealing of this shift was the noticeable change in those who rioted under the rubric of Demoiselles. On 13 December 1834, a brigadier of the forest administration surprised ninety peasants from the commune of Massat cutting wood in a prohibited area; the peasants turned on the guards, throwing rocks and waving their hatchets, and the guards withdrew to report on this insurrection of "Demoiselles." Yet according to the testimony of the guards, more than a dozen women had taken part in the action. And on 24 April 1834, in another reported appearance of "Demoiselles," about forty peasants gathered around the forest guard Lavivier, insulting him and pelting him with stones. According to the mayor of Castillon, the crowd was spontaneously formed—and composed mostly of women.

EPILOGUE

n the summer of 1979, the 150th anniversary of the outbreak of the War of the Demoiselles went largely unno-
ticed in the Ariège. I was a little surprised, perhaps even
disappointed, since I was spending my days with the
Demoiselles in the archives, listening as their strange doings were described and filtered through the reports of sub-prefects, forest inspectors, and the courts. In the evenings, their descendants in the nearby
mountain villages told me much about themselves and their forests,
but nothing of the Demoiselles. I did not discover, in 1979, any collective memory of the event: for the Ariégeois, the story seemed as bi-
zarre as it first does to outsiders. Thus when an older peasant from
the village of Serres proudly declared his kinship with the rioters
("My brother was a Demoiselle") I was astonished, at least until I
learned that the man was referring to the role of a Demoiselle which
his brother had played in a 1976 film about the revolt, shot on location in the forests of the Ariège.

The first fictional rendition, in the narrower sense of the term, of
the War of the Demoiselles was in 1830, but it has really only been
since the mid-1970s that the story of the Demoiselles has lent itself
so extensively to a range of artistic creations. These creations became
part of a larger cultural revival of representations of traditional life—
of "folklore"—in southern France. As such, they can be linked to the
movements of localism, regionalism, and cultural nationalism that
animated political life in France in the decades after 1968. In 1975,
Guy Vassal wrote a play for a summer theater festival in Car-
cassonne, Albi, and Aigues-Mortes which captured the relation between festivity and revolt as a drama—in ways, it might be added,

that could not be done within the bounds of the historical record. In 1976, the Occitan author Jean Boudou published *Les Demoiselles,* a satirical and sometimes romantic novella about the contemporary decline of peasant culture and the creation of a national park, based on the events of the Ariège, but transposed to the Espinergue region of Languedoc. After Gérard Guillaume's 1976 film made for French television—a deeply sympathetic rendition of the War of the Demoiselles—Jacques Nichet shot a second film about the Demoiselles in 1983, in which the peasants spoke their own Occitan dialect, and which was subtitled in French. In 1985, Nichet's screenplay was used as the basis for a comic book—a *bande déssinée*—about the revolt. In 1989, Louis Pujol published his novel *Le temps des fleurs,* which used the War of the Demoiselles as the backdrop of the love trials and tribulations of a young shepherd girl, whose diary the author supposedly transcribed. Meanwhile, in 1982, a traveling exposition organized by the departmental archives included documents, contemporary drawings, objects of traditional material culture (including the one remaining shirt purportedly worn by a Demoiselle), and a puppet show. In the summer of 1982, the exhibit traveled widely throughout the department. If in 1991 the people of the Ariège knew much about the young men who partially disguised themselves as women to chase guards and workers from the forest—as I can testify in return visits to the area—it is due in large part to these dramatic and fictional reconstructions of the War of the Demoiselles.

These reflections point to the ways in which the memory of the revolt in the Ariège today is mediated by its fictional recreations. But the history of the War of the Demoiselles will also be mediated, not by one fiction, but two. The archival sources are a filter, which offers only second-hand (and outsiders') interpretations of what the peasants thought and did. My own interpretation of the events and their meaning from these long-silent texts is itself a work of fiction, in the sense of an imagined reconstruction which, because this is a work of history, has been held in check by the archival sources, however fragmented and imaginative they may be.

Since 1830, the War of the Demoiselles has lent itself easily to dramatic and fictional renditions, for at the core of the events themselves was a fiction and a drama. The fiction was the disguise itself: the peasant men were not really women, nor were they really trying to disguise themselves as women; rather, they were men—many young and unmarried, some soldiers, deserters, and others—who represented themselves in an abbreviated fashion as women while they maintained, even deepened, their masculine identities. And the idea of drama came not so much from the official voices at the time, military commanders who frequently invoked the "theater" where the events took place, as from the sense that the events were about a peasantry's self-consciously dramatic enactment of its claims to the forest.

In telling this story, I have tried to evoke this fiction and this drama in the forests of the Ariège while making sense of the war within the wider world beyond the forests of the Ariège. Each interpretive path moved away from the events in a different direction in order to look back on them with new insights. From deep within the feminized forests of the Ariège, from the calendrical rituals of Carnival during the early modern period, and from the wider political world of nine-teenth-century France, I have tried to give new perspectives on the War of the Demoiselles.

In the process, I suggested how our understanding of these rich and complex events must consistently and self-consciously abandon the language of utility and practical reason—of the functions which the disguise played—as the final explanation of its meaning. The War of the Demoiselles needs to be resituated within a world of peasant culture; in particular, within the complex, inherited beliefs and prac-tices, symbolic and instrumental, about and in the forest. The lan-guage of festive rebellion, drawn from their local culture, structured the goals of the rioters' collective action—to dramatically reclaim possession of the forests from the guards and workers. But the lan-guage of festive rebellion also provided the means to achieve those goals, the ritualized actions and the "disguise" as women.

I have maintained throughout this book that the very language of "disguise," and the recurrent phrase "armed and disguised as women," are misleading. When contemporary historians use the lan-guage of "disguise" (just as when they are content to describe the events as a "revolt" or a "protest") they offer a thin version of the events, one which recovers implicitly the nineteenth-century bour-geois discourse. That discourse, organized around the ideas of utility and practical reason, was in fact much older: as I have suggested, it took shape in the thought of Descartes in the seventeenth century, and has taken many forms and variations since then.

The War of the Demoiselles makes clear, however, that there are no evident, straight lines out of the forest, no easy shorthand to ex-plain the peasants' revolt. I have suggested the need to proceed instead along a set of paths which takes seriously the event as an expressive enactment of claims to the forest: these paths lead toward the drama, the play of metaphors, the symbolic action, and the cultural values that shaped the goals of the revolt and gave the rioters the necessary tactics to achieve them.

The "disguise," as an abbreviated and caricatured representation of women, signified many things. It represented the unruly and excusable power of women, past and present. It made reference to a notion of a feminized conception of the forest in peasant culture, and thus was part of a set of metaphors by which peasant men took possession of and defended their forest. The "disguise" drew on the rites of the calendar year, especially on those of May and Carnival: the War of the Demoiselles was a festive rebellion which narrated the interests and prerogatives of local communities against the attempted usurpations by the forest administration and the rural forest and forge owners.

But the "disguise" was also a tactic: it was useful within a world of action, functioning in extremely practical and instrumental ways—to disguise identities, to express community, and to scare off the forest guards. Thus in March 1831 at Croquier, during a house search by the local forest agents for illegal wood, several peasants were overheard whispering that "now if we were masked, all would go well." At the end of the guards' search, a half dozen Demoiselles with blackened faces and shirts pulled out appeared, threatening the guards. In the commune of Bosc during May 1830, the mayor wrote to the prefect that "until now, the Demoiselles had not appeared on the Andronne mountain. There were many delinquents, unmasked, cutting wood from the prohibited areas, but without bothering to dress up. It was only to receive the forest inspector that they dressed up as Demoiselles." Peasants dressed up as Demoiselles for a variety of practical reasons. Simply to list these, or to enumerate the functions of the disguise, would be an insufficient explanation of the War of the Demoiselles. The utilitarian dimension of the "disguise" cannot disclose its meaning, drawn from peasant culture but treated as well in the confrontation with outside authorities.

But is the distinction between function and meaning, an age-old quarrel repreated among the competing approaches of the social sciences in the 1960s and 1970s, still relevant? As I have tried to describe in the War of the Demoiselles, the stark dichotomy of function and meaning, of "disguise" and "drama," vanishes, like the white lady in the forest, the closer one approaches. Function and meaning are not alternatives, but stand in relation to each other: the practical reason of an act is an interested deployment of meanings. Explanations based on functions, on the logic of utility, can thus never recover the cultural specificity of the event: in 1829 Ariège, that the peasants disguised themselves as (caricatures of) women; that the timing of their revolt was related to the festive calendar; that their adoption of the language of liberty in 1830 and the abandonment of the disguise were meaningful acts, as were the republican uses of charivari.

Part of the fascination with the War of the Demoiselles, and much of the inability to make sense of the disguise in a language other than that of utility, come from the fact that the events took place, not in the early modern period, but at the heart of the nineteenth century. It was, after all, *the* century of utility, a mode of discourse which fit the processes of massive urbanization, the quickening pace and pervasive reach of capitalism, the social disruptions of industrialization, the extended authority of the administrative state, and even the birth of (modern electoral) politics. In one sense, the War of the Demoiselles stood poised on the brink of a great historical rupture in Europe (although the change sometimes came much earlier in France than elsewhere)—the revolutions in communications of the later nineteenth century and the forced participation of rural communities in the life of the nation through universal conscription and mandatory primary education.

In this way, it has been argued, the War of the Demoiselles represents the last gasp of a peasant culture about to be annihilated, with its remains assimilated into the modern cultural, economic, and political life of the nation. The Ariège peasants stood on the brink of entering the modern world, of losing their distinctive identities and cultures. The revolt, in defense of that culture, was backward-looking and conservative: in the typology of political modernization theory, it was communalist, not associational; traditional, not modern; folkloric, not political. According to this logic, what could be more inevitable than a backward, conservative peasantry reaching into the irrational depths of its culture to prevent its own demise?

This is the language of modernization, which has deep roots in European thinking about its own modernity, but which developed as an academic model as well in the social scientific and historical studies of the 1960s and 1970s. At the same time, social historians more sympathetic to the plight of the "victims" of modernization nonetheless accepted much of the same terminology: thus the Demoiselles of the Ariège would certainly have been considered "primitive rebels" (Hobsbawm 1959) whose uses of ritual in movements of social protest would disappear with the arrival of trade unionism and modern electoral politics. In nineteenth-century French historical studies, a generation of social historians heralded, in a similar fashion, the presence of the "Republic in the Village" (Agulhon 1982), the penetration of national political ideals and values into a peasant culture, where they coexisted with—but were ultimately adopted in place of—traditional folkloric practices and beliefs.

Much of the problem with such models is an excessive dualism that seems destined to be repeated endlessly about nineteenth-century France. Although historians debate the timing and mode of the transformation, at some point they agree that peasants became Frenchmen: modern electoral politics eliminated local struggles, shifting the arena from the village to the nation; peasants abandoned local and adopted national identities; folkloric practices were transformed into the unmarked acts of modern daily life. Some consider the French Revolution the critical moment of these transformations; others point to the political experiences of the Republic of 1848; still others, more famously, point to the transformations wrought by the railway, primary schools, and military conscription in the first part of the Third Republic (1871–1914). But all agree that the movement from peasant to Frenchman was a movement from tradition to modernity.

One problem with this formulation lies in the false idea of the nature of "modern" practices, especially political practices. No one who studies modern political life, whether the electoral campaigns of American presidents or revolutionary upheaval in Eastern Europe, can fail to be struck by the symbolic dimensions of political beliefs and practices. Nor can those who investigate the struggles and protests of local communities in the late nineteenth and twentieth century deny the continuing manner in which abstract, national issues take on form and meaning in local terms.

But a larger part of the problem is tautological: the scholarly and commonsensical notions of modernization consider the categories of "folklore" and "tradition" as part—by definition—of a "pre-political" world. These were already the constructions of official culture in 1830, whose narrow (or thin) definition of politics excluded the political from the Demoiselles and vice versa, as I suggested in Chapter 4.

Definitions aside, the notion of a fixed and unchanging "tradition" suggests far too much immobility and stagnation. It is true that much of peasant culture among the mountain communes of the Ariège was founded in the constantly renewed attempts to reproduce an inherited way of life adapted to the harsh conditions of the mountain environment and its agro-sylvo-pastoral economy. To outsiders, such as the prefect writing in 1806, this could only mean an archaic and conservative outlook in desperate need of revision: "The inhabitants of the Ariège hold tenaciously to the cult of their fathers . . . habit alone directs them in their daily work . . . they hold onto the soil as well as the customs of their fathers, and one is at great pains to tear them away." Yet this was not the blind and mindless attachment to the past seen by the prefect and others. Rather, the Ariège peasantry acted in ways that deliberately and self-consciously denied the historical "forces" to which they were subjected, and the structural transformations which they experienced. Such was the basis of the cult which they made of their written charters, titles, and notarial acts of the later Middle Ages, documents which guaranteed their possession and use of the forests, waters, and pastures of the high mountains.

Throughout the Old Regime, and especially during the nineteenth century, peasants sought to restore what they believed was their primitive condition of possession, affirmed by their experience of the French Revolution, then transformed by the state and by seigneurs and forest owners. This is not to claim that in seeking to restore the past, the peasants were another "people without history" (to adapt a phrase from Eric Wolf, 1986). It would be misleading as well to think of peasants as a "cold" society, structurally resistant to change, as opposed to a "hot" society such as our own (Lévi-Strauss 1966). But it is true that societies experience and make history differently: Marshall Sahlins (1985) has characterized some non-western cultures such as Hawaii as "prescriptive," in that people acted in these cultures to incorporate the meaning of events into inherited structures of meaning, denying as much as possible the ways in which those structures were transformed by events.

But such questions about "meaning," "structure," and "event" are perhaps better left to the social scientist. The historians' job is, after all, less to construct models than to make sense of their informants' lives, however distant in time, and even when they cannot speak for themselves. In rare instances, however, they do, as when the inhabitants of Aix in 1841 explained their own relation to history, claiming that they were only seeking "to maintain the practices of the commune, practices passed on to us from our ancestors that we could not change without altering our existence and making life impossible."

This way of life, adapting a culturally organized set of needs to the harsh material conditions of the mountain environment, amounted to a dexterous and flexible traditionalism. And the modes of protest used to defend the peasant's way of life, as we have seen, involved as much a self-conscious and dramatic play with "folklore" and "tradition" as the unself-conscious expression of these categories.

The Ariège peasantry's "traditionalism" was not unilaterally opposed to the dictates of state-building and capitalism. Rather, these processes had long been part of their lives; by the early nineteenth century, the peasants of the Ariège were actively taking part, through their own strategies, in the world of states and in the wider economy. The "cake of custom"—a metaphor used frequently to describe a traditional way of life—had long been broken, if it had ever existed at all. The structures of capitalism, in the form of ironworks and the commercialization of the rural economy, had been in place since the seventeenth century, and the Ariège peasants in the nineteenth century were participating in a cash economy, and willing to make the most of it. The French Revolution of 1789 had already inserted the struggles of local communities into a wider political context, providing new opportunities and new constraints in the peasantry's claims to possess and exploit the forests.

More remarkably, the peasants largely failed to challenge the most dramatic "intrusion" of the state into village life: military service. Indeed, even as the Demoiselles fought and played hard in 1829 to preserve the communities' rights to the forest, the age cohort drafted in 1829 went quietly, and even, according to the prefect's report, enthusiastically. This is all the more surprising since the Ariège, like many peripheral regions of France, had strongly resisted the repeated demands for men by the Napoleonic state, such that by 1811 and 1812, few if any soldiers could be secured for the Grand Army. But in the next two decades, male youths showed themselves increasingly compliant, even willing volunteers for the army. Indeed, by 1829, the government had no problems whatsoever raising the military conscriptions, even in the outlying mountain hamlets of the department.

Far from immobile, the peasant society and culture in the nineteenth century was constantly adapting itself to and complying with some of the demands of the modern world. And far from merely "traditional," the peasant communities used the traditions and elements of their culture as resources to defend themselves against the imposed demands of government officials and others.

This is not to deny that in the second half of the nineteenth century the peasants of the Ariège, as those elsewhere in France, experienced a profound transformation. The evidence is, above all, demographic. After 1845, the population of the mountain communes reached its highest density, and permanent out-migration from the villages to the cities and the plain began in earnest. The population of the Ariège Pyrenees has declined slowly but steadily ever since, both a result and a cause of changes in the peasant communities' relations to the forest. The shortage of wood and pasture and the devastation of the forests became hotly contested political issues during the Second Republic (1848–1851), just at a moment when mountain communes changed their strategies in the fight over the forest. The closing down of the Catalan forges after the 1850s (the last was shut down in 1875) and the new reforestation laws imposed by the forest administration beginning in 1869 further transformed the character and terms of the struggle between peasant communities, local forest owners, and the state, the authority of which had been confirmed by the 1827 Forest Code. When the mountain peasantry resisted new attempts to restrict possession of "their" forests, they did so by means other than the disguise and drama of the War of the Demoiselles.

With their access to the forests restricted by the Code, the peasants shifted their struggle toward individual acts of delinquency. Already between 1832 and 1844, the number of forest infractions in the district of Saint-Girons rose from 506 to 2340, and it continued to grow throughout the nineteenth century as individual peasants struggled to survive by stealing firewood and building materials, or pasturing their few goats and sheep in prohibited areas of the forest. The battle also shifted into the courts, as the communities, led after the 1850s by their syndicates, or associations of the richer household heads, attempted to salvage what remained of their rights within the legal suits of *cantonnement*. Such court-ordered divisions of property per-

mitted proprietors to gain full possession of portions of their mountains and forests by giving up other areas to the peasant communities
who previously held use-rights. These legal sales became the central
struggle of the mountain peasant communities after 1850, and in the
Massat "Affair of the Mountains" after 1832. Into the early twentieth century, the peasant communities and syndical associations debated, sued, dragged their feet, openly rebelled (killing a forest guard
in 1867), and manipulated (and were manipulated by) political parties within the national arena. In all these newer forms of struggle
over the forest, the threat that the Demoiselles would reappear in the
forests was consistently a useful tactic.

To look back from the later nineteenth and twentieth century is to
see the War of the Demoiselles, not as the last gasp of a dying peasantry, but as the beginning of a different struggle over the mountains
of the Ariège. The War of the Demoiselles opened up a new era of
contention among peasant communities, forest owners, and the state.
In 1973, the peasants of the Ariège—men and women who still
worked the land and earned their livelihood from stockraising—organized themselves and successfully opposed a governmental pro-
posal to create a national park in the mountain communes. The association defended their inherited rights against the threat of an
invasion of tourists and further restrictions of their pasturing rights.

Yet the disguise as women was not part of their language of struggle, which instead consisted of mass meetings, petitions, press re-
leases, and the mobilization of public opinion. Even as they learned
about their ancestors' struggles, they found the War of the Demoiselles quaint, faintly embarrassing, and even childish. Like the world
of Carnival and other folkloric practices which it evoked, the masquerade and disguise as women belonged to a forgotten youth. So it
was more generally, in nineteenth- and twentieth-century France, that
as the inherited practices of village life were transformed and disappeared, Carnival became a matter for children.

But if the tactics have changed, if the repertoire of collective actions
has shifted, if the terms of defeat and victory have evolved, the basic
struggle nonetheless remains the same: more than a century and a
half after the War of the Demoiselles in 1829, peasants of the Ariège
continue to battle the state and outsiders for possession of their forests.

BIBLIOGRAPHIC ESSAYS

SOURCES

ACKNOWLEDGMENTS

INDEX

BIBLIOGRAPHIC ESSAYS

Preface

For historians of the War of the Demoiselles, a large part of the archival record of the events themselves has already been collected, first by the forest administration, then by those working at the departmental archives in Foix. Most of the descriptive material can be found in three boxes, Archives départementales de l'Ariège, hereafter ADA 7P 10–7P 12. The boxes contain much of the administrative correspondence with the department, within the forest administration, and between the administrative authorities in the department and the ministries of war and the interior in Paris. The quality of these reports and correspondence is uneven. The most careful descriptions of the Demoiselles' appearances tend to be the written reports by the forest guards who were their victims. These "verbal proceedings" then suffered a common fate: forest inspectors excerpted from them in their own reports, while officials in the local civil administration, sub-prefects, and the prefect himself relied mostly on these descriptions in their accounts to the national authorities. (Some of this correspondence is duplicated in reports of the *gendarmerie* found in the Archives nationales, hereafter AN BB18 1308–18 1309, which also contain a few original letters.) Along the way, the descriptions became more abbreviated and stylized, so that by the time the accounts reached Paris, they were themselves almost caricatures of the original, and they relied heavily on the shock value of the phrase, repeated throughout this book, "armed and disguised as women."

At the same time, the background reports of prefects and sub-prefects, as well as those of the district attorneys of the royal courts, which describe the conditions of the mountain peasantry and their relations to the forest administration, are frequently perceptive, often sympathetic accounts of the plight of the peasantry. Yet almost universally, the administration's ultimate interests in and concerns with repressing the rioting and restoring "order" inevitably lead to misinterpretations of the events, as I have described in the text. Repression was also the singular concern of the military commanders in charge of troops in the Ariège, whose correspondence concerning troop movements—revealing much about the perceptions of the events the military establishment shared with the civil authorities—can be found in the archives of the war ministry at Vincennes (Archives du Ministère de la Guerre, hereafter AG) D(3), and E(5).

More useful, perhaps, in getting closer to the peasantry's perspective are the judicial records of the departmental archives (ADA 3U65–3U67), which contain the record of the five major trials of Demoiselles in 1829 and 1830, as well as descriptions and denunciations of the property damage inflicted throughout the revolt. In these records may be found oral testimony both from the villagers and from the victims (forest guards and charcoal-makers). The former, as I have suggested, tend to be complicitous and sometimes frightened into silence, although the occasional denunciation and description of the costumes and actions offer revealing detail. Testimony from the guards and charcoal-workers, not surprisingly, is invaluable in reconstructing the pattern of the festive rioting.

Published sources on the War of the Demoiselles from the time of the riot include the newspaper accounts in the court paper *Gazette des tribunaux,* nos. 1432 and 1433 (14–16 March 1830), reporting on the more publicized judicial trials of several captured Demoiselles in the spring of 1830, and other mentions in the national press during that time. More intriguing is the first literary and dramatic reconstruction of the events in the melodrama *Les Demoiselles,* by Brazer and Carmouche, which ran for two weeks in Paris beginning on 15 March 1830, and which I discuss at the beginning of Chapter 4. Subsequent literary and historical accounts continue with the short, romantic, but not always inaccurate, vision of Prosper Barousse in 1839, and the nostalgic recollections of the events by Hippolyte Cabannes in a local newspaper article in 1857, which included the first written use of the title "War of the Demoiselles."

There were sporadic reappearances of the Demoiselles between 1834 and 1900, with a total of approximately 80 individuals sighted (of the 8100 Demoiselles reported since 1829). But there were no other literary or historical accounts until the Demoiselles found their first historian in Marcel Dubédat, who published an article on the rioters in 1900. Dubédat, himself a lawyer, was particularly interested in the legal personalities and processes of the trials; the social and economic background of the revolt was not reconstructed until René Dupont's study in 1933. The explanation of the rioting exclusively in terms of the peasantry's resistance to the National Forest Code (with no particular attempt to make sense of the "disguise") was most elaborately documented in the university thesis of Louis Clarenc in 1963, the results of which were published in a short article in 1967. The revolt made itself known to an English-reading public in John Merriman's useful summary of the events, "The Demoiselles of the Ariège, 1829–1831."

Literary accounts, in the strict sense of the word, disappear after the 1830 play, and they do not reappear until the 1947 novel by Louis Bourliaguet entitled *La guerre des Demoiselles.* Sympathetic to the claims of the rioters, Bourliaguet focuses on the love of a fictional young peasant leader for the daughter of a local seigneur. Then, as I describe in the Epilogue, the revival of local culture in the post–1968 political world produced a number of texts.

In 1989, Louis Pujol published his novel *Le temps des fleurs,* which used the War of the Demoiselles as the backdrop of the love trials and tribulations of a young shepherd girl, whose diary the author supposedly transcribed. Meanwhile, in 1982, a traveling exposition organized by the departmental archives brought documents, drawings, and a puppet show to the public and resulted in the publication of a useful catalogue. It is these recent literary and historical accounts, discussed briefly in the Epilogue, that have made the Demoiselles known to the Ariégeois, and others, today.

One of the most important of these was Guy Vassal's 1975 play, *La guerre des Demoiselles,* which captured the creativity and symbolism of festivity and folk culture in revolt. Vassal's work was largely inspired, he himself claimed, by the remarkable university thesis of François Baby, published in 1972 as *La guerre des Demoiselles en Ariège, 1829–1872.*

Baby's work is by far the most important scholarly account of the War of the Demoiselles. Baby was the first to sort systematically through the vast archival record and document extensively the appearances of the Demoiselles in space and time, as well as their gestures and costumes. Baby's concerns centered around the uses of folklore within the revolt: he astutely identified the ritual gestures of a "Carnival in action" and offered, among other insights, a psychoanalytical interpretation of this "dramatic game." (Baby also reproduced, in his appendixes, the extant writings signed by Demoiselles, as well as precious testimony about the costumes and collective actions of the rioters.) My earlier treatment of the War of the Demoiselles, "Rites of Revolt: The 'War of the *Demoiselles*' in Ariège, France (1829–1867)," drew heavily on Baby's work. I had returned to the archival record for further details, and I put more emphasis than he on the background of the revolt in local peasant culture and economy. When I revisited the archives in 1989 and 1991, I delved further into the relations of peasant communities and their forests, especially during the eighteenth century, and spent more time trying to understand the meaning of the forest in nineteenth-century peasant culture. Nonetheless, this book owes a great intellectual debt to the work of François Baby and to that of other local historians and archivists of the Ariège, without whose labors this text could not have been written.

1. The War of the Demoiselles

THE ARIÈGE

The principal published work on the mountain districts of the Ariège department during the nineteenth century is Michel Chevalier's monumental disser-

tation, *La vie humaine dans les Pyrénées ariègeoises au XIXe siècle*. Chevalier gives detailed information on the geography and settlement patterns of
the mountain villages, as well as solid descriptions of the agro-pastoral economy and a sensitive interpretation of the "forest question"—extreme demographic pressure, limited arable land, and lack of wood—in the middle decades of the nineteenth century. Jean-François Soulet's two-volume study
Les Pyrénées au XIXe siècle is a vast descriptive account of the social organization and mental world of the Pyrenean peasantry, with excellent material
on dissidence and protest. Readers will find much information about marriage, family, property owning, sociability, as well as the economic and demographic "conjuncture," criminality, delinquency, and other forms of resistance to a dominant French culture. Soulet's massive study of the
nineteenth century is founded largely on a systematic use of judicial archives,
which somewhat limits his interpretation, especially since he frequently does
not elucidate the conditions under which the ethnographic record was generated, or fully sort out the perspectives of those who prosecuted village culture. Like his slighter, but still useful, earlier book on daily life under the
Old Regime, *La vie quotidienne sous l'ancien régime (du XVIe au XVIIIe
siècle)*, the work is a valuable compendium of material, but it often fails to
get "below" the surface content of the documents.

When I began thinking about the meaning of the "disguise as women,"
my earlier instinct was to take the term rather literally and examine the
status of women in the mountain peasant communities during the nineteenth
century. This yielded some interesting material on the relative empowerment
of women household heads in the medieval period and during the Old Regime, but ultimately it did not lead to a satisfactory account of the "disguise"
in 1829. On the status of women within family law in the central and western
Pyrenees, with its emphasis on the integrity of the household, see, for the
medieval period, the work of the legal historian Jean Poumarède, *Les successions dans le Sud-Ouest de la France au moyen âge*. For the Old Regime,
Anne Zink has recently published an exciting part of her massive study of
the institutions and practices of the family in southwestern France, including
the central and western Pyrenees, *L'héritier de la maison*. The fact that
women in the Pyrenees could inherit property and act as household heads
in the public domain led to a certain notoriety not unlike that of the Demoiselles. For more popular accounts of this exceptional status of women in the
Pyrenees, see Latour, "D'un ancien féminisme du côté des Pyrénées et d'un
anti-féminisme venu d'ailleurs," and Gratacos, *Fées et gestes—femmes pyrénéennes: Un statut social exceptionnel en Europe*. For the reform of family
law during the Old Regime and the Revolution, see Traer, *Marriage and the
Family*. The resulting peasant practices have been insightfully analyzed for
the central Pyrenees by Rolande Bonnain, "Droit écrit, coutume pyrénéenne,
et pratiques successorales," and by Pierre Bourdieu for the Béarn, "Les stratégies matrimoniales."

Useful contemporary descriptions of the mountain peasantry in the Ariège include Mercader, *Ebauche d'une description abregée du département de l'Ariège* (an IX [1801]); the remarks by Berges, *Lectures morales suivies de la description du département de l'Ariège* (1839); Laboulinère, *Itinéraire descriptif des Hautes Pyrénées françaises* (1825); and "Mémoire sur la reconnaissance du pays de Foix," 22 February 1828, in Ministère de la Guerre, Archives de l'Armée de la Terre, Mémoires et Reconnaisances 1224, nos. 42–43. (Frequently, the military engineers and officials sent to the provinces on reconnaissance missions proved to be the best ethnographers of rural society in early-nineteenth-century France. Their perspective enunciated a kind of proto-nation-building, and as such deserves further study.) Detailed reconstructions of the agro-pastoral economy and way of life among the communities of the Ariège and the central Pyrenees can be found in the works of social geographers such as Chevalier and Henri Cavaillès, *La vie pastorale et agricole dans les Pyrénées des Gaves, de l'Adour, et des Nestes.* Population statistics for the Ariège can be found in ADA 10 M 1–5; for the nineteenth century (to 1936), see the analysis by Gadrat, "Le mouvement de la population en Ariège."

THE QUESTION OF THE FORESTS

The Question of the Forests—the struggle between peasant communities, forest owners, and the state over decreasing forest lands—at the time of the Demoiselles has long preoccupied historians and geographers of the Ariège and the Pyrenees. Some useful summaries include Campagne, *Les forêts pyrénéennes;* Dupont, "Les forêts du Saint-Gironnais"; Gaussen, "La question forestière aux Pyrénées"; and Bonhôte, "Forges à la catalane et grandes essences forestières" and "La destruction des forêts." The question of the extension of the forest is a vexing one for historians and social geographers: at once semantic and political, it is an issue intimately linked to the responsibility for the destruction of forest lands. Does the forest include "brushland" and "empty lands"? Chevalier's own estimate of forest lands in the Ariège (100,000 hectares) is lower than mine, which is somewhat lower than the figure of about 175,000 hectares given by Lucien Daubrée in *Statistique et atlas des forêts de France* and adopted by others. My own statistics, enumerated in the text, have been worked out through a comparison of a more contemporary atlas (France. *Statistique forestière* [1878–1879]) and some tabulations compiled by the forest administration at the beginning and middle of the nineteenth century, including the figures published by Alexandre du Mège, *Statistique général des départements pyrénéennes* (1828–1829), and Arbanère, *Tableau des Pyrénées françaises* (1828).

Unpublished statistics of the extension and condition of the forests can be found in the writings of Etienne Dralet (1757–1844), dating from his service as inspector for the district of Saint-Gaudens during the Imperial

Reformation in 1807 and 1808. His memoranda from those years, based on extensive visitation of the sites, can be found in the Archives départementales de la Haute-Garonne (hereafter ADHG), P 334 (Pamiers) and P 335 (Saint-Girons). Some of this material was later published in *Description des Pyrénées* (1813), and he makes extensive reference to his Pyrenean experiences in his general treatises of forest management cited in the bibliography. Other unpublished discussions of the surface extension and condition of the forests in the Ariège can be found in "Aperçu sur le service forestier de l'arrondissement de Saint-Girons," 9 September 1830, in ADA 7P 11; ADA 7P 3, "Tableau des situations des forêts" (1848); and "Rapport sur l'administration des forêts" (1849). Finally, a series of official accounts of the condition of the forests in the early-nineteenth-century Ariège remains useful: the accounts include "Rapport sur les forêts du département de l'Ariège," 24 September 1819, by the General Director of Registration, Domains, and Forests (ADA 7 P 3), an enormously sympathetic account of the plight of the peasantry that nonetheless points to their pasturing rights as the "permanent cause of the ruination of the forests."

The Imperial Reformation of 1806–1807 generated much important and detailed information about the peasantry's uses and management of the forests, but there was also much detail that surfaced during the initial application of the 1827 Forest Code, when communities were given the opportunity to identify and justify their age-old use-rights to the forest. In particular, ADA 7P 85 is a tabular formulation of communal and private usufruct rights in the forests of the Ariège, drawn up in May 1828 by Dralet. A further description of these rights and their legal status in the nineteenth century, which includes many excerpts from the reformations of 1669 and 1806–1807, can be found in the Archives Nationales F10 1664 ("Cantonnements, Ariège"). The dossier was assembled in the 1860s, at a moment when many forest and mountain owners took advantage of article 63 of the Forest Code, which allowed them to free their possessions of all use-rights by assigning to the communities as property a portion, generally one-third, of their forests. Not surprisingly, the descriptions of use-rights and practices of the 1860s confirm the observations of the first forest reformation following Colbert's Ordinance of 1669.

Louis de Froidour (1630–1685), who became a *grand maître* in Toulouse, visited the forests of the central Pyrenees after the passage of the ordinance in 1669. (See his published treatise, *Ordonnances des eaux et forêts*.) His rich and detailed observations can be found in ADA 2B 31, fols. 739–756 (*maîtrise* of Pàmiers, 6 May 1670); some of his letters were published by Paul de Casteran in *Les Pyrénées centrales au XVIIe siècle;* and much relevant material was used by M. Durand Barthez, "La maîtrise des eaux et forêts de Comminges avant 1789," although this thesis from the Ecole Nationale de Chartres is difficult to consult. See also the older but still useful account by J. Bourdette, "La maîtrise des eaux et forêts de Comminges avant 1789."

Secondary sources on the history of French forests and the French forest administration abound. The best orientation to the primary sources and secondary literature is *Histoire des forêts françaises: Guide de recherche,* put together by the Groupe d'Histoire des Forêts françaises, which complements the older guide by Georges Plaisance, *Guide des forêts de France.* Within the vast literature on French forests, I learned the most from Georges Huffel, *L'économie forestière,* which contains a wealth of useful information on the history of state forest management; the social geography of Pierre Deffontaines, *L'homme et la forêt,* and the collected articles of Michel Devèze, *La forêt et les communautés rurales, XVI-XVIIIe siècles,* which concentrate largely on the forests in the north and east of France; the excellent recent work on Burgundy by Andrée Corvol, *L'homme et l'arbre sous l'ancien régime,* and her more general work, *L'homme aux bois: Histoire des relations de l'homme et de la forêt, XVIIe-XXe siècle;* the acts of the colloquium *Des arbres et des hommes;* and the recent volume *Les eaux et forêts du 12e au 20e siècle,* which includes sections on Colbert, the Imperial Reform, the French Revolution, and the 1827 Forest Code. On the occasion of the Bicentennial celebration of the French Revolution, Denis Woronoff edited an excellent set of articles about forest management and forest exploitation between 1789 and 1799, *La Révolution et l'espace forestière.* The major legislative texts of the Revolution concerning the forest can be found in Georges Bourgin, *La Révolution, l'agriculture, la forêt.* A valuable work on the forests of the Pyrenees east of the Ariège is Christian Fruhauf, *Forêt et société: De la forêt paysanne à la forêt capitaliste en pays de Sault sous l'ancien régime (vers 1670–1791).* A good introduction to the problem of forest administration in the later nineteenth and twentieth century is B. Kalaora, *La forêt pacifiée.*

On the 1827 Forest Code, see the Chamber of Deputies' report of 26 December 1826, which can be found in AN C*1 232, while Chevalier, "Le vote du code forestier de 1827 et ses implications politiques," considers the Code within the nineteenth-century liberal project. A more detailed contemporary explication of the provisions of the Code can be found in Brousse, *Le code forestier* (1827); for a complete account of the regime preceding the 1827 Code, see Dralet, *Traité des délits, des peines, et des procédures en matière d'eaux et forêts,* 4th ed.

"Disguised as Women"

The history of peasant resistance to state forest legislation during the Old Regime in the districts which made up the Ariège can be reconstituted from the dossiers in the judicial archives of the forest administration, the series

2B in the departmental archives of the Ariège, *Maîtrise du pays de Foix* (Pamiers and Foix). A detailed inventory, available at the archives, was prepared by E. Laval, R. Jolibert, and C. Pailhès in 1983. For the early-nineteenth-century precedents of the War of the Demoiselles, I consulted the judicial archives of the criminal and appeals courts in the Ariège (series 2U and 3U), as well as a dossier of incidents of resistance to the forest administration in ADA 7P 9.

In all this, I found many precedents of the Demoiselles, bands of "armed" peasants who chased off forest inspectors, but who more frequently fought among themselves over the mountains and pastures. Like Soulet *(Les Pyré-nées),* I believe that the War of the Demoiselles was but the most dramatic and elaborate instance of revolt drawing on a widespread popular political culture in the central Pyrenees. Nonetheless, in scouring the archives for precedents of the "disguise," though I uncovered much relevant material on local forest management and resistance to the state administration, I found only one instance, discussed in the text, of peasants "disguised" (not even as women) in 1767: ADA 2B 224, nos. 26–27. Soulet, *Les Pyrénées* (ii, 595–636), mentions in passing the other Pyrenean examples discussed in the text.

In many of these forest riots, from the seventeenth to the nineteenth century, women were active participants. The more general historical literature that treats the meaning and participation of women in riots and revolts during the early modern period and the French Revolution is vast. In her now classic 1971 article "Women and the French Revolution," Olwen Hufton established a research agenda of the experiences and roles of women in a revolutionary context, and a generation of scholarly research has revealed the extensive participation of women in a wide variety of protests and rebellions. These are usefully synthesized by Arlette Farge in "Protesters Plain to See." A good local study for France is Maurin, "Le role des femmes dans les émotions populaires dans les campagnes de la généralité de Lyon de 1665 à 1789." For a synthesis of work on the social basis of women in popular protest in the Netherlands during the Old Regime, see Dekker, "Women in Revolt." Dekker has also co-authored a fascinating study of women disguising themselves as men in early modern England, Germany, and Holland. According to Dekker, the women donned the disguise on a variety of occasions, including to participate in riots and revolts. See Dekker and Van de Pol, *Tradition of Female Transvestism.*

Other incidents of men dressing as women in acts of revolt are described by Davis, "Women on Top," in *Society and Culture,* and by Bercé, *Fête et révolte,* drawing in part on his monograph of the sixteenth-century revolts in the southwest, entitled *Histoire des croquants* (an abbreviated version of which appeared in English as *History of Peasant Revolts*). Specific monographs include Williams, *Rebecca Riots,* and, most recently, Jones, *Rebecca's*

Children, on the Welsh turnpike riots in the 1830s; Hours, "Les fayettes de Saint Just d'Avray," for an account of the "fairies" of the Beaujolais in 1774; Sonenscher, "La révolte des masques armés," for an account of masked revolt in Vivarais in 1783, recently reconsidered by Sabatier, "De la révolte de Roure (1670) aux masques armés (1783)." But the most striking parallel to the War of the Demoiselles, was the so-called Revolt of the Demoiselles, which took place in a Burgundian forest in February 1765. The incident is described in Gresset, "Identité provinciale et mouvements populaires en Franche-Comté." This, too, was a forest riot, involving bands of armed peasants "disguised as women"—inspired in part by the kinds of festive rituals of Carnival and the calendar year described here in Chapter 3—who for several months managed to keep guards out of the royal forests of Chaux. The War of the Demoiselles in the Ariège from 1829 to 1831 was singular, but it was not unique.

2. Deep Play in the Forest

FOLKLORE

Nineteenth-century peasant culture, in its most encompassing definition, left traces throughout the judicial and administrative archives. Yet when we search for descriptions of customs, beliefs, and ceremonies of peasant culture, our principal sources are the accounts and descriptions which I have called "folkloric inquiries" or simply "folklore"—the lore of the people. The formal (conceived as "scientific") study of folklore in France began in the early nineteenth century, although members of learned, literate culture had long investigated the culture of the "people" in early modern France (see the important essay by Natalie Zemon Davis "Proverbial Wisdom and Popular Errors," in her *Society and Culture*). Yet the "Golden Age" of French folklore came somewhat later (roughly the period ca. 1870–1914, and particularly in the 1880s, which saw the founding of *Revue des traditions populaires* by Paul Sébillot), at the moment in which "traditional" peasant culture was undergoing profound change. Eugen Weber's *Peasants into Frenchmen: The Modernization of Rural France* described the decline of local communities and ways of life under the impact of railroads, road networks, universal primary education, and compulsory military service; as such, he largely adopts the worldviews of his sources—prefects, schoolteachers, antiquarians, and others who were generally content to witness what they believed was the passing of an era.

Such was, in part, the impulse behind the study of folklore, created as "a part of anthropology" or "popular ethnography," but whose first goal was preservation: to document and record the diversity of local cultures as they were believed to be disappearing. (For a good overview, see Marrus, "Folklore as an Ethnographic Source.") The substance of this local culture, and the definitions of folklore itself, varied greatly. Some understood peasant culture to be a popular version of "high" culture: thus they collected popular songs, dances, poetry, and examples of material culture. Others focused on the myths and legends of the rural world. Still others were more inclined to center on the rituals and ceremonies surrounding the life-cycle of an individual, as well as those of the calendar year. The most important synthesis of these could be found in the indefatigable Arnold Van Gennep, whose monumental multivolume work *Manuel de folklore français* remains an essential and inexhaustible source for the study of popular culture. Other synthetic compilations include Paul Saintyves, *Manuel de folklore,* and Paul Sébillot, who in his encyclopedic *Folklore de France* understood folklore as the study of beliefs—including legends, proverbs, songs, tales, and "superstitions" about the natural world. Finally, a few folklorists attempted to understand folklore in terms of an entire agrarian civilization, incorporating social structure, popular beliefs, agricultural practices, and modes of life: the most original of these was André Varagnac, *Civilization traditionnelle et genres de vie.* For his contemporary reflections on the study of folklore, see "Folklore et histoire des civilizations"; for some contemporary reflections by a sympathetic historian, see Febvre, "Folklore et folkloristes."

The use of these sources presents certain problems. For one, they can hardly be read as transparent, unmediated accounts of rural life and beliefs. Not only could they become engaged in specifically national and political projects, as Sébillot clearly was (and as recently described by Herman Lebovics in his study *True France: The Wars over Cultural Identity, 1900–1945*), but these accounts were also unself-conscious: their authors made no attempt to describe the conditions—material, moral, political—under which the data was gathered. Although folklorists such as Van Gennep could specify the variations of a belief or practice, even at the village level, they would rarely describe or identify what anthropologists call their "informants" sufficiently, nor would they consider, as post-modern anthropologists do, the meaning of their intervention. Moreover, the social and geographic unities of folkloric inquiry were often problematic. Whereas Van Gennep relied largely on the historical and cultural identity of provinces, others made often sweeping claims about regional usages based on single village examples. More rare are the folkloric inquiries which specify the moment, place, and social origin of the informant: these were made much later, in the 1950s, and were already contaminated, perhaps, by the practices of ethnography.

The issues of contamination and purity are central to our understanding of "folk" culture. It is clear that much of what we intuitively grasp as popular has a long and sometimes tortured history of circulating between different social groups, between high and low culture. The case of fairy tales is one of the most obvious examples of the circulation of beliefs and texts. In Chapter 4, I show how the codes of charivari passed between popular and print culture during the nineteenth century.

YOUTH GROUPS AND CHARIVARI

The most useful folkloric source for information on youth groups, the festive calendar, and charivari is Van Gennep, *Manuel de folklore français contemporain,* vol. 1, pts. 2 ("La Jeunesse") and 5 ("Les cycles de carnaval et carême"). For the Ariège, in addition to De Nore's description of youth group participation in marriage rituals, see Van Gennep, "Coutumes et mariage dans l'Ariège." Secondary works on the structure and activities of youth groups in early modern France include Davis, "The Reasons of Misrule," in *Society and Culture,* and Nicole Pellegrin's excellent study of youth groups and culture in southwestern France, *Les Bachelleries.* Gutton, "Reinages, abbayes de jeunesse, et confréries"; Rossiaud, "Fraternités de jeunesse et niveaux de culture"; and Vaultier, *Le folklore pendant la guerre des cents ans,* all consider youth groups during the Middle Ages. For the Old Regime, there is much material dispersed in Agulhon, *Pénitents et francs-maçons de l'ancienne Provence.* Important secondary works on southern French youth groups around 1830 include Mazoyer, "La jeunesse villageoise," Fabre and Lacroix, *La vie quotidienne,* for nineteenth-century Languedoc, and the recent useful synthesis by Farcy, "Jeunesses rurales."

"Charivari is à la mode," reported the judicial newspaper *Gazette des tribuneaux* on 16 March 1829, referring to an incident in the town of Pau. But the report might just as well have been made with reference to the concerns of French cultural historians and others since the late 1960s, who often fixed on the practices of charivari to interpret a variety of concerns about popular culture and its transformations between 1500 and 1900. The questions asked of charivari concerned a range of issues: the identities and roles of urban and rural youth groups in the enforcement of customary norms of marriage; the functions and symbolism of discordant noise and ritual inversion in the articulation and contestation of power and authority within and beyond the community; and the ecclesiastical and secular attempts to control and reform village and urban popular culture. Important earlier studies of charivari include Saintyves, "Le charivari de l'adultère," and Alford, "Rough Music or Charivari." The French anthropologist Claude Lévi-Strauss saw the discordant noise of charivari as the key signifier of a "rupture in the ideal continuity of a chain of marriage alliances" (*The Raw and the Cooked,* 288). Recent historical work includes Davis, "The Reasons of Misrule," in *Society and Culture;* Davis, "Charivari, Honor, and Community"; Margolin, "Charivari et mariage ridicule"; Fabre, "Families: Privacy versus Custom"; Desplat, *Charivaris en Gascogne;* and Rey-Flaud, *Charivari,* which treats the charivari psychoanalytically as a ritual of sexuality. Finally, the contributions to the conference on charivari in 1977, edited by Le Goff and Schmitt, bring together a wide variety of concerns in the study of charivari in other times and cultures.

On the discipline and distortion of charivari in the Ariège, see Lalou, "Des Charivaris." Brillon, *Dictionnaire des arrêts,* lists the condemnations of charivari by the Toulouse parlement; see also Merlin, *Receuil des arrêts.* ADA G 143 contains the ecclesiastical denunciations of charivari in the dioceses of Pamiers during the 1660s and 1670s. On the ecclesiastical condemnations more generally, see Burguière, "Pratique du charivari." Further details for the Ariège were culled from the records of royal courts in Foix, for example, ADA 1B 170, fols. 165–169, on the charivari performed during Carnival in January 1761 against the remarriage of a widow in Labastide de Sérou. In Chapter 3's essay, I treat further the domestication of charivari in the context of the fate of carnival culture during the early modern period.

FOREST CULTURE

My interpretations of forest culture, of both the world of the fairies and the feminine symbolism of the forest, are derived from a variety of sources. The linguistic evidence for the gendering of the "forest" and "matter" comes from Robert Pogue Harrison's enchanting study *Forests,* which appeared as I was completing my work on the idea of the feminized forest. I also gained insight from Marcel Mauss, "Conceptions qui ont précédé la notion de matière," in *Oeuvres,* ii, 161–168.

General treatments of learned and literate perceptions of the natural world and the forest before the Scientific Revolution of the seventeenth century are suggested in Merchant, *Death of Nature,* esp. 1–41, though she tends to emphasize the creative vitalism of nature, not its destructive and disorderly qualities. On the latter, there are some remarks in Thomas, *Man and the Natural World,* esp. 192–223, concerning the "disorderly" and "savage" attributes of the forests in early modern England. For the "disenchantment" of the natural world during the course of the eighteenth century, see the essential work by Ehrard, *L'idée de la nature.*

Clues pursued in my study of the feminized forest in France derive from forest folklore, which I described in the text. Sébillot's multivolume work *Folklore de France* has been recently reprinted in sections: *La terre et le monde souterrain* and *La Flore* contain a wealth of references to the fairy world, the legends and myths of specific forests, and so forth. Some of this material also appears in Sébillot's "Légendes des forêts de France." Crampon, "Le culte de l'arbre et de la forêt," explores attributes of the forest in Picardy; Maury, *Les forêts de la France,* emphasizes the feminine attributes of the inhabitants of the forests. Gubernatis's 1878 study *Mythologie des plantes* provides a wealth of valuable material on specific species and kinds of plants and trees, what might be called an "ethnobotanical" account of the natural world; it is "modernized" synthetically in Brosse's recent *Mythologie des arbres*. In the accounts of the mythology of "enchanted nature," the work of the Society of French Mythology in 1948–1950 crossed the difficult line between folklore and mythology. See, under the direction of Dotenville, *Histoire et géographie mythiques de la France* and *La France mythologique*. More recently, Barrier's study of forest stories, legends, and customs in France, *Forêt légendaire*, makes much of the feminized qualities of the forest.

More general discussions about attitudes and beliefs concerning the forest include "La forêt entre la réalité et l'imaginaire," in *Histoire des forêts françaises*, 176–181; Bechmann, *Des arbres et des hommes*, brings out certain dimensions of the medieval imagery; and Bozonnet, *Des monts et des mythes*, discusses the mythology and representations of the mountain in contemporary French culture. Other recent works have also examined the images of trees and forests in learned writings and iconography: examples include Davies, "Evocative Symbolism of Trees," and Daniels, "Political Iconography of the Woodland."

Fairies and "Gardening" in the Forests

With the range and depth of material on fairies in French culture, the historian is in the difficult position of sorting through learned appropriations, popular conceptions, and everything in between. For an overview of sources (not restricted to France), see Marshall, "Fairies." For the medieval period, see Maury, *Croyances et légendes du moyen âge*, who saw fairies as the last vestige of paganism; Harf-Lancner, *Les fées au moyen âge*, esp. 11–78, concerning the elite's reading of popular tales; and for a study of the early modern transformations of the legendary fairy Mélusine, see Le Roy Ladurie, "Mélusine down on the Farm: Metamorphosis of a Myth," in his *Territory of the Historian*, 203–222. More generally, on the uses of fairy tales at court, and the shifting relations between learned culture and popular traditions, see Soriano's classic account *Les contes de Perrault*.

The folkloric inquiries for the south of France were useful in confirming the general and specific character of forest fairies; see especially Laisnel de la Salle, *Croyances et légendes du centre*, and Du Mège, *Statistique générale des départements pyrénéennes*, ii, 373, noting that fairies were called *hados* and *blanquettes*. But the indispensable source for the Ariège is Charles Joisten, "Les êtres fantastiques dans le folklore de l'Ariège." Gratacos, *Fées et gestes*, 25–75, has some suggestive if at times misleading remarks. On the legendary reformulations of such beliefs, see Moulis, *Légendaire de l'Ariège*. Moulis links the "White Lady" to the Esclarmonde, daughter of a leader of the Albigensian heretics captured in 1244, who reappears at night around the Black Pond. A modern ethnographic account linking the activities of washing and fairies (in Burgundy) can be found in Verdier, *Façons de dire, façons de faire,* 83–155.

Part of my strategy in identifying certain feminized characteristics of the forest was to look beyond (or "below") fairy beliefs and tales and reconstruct the peasant mode of production, *jardinage.* This meant taking into account the conflict between peasant and state forms of forest management, and opening the interpretation to a variety of sources. The feminine character of household gardening and the garden as a privileged site for women are suggested in Fabre and Lacroix, *La vie quotidienne,* 172–173; Segalen, *Love and Power in the Peasant Family,* 43, 93; and Zonabend, *The Enduring Memory,* 22–36. The technique of gardening in the forest is described by Campagne, *Les forêts pyrénéennes,* 104–110; and by the republican deputy from the Ariège, Latour de Saint-Ybars, who ran on a platform supporting peasant access to the forest, and who published a pamphlet in 1849 entitled *On the Forest Question in the Ariège (De la question forestière en Ariège).* This pamphlet was criticized for political opportunism and ignorance of local practices in an unpublished response by a forest guard in 1849 (ADA 7P 11). Etienne Dralet makes some critical remarks throughout *Description des Pyrénées;* more positive assessments are unpublished pieces such as the anonymous "Observations sur les moyens d'améliorer et de multiplier l'espèce bovine," 1819, in ADA 12M 97, and a letter by M. Gomma, justice of the peace of Ax to the director of domains and forests, 27 April 1820, in ADHG P 381. On the vocabulary and history of state forest "management," see Huffel, *L'économie forestière,* iii, 4–7, and Mormiche, "La notion d'aménagement forestier."

DEEP PLAY IN THE FOREST

Clifford Geertz's 1973 essay "Deep Play: Notes on a Balinese Cockfight," in his *Interpretation of Cultures,* set many historians in search of their own thickly describable "cockfight" in Europe and America in the hopes of enriching the cultural and symbolic dimensions of their chosen societies and historical periods. A good example would be Robert Darnton's "Great Cat Massacre," a tale of a festive rebellion of a different kind in the print shops of eighteenth-century Paris: *Great Cat Massacre,* 75–104. In borrowing the notion of "Deep Play," I do not claim to interpret the War of the Demoiselles through a Geertzian universe of symbolic anthropology, where groups and individuals move through (are caught in?) Weberian and overly consistent "webs of meaning" which give sense to "pre-established, non-symbolic system[s]" (in *Interpretation of Cultures,* 93–94). Rather, my invocation of deep play is intended to capture the cultural frames of reference that organized the goals of the peasants in revolt, and that provided the tactics with which to achieve them.

3. Festive Revolt

THE *FÊTES* OF THE CALENDAR YEAR

The French word *fête* unfortunately does not translate well: "festival" suggests a more organized and structured celebration, whereas "feast" suggests too alimentary an event, and "feast day" seems awkward. The *fête* was, potentially, a feast, a festival, and festivity all at once. French sociologists and others have meditated on the more general meanings of festivity. For example, Callois, *Les jeux et les hommes,* stressed the crucial role of festivity in providing release from the rules of daily life, a functional view also shared by Villadary, *Fête et vie quotidienne.* For related views, see Mesnil, *Trois essais sur la fête,* and the contributions to the collective reviews "Festivals and Carnivals: The Major Traditions" and "Festivals and Cultures." More concretely, the *fêtes* of southeastern France at the turn of the eighteenth century have been the object of careful historical study, including Agulhon, *Pénitents et fránc-maçons,* and Vovelle, *Les métamorphoses de la fête en Provence,* which covers the transformations of the revolutionary period. The best general study of festivity during the French Revolution is Ozouf, *Festivals of the French Revolution.*

For the French peasant calendar, and all its regional variations, the most useful source is Van Gennep, *Manuel de folklore français contemporain.* The compendium was never completed, although Van Gennep did cover the winter and spring festivals, as well as the calendrical folklore of youth groups. Much of the impulse of Van Gennep's work was to identify folkloric "zones" where certain customs were practiced (for example, the May "Queens"), areas which did not reproduce administrative or cultural regions. Thus he paid more attention to the geographic specificity of calendrical rites than other folklorists, who tended to generalize on the basis of departments or regional cultures. In my reconstruction of the Ariège calendar, I relied heavily on Van Gennep, on Rivière's more contemporary study, "Fêtes et cérémonies," and on a wealth of local folkloric studies, including: Moulis, *Croyances, superstitions, observations* and *Traditions et coutumes;* Nelli, *Le Languedoc;* Pouleigh, *Folklore des pays d'Oc;* Ruffié and Pasquier, *Massat;* Seignolle, *Folklore du Languedoc;* Fabre and Lacroix, *La vie quotidienne,* and others. To reconstruct the "season" of patron saint festivals, I used the 1877 list "Fêtes locales des diverses communes de l'Ariège." Interesting references to specific calendrical customs include Lévi-Strauss's reflections on Christmas, "Le Père Noël supplicié." On the rites of May trees, see

Sébillot, "Des usages des mois de Mai," Ozouf, "Du mai de liberté," and Corvol, "The Transformation of a Political Symbol," for her account of the nineteenth-century uses of the May trees. Other reconstructions of specific festive calendars in medieval and early modern Europe include Gaignebet, "Le cycle annuel des fêtes à Rouen," as well as his study of Carnival with Florentin; and Pythian-Adams, "Ceremony and the Citizen."

CARNIVAL

The study of European Carnivals has produced a vast if uneven literature, from anthropological and folkloric inquiries of the late nineteenth century to post-structuralist interpretations of the late twentieth century. Sir James Frazer's massive collection of collateral material in *The Golden Bough,* centering on the myths and practices of priestly sacrifice in the grotto at Nemi, included a developed "survivalist" theory about the calendar year and the European peasant Carnival in the nineteenth century. Frazer, and others since, treated the meaning of calendrical celebrations as if they were fixed by their supposed origins. In this view, the peasants' celebration of May rites—already, by the time he was writing, in abeyance—and the May Queens and May trees were shadowy evidence of a religious worship of a vegetation spirit, a deity whose functions complemented those of the winter carnival mannequin. Carnival was considered a distant and pallid heir of the ancient Saturnalia or the Roman Lupercales; the Christmas feast and the fires of Saint Jean were rites celebrating the winter and summer solstices, survivals of pre-Christian solar cults; All Hallow's eve was descended from the solemn festivities which marked the end of the Celtic year; and so forth.

The "survivalist" interpretation is ancient and forms part of the Christian discourse against paganism during the Protestant and Catholic reformations. Indeed, the denunciation of pagan survivals in dancing, singing, masking, and charivari forms one of the most important sources of these practices and also explains the attitudes of clerical and learned culture toward Carnival. These perceptions survived into the nineteenth century in a more secularized version (for example, Raepsaet's 1827 book *Anecdote sur l'origin et la nature du carnaval*), and have been available to Frazer and others since.

Folklorists of the early twentieth century, and especially Arnold Van Gennep, understood, however, that such "survivals" or "residues" of early times made sense to observers and participants only as part of a vital, meaningful set of cultural practices. Yet Van Gennep's project, like that of other folklorists, lay much more in describing the variations of these practices than in elaborating systematic theories about their meaning.

By contrast, more recent treatments of Carnival, informed by a structural study of myth and ritual, have interpreted the peasant Carnival accordingly.

Gaignebet and Florentin, *Le Carnaval,* is a sustained interpretation of Carnival and the peasant calendar as focal points of a truly "popular or folkloric religion," at once rural and prehistoric, with mythical and ritual expressions. The thesis has been severely criticized from a more historicist point of view by Daniel Fabre, "Le monde du carnaval," which draws attention to the specific historical and cultural contexts that informed the enactment of carnival rites within communities. See also, along these lines, Casanova, "Culture populaire et société rurale traditionnelle: Les problèmes du carnaval."

For the Ariège itself, some local studies provide precious details on Carnival: Cocula, "Trois siècles de carnaval à Sarlat," Delaye, "Comment, autrefois, on fêtait le carnaval à Pamiers," describing all the classical components of the festivities, including masking, balls, ritual solicitations of "fat" foodstuffs, and the burning of the carnival mannequin; Moulis, "Le carnaval à Vernajoul autrefois," Baby, "L'invective et la satire en languedocien ariégeois," Pasquier, "Un épisode de carnaval à Belesta Ariège en 1753," and Blazy, "Le carnaval à Foix en 1492." Caro Baroja, *El Carnaval,* is founded on Carnival in the Spanish Basque Pyrenees, but is nonetheless a useful general introduction to the story of Carnival. Recent essays include Ayala and Boiteux, *Carnavals et mascarades,* Feuillet, *Le Carnaval,* and Fabre, *La fête en Languedoc* (with photographs of contemporary Carnivals).

Secondary works on the late medieval and early modern Carnival and Feast of Fools in France and England include Swain, *Fools and Folly during the Middle Ages and the Renaissance;* Grinberg, "Carnaval et société urbaine"; and Heers, *Fêtes des fous et carnavals* (with a useful bibliography).

The "discovery" and interpretation of Carnival and popular culture by historians of early modern Europe, as well as their reflections on festivity and revolt, undertaken in the late 1960s and 1970s, seem to have had three distinct sources of inspiration. First was the Russian literary critic Mikhail Bakhtin, whose work *Rabelais and His World* was translated into English in 1968. Bakhtin saw the gradual elimination of the festive, boisterous laughter of the people and the marketplace after their literary recreation in the work of the great Renaissance humanist Rabelais. A generation later, scholars are dubious about the lyrical utopia created by Bakhtin, but they have preserved his insights into the transgressions of a world upside down. See, for example, Stallybrass and White, *Politics and Poetics of Transgression,* and Kinser, *Rabelais's Carnival.*

The second influence on the first wave of scholars of popular and festive culture in Europe was anthropologists in other fields working on the problem of symbolic inversion in ritual and theater. The collection of essays edited by Babcock and entitled *The Reversible World* shows an exemplary range of topics. In a complementary approach, the cultural anthropologist Victor Turner (*The Forest of Symbols* and *Dramas, Fields, and Metaphors*) explored the expressions of *communitas* in the "liminal" moments of ritual reversal, a model ultimately inspired by Van Gennep's general study *Rites of Passage*.

The third influence, specifically on the models of festivity and revolt, was the structural-functional social science of the 1950s, most notably the study of ritual reversals in Africa by the English anthropologist Max Gluckman, *Rituals of Rebellion in South-East Africa*. Gluckman founded his model on the Swazi Incwala ceremony, subsequently provoking a minor debate, a template on which the tools of anthropology since the 1950s have been forged. For the latest installment, see Lincoln, "Ritual, Rebellion, Resistance: Rethinking the Swazi Incwala," in *Discourse and the Construction of Society*, 53–74. By the mid-1970s, historians, too, had reacted against the idea that Carnival was only a temporary dissolution of hierarchies and norms. As discussed in the text, historians of French popular culture have argued for the subversive character of Carnival, but at the cost of reproducing the same functional linkages between culture and revolt. In addition to the work of Natalie Davis, Yves-Marie Bercé, and Gaignebet, see the study of Le Roy Ladurie, *Carnival in Romans*. A recent transhistorical account of the subversive functions of Carnival can be found is Scott, *Domination and the Arts of Resistance*, 172–182.

The sources for what I have called the "domestication" of Carnival in the early modern period are widely diffused. It is worth noting several major texts of both Protestant and Catholic writers in the sixteenth and seventeenth century in their efforts to "reform" various dimensions of popular culture: Lambert Daneau, *Traicte contre les baccanales ou mardigras* (1584); Jean Savaron, *Traitté contre les masques* (1608); Claude Noirot, *L'origine des masques, mommeries, bernez, et revennez es iours gras de caresme prenant* (1609), reprinted and edited by C. Leber, *Collection des meilleurs dissertations*, 9: 50–53; Abbé Thiers, *Traité des superstitions* (1679); and M. du Tilliot, *Mémoires pour servir à l'histoire des fêtes des Fous* (1751).

The secondary literature on early modern popular culture has been attentive to the ways in which the purveyors of a dominant, literate culture both disciplined and distorted the popular rite. Historians disagree widely about the relative success of such attempts in early modern France. I have already discussed the attitudes toward charivaris in the essay to Chapter 2. More general studies of the discipline and reform of popular culture include the classic works by Muchembled, *Popular Culture and Elite Culture in France;* Mandrou, *De la culture populaire* (on the popular chapbooks of the seventeenth and eighteenth century), and, to a lesser extent, Bercé, *Fête et révolte*, who argue that political and ecclesiastical elites were generally successful in reforming popular culture, a thesis laid out more equivocally by Burke, *Popular Culture in Early Modern Europe*. Davis, "Proverbial Wisdom and Popular Errors," in *Society and Culture,* 227–267, emphasizes by way of contrast the vitality and flexibility of popular beliefs and practices faced with such attempts at reform. Elias, in *The Civilizing Process,* attempted to understand the "domestication" of folk culture in relation to the sociogenesis of an aristocratic and courtly culture. Recent accounts of the relation between popular festivity and print culture include Chartier, "Ritual and Print," in *The Cultural Uses of Print,* 13–31; Revel, "Forms of Expertise"; and Briggs, *Communities of Belief.* Finally, the entire concept of "popular culture" has been subjected to a number of critical inquiries: see, for example, de Certeau et al., "La beauté du mort"; Chartier, "La culture populaire en question"; and Davis, "The Historian and Popular Culture."

CARNIVAL IN COMPARATIVE CONTEXT

The attempt to understand the languages of Carnival by drawing parallels with non-European examples of calendrical festivals of symbolic inversion is a project fraught with difficulties. Few historians have taken seriously the comparison between the European popular Carnival and calendrical rites of other cultures, including the Roman Saturnalia, although the research group coordinated by Carlo Ginzburg in Bologna suggested certain affinities (see Ginzburg, "Ritual Pillages"). The structuralist approach in anthropology is comprised of the studies of the Hawaiian Makahiki, or New Year ceremony, in Valérie, *Kingship and Sacrifice,* and M. Sahlins, "The Stranger-King; or, Dumézil among the Fijians," in *Islands of History,* 73–103. M. Sahlins was inspired, in part, by Dumézil's own comparative study, drawing on examples from India and Rome, of Indo-European representations of sovereignty, *Mitra-Varuna,* as well as Frazer's countless examples of the carnivalesque rituals of inversions during New Year ceremonies in *The Golden Bough.*

4. Revolution Unmasked

To research the play by Brazer and Carmouche *Les Demoiselles* (1830) and to make sense of the representations of Carnival and charivari as well as revolt within bourgeois culture, I had to enter another world, and another set of archives. For a discussion of the Théâtre de la Gaité, where the play was shown, and its socially mixed audiences, see Klotz, *Le Théâtre de la Gaité de 1808 à 1835.* I looked through the censor's reports, in the national archives F series. Surprisingly, at the moment—in March 1830—when censorship was clearly being reimposed and other apparently innocuous plays were severely censored, *Les Demoiselles* failed to interest the censors. Yet the reception and reviews of the play were tepid at best; see, for example, the review in *La Pandore,* 16 April 1830.

The 1830 Revolution

The 1830 Revolution has produced a comparatively small literature—compared, at least, with the events of 1789, 1848, and 1870—and is due for a major reinterpretation. The best recent narrative of the Revolution in Paris remains Pinkney, *The French Revolution of 1830,* but see the recent essay by Pamela Pilbeam, *The 1830 Revolution in France.* An excellent survey of the economic crisis surrounding the political revolution is given by Gonnet, "Esquisse de la crise économique en France de 1827 à 1832." Work on the impact of the Revolution in the provinces includes the contributions to Merriman, ed., *1830 in France;* Prince, "Popular Disturbances in the French Provinces after the July Revolution of 1830"; and Pilbeam, "Popular Violence in Provincial France after the 1830 Revolution." Secondary sources on the impact of the 1830 Revolution in the Ariège include Merriman, "The *Demoiselles* of the Ariège," and Combes, "L'esprit publique en Ariège au lendemain de la Révolution de 1830." Archival sources for the Ariège include the already-cited dossiers on the Demoiselles themselves, especially 7 P 12; the reports of the Ariège mayors to the provisional administration in Foix in ADA 5 M 53/1 and ADA 5 M 44; correspondence between the new administration in Foix and the interior ministry in AN F(9) 158; and the local correspondence between the sub-prefectures and the provisional administration in Foix in ADA 5 M 57.

To make sense of the 1830 Revolution, it was necessary to reconstruct the meaning and memories of the revolutionary tradition in the Ariège. The older, historical narratives describe the main stages of the revolutionary process as they were experienced in the Ariège, and they include occasional details about the mountain peasantry's relation to the forest. See Arnaud, *Histoire de la Révolution française dans le département de l'Ariège;* Casteras, *Révolutionnaires et térroristes du département de l'Ariège;* and Cau-Durban, "La période révolutionnaire à Castelnau-Durban, 1790–1802." The catalogue of a recent exhibition of documents at the departmental archives, *Images de la Révolution française en Ariège,* provides a useful orientation. Archival sources include the L series of the departmental archives, usefully inventoried by M. Thieron and M. Rivière, including 8 L 32 (on the revolutionary devastation of the chateaux of Brassac, Bonac, and Ganac, January-February 1793). I also consulted extant municipal archives, deposited in the E series of the departmental archives in Foix, and listed among the "primary sources consulted." There is no evidence, in the Ariège, of the infamous "masquerades" which made their appearance at the height of the popular dechristianization campaign in the southeast and in Paris during the winter of 1792–1793. A useful summary of those events can be found in Bianchi, "Les mascarades de l'an II dans la région parisienne." A copy of the Convention's decree condemning gatherings involving men "disguised as women" can be found in AN DXXXIX, 9. I'd like to thank Carla Hesse for the reference. The report which sparked the decree is discussed in *Moniteur de la Révolution,* vol. 17, p. 336 (9 August 1793).

CHARIVARI IN THE NINETEENTH CENTURY

As Maurice Agulhon and others have long pointed out, the problem of disciplining charivari was not just a problem for the Old Regime; indeed, the mock serenade and related festive rites flourished in French rural culture during the first half of the nineteenth century. Agulhon described this "efflorescence of popular culture" in his seminal study of the Second Republic in the Var, *The Republic in the Village,* esp. 85–176. The high visibility of such rites was in part the result of a repressive gaze: in the 1820s and 1830s, governmental officials, priests, and members of the urban middle classes—heirs of the religious reformers and parlementary officeholders of the Old Regime—continued to dismiss and discipline charivari as an "archaic," "barbaric," and "scandalous" popular custom; an important article on this subject is Bonnain-Moerdyk and Moerdyk, "A propos du charivari: Discours bourgeois et coutumes populaires." An important source for the study of charivaris in the decade before the 1830 Revolution is the dossier created by the interior ministry entitled "Charivaris," which consisted of administrative correspondence concerning some twenty-two separate incidents from villages and small towns all over France between 1824 and 1830 (AN F(7) 9328). On the legal status of the rituals within nineteenth-century jurisprudence, see Sourioux, "Le Charivari: Etude de sociologie criminelle."

The vitality of charivari in early-nineteenth-century France has generally been understood as part of the "politicization" of folk culture before its "decline" during the Third Republic. Charles Tilly has argued that such a politicization, especially in the years surrounding the 1830 Revolution, occurred during the transition from traditional, local, and folkloric repertoires of collective action to modern, national, and political ones; see his article "Charivaris, Repertoires, and Urban Politics," and also *The Contentious French.* Maurice Agulhon and Alain Faure have pointed to the political "infiltration" of popular life in this period, whereas Yves-Marie Bercé and Eugen Weber emphasize the transformations of local communities that underlay the novel links between folklore and politics in the nineteenth century. See Faure, *Paris carême-prenant,* esp. 95–96; Bercé, *Fête et révolte,* 40–44; and Weber, *Peasants into Frenchmen,* 399–406. Despite their differences, these historians share an implicit model of modernization that places the politicization of charivari at the center of a struggle between the traditional and the modern, folklore and politics, and rural and bourgeois cultures in nineteenth-century France, issues I take up in the Epilogue.

On the political charivaris of 1832, the single best source is Gabriel Peignot, who wrote, under the pseudonym Docteur Calybariat, *Histoire morale, civique, politique, et littéraire du charivari,* printed together with *Tableau des charivaris modernes, ou complément de l'histoire des charivaris du Docteur Calybariat,* by Eloi Christophe Bassinet (Paris, 1833), which usefully listed the charivaris by place and date. The *Gazette des tribunaux* allowed me to reconstruct the arguments at the more celebrated trials, as did the accounts of other newspapers. Two of the trials were later reprinted in pamphlet form: *Procès du charivari à grand orchestre donné en l'honneur de M. Fossau-Colombel* and *Procès du charivari, donné a M. le Baron de Talleyrand.* Kastner, *La parémologie musicale de la langue française* (i, 45–57), gives another list of political charivaris during 1831 in Normandy; see also Lavalley, "L'art du charivari en 1831." For an account of the uses of charivaris around 1830 in the western Pyrenees, see Desplats, *Charivaris en Gascogne,* esp. 132–157, who argues against the idea of a (permanent) "confiscation" of charivari in bourgeois milieux. For accounts of the charivaris in the towns of the Ariège plain in 1832 and 1833, I consulted the dossiers in ADA 5M 53 (1) and 5M 57. Tilly, "Charivaris, Repertoires, and Urban Politics," discusses these charivaris in relation to the changing repertoires of collective action during the nineteenth century.

Caricature and Charivari against the Juste Milieu

For background on the early years of the July Monarchy, see Collingham with Alexander, *The July Monarchy,* and, of course, Marx's critical account in *Class Struggles in France.* Particularly useful summaries of the cultural politics of caricature include Weisberg, "The Coded Image: Agitation in Aspects of Political and Social Caricature"; Blum, "La caricature politique sous la Monarchie de Juillet"; Schrenk, "Le mouvement artistique au sein de l'opposition de la Monarchie de Juillet"; Goldstein, *Censorship of Political Caricature in Nineteenth-Century France;* and Terdiman, *Discourse/Counter-Discourse,* 149–197.

Good accounts of the founding and early years of *Le Charivari* include Vincent, *Daumier and His World,* 10–33; Cuno, "Charles Philipon and La Maison Aubert," parts of which are summarized in his article "Charles Philipon, La Maison Aubert, and the Business of Caricature in Paris, 1829–1841"; and Bechtel, *Freedom of the Press and "L'Association Mensuelle."* On the youthfulness of the opposition to Louis-Philippe, see Mazoyer, "La jeunesse villageoise"; and on the French "Generation of 1830," see Esler, "Youth in Revolt." On the republican press and secret societies in the early July Monarchy, see Perreux, *Au temps des sociétés secrètes;* Tchernoff, *Le parti républicain sous la Monarchie de Juillet,* 142–156; Weill, "Les républicains français en 1830"; and Plamenatz, *The Revolutionary Movement in France,* 35–54. On the imagery of the "people" in early republican thought, see especially Fritz, *L'idée de peuple en France du XVIIe au XIXe siècle,* esp. 93–136.

Epilogue

Social historians of the French peasantry have produced, over the last thirty years, innumerable monographs on the transformations of the nineteenth-century peasantry, several of which have already been discussed in passing. For a recent survey of the field, see Moulin, *Peasantry and Society in France.* One focus of attention was the political transformations wrought by the Second Republic (1848–1851), including the politicization of the rural world during France's first experiment with universal male suffrage in 1849, and resistance to Napoleon's coup d'état of December 1851. Agulhon's seminal study of the "Démoc-soc" movement in the Var, *Republic in the Village,* established a "trickle-down" model of politicization which continued to insist on the opposition of local/folkloric and national/political life during the first half of the nineteenth century. Combining a synthesis of the vast literature on the Second Republic with his own research in the Pyrénées-Orientales, McPhee in his recent study of political mobilization, *Politics of Rural Life,* demonstrates how far the field has come. Local studies of the Second Republic in the Ariège include Clarenc, "Riches et pauvres," Coquerelle, "Les droits collectifs," and Morère, "La Révolution de 1848."

Weber's *Peasants into Frenchmen* focused instead on the early Third Republic as the critical moment of nation-building in which "traditional" peasant society was transformed. This model has been criticized by Tilly, "Did the Cake of Custom Break?" and also by P. Sahlins, *Boundaries,* 7–9 and passim, which develops a more general critique of models of nation-building, considering the earlier and more complex development of national identities in the Pyrenean borderland. On the increasing responsiveness of the Ariège mountain communes to conscription in the decades before the Demoiselles, see the reports sent to the interior minister in AN F 9 158. For an overview of the socioeconomic transformations of the Ariège during the nineteenth century, see Chevalier, *La vie humaine.* Tamara Whited's Ph.D. dissertation, "The Struggle for the Forest in the French Alps and Pyrenees, 1860–1914," treats the shifting character of politics in the evolution of the "forest question" after the War of the Demoiselles.

SOURCES

Archival Materials

I. Archives départementales de l'Ariège (ADA), Foix, Ariège.

Researchers should consult the indispensable *Guide des archives de l'Ariège* (Foix, 1989), under the direction of Claudine Pailhès.

Series B (Cours et juridictions avant 1790)

    B Sénéchaussée de Foix puis Pamiers, documents: 207

    1B Sénéchaussée de Foix puis Pamiers, dossiers: 113, 170, 224

    2B Maîtrise des eaux et forêts du pays de Foix: 3, 4, 5, 20 [use-rights], 25, 31, 34, 35, 40–41

Series C (Administration provinciale, pays de Foix): 1, 3, 6, 18, 19, 34, 35, 234 [forest questions concerning use-rights in 1690], 239, 268

    1C 234 (Eaux et forêts)

Series E (Communes): 80–81

    4E (Etat civil depuis l'an XI): Antras, Argein, Aucazein, Audressein, Balaguère, Bethmale, Bonac, Bordes, Buzan, Castillon, Cescau, Irazein, Orgibet, Saint-Jean, Saint-Lary, Salsein, Sentein, Villeneuve (1820–1822 and 1830–1832)

Series G (Clergé séculier avant 1790): 143

Series J (Varia)

    1J 57, 91, 335, 353, 438

Series K (Administration et comptabilité)

    Archives du Cadastre

Series L (Révolution)

    1L 136, 139, 158

    8L 32 [Devastation of chateaux of Brassac, Bonac, Ganac, Jan.-Feb. 1793]

    11L 48

Series M (1800–1940)

    2M (Elections)

    5M (Police politique): 21, 25, 26/1, 31, 44–46, 53/1–2, 54, 57, 59

7M (Police administrative): 2(10)

10M (Population et état civil): dénombrements de la population, an XII–1900, arrondissements de Foix et Saint-Girons

12M (Agriculture): statistiques agricoles, 1812

13M (Commerce): 18, foires et marchés

15M (Travail): 2(1), enquête sur le travail, 1848

Series O (Affaires communales)

2042–2043 (Massat)

Series P (Eaux et forêts)

7P 1 (Instruction générales, 1819–1861)

7P 3 (Rapports du conservateur, 1817–1918)

7P 4–13 ["War of the Demoiselles," 1809–1917]

7P 85

old P244–248 (Droits d'usage)

Series U (Justice)

2U (Tribunal criminel de l'Ariège, 1791–1810)

3U (Cour d'assises de l'Ariège) 64–67 [trials of Demoiselles, 1830–1831]

4U (Tribunal criminel spécial), an IX–1811

6U (Tribunal de primièrc instance de Foix, Pamiers, Saint-Girons)

716 (1832–1835)

717 [includes documents on the Demoiselles], 1844–1848

7U (Tribunal de première instance de Foix, Pamiers, Saint-Girons)

703 (1821–1824)

704 (1825–1829)

705 (1830–1833)

8U (Tribunal de première instance de Foix, Pamiers, Saint-Girons): 721

II. Archives Communales

Deposited in the ADA, Foix: 102 E suppt. D1 (Audressein); 104 suppt. D1 (Sentein); 107/2 (Ercé); 131 suppt. D1 (Moulis); 120 suppt. D1 (Ir-azein); 220 E suppt. 4–5 (Ax les Thermes); 169 E suppt. 2–3 (Bonnac); 136 E suppt. BB1 (Seix); 199 E suppt. DD1–3 (Alos)

Archives communales de Massat (Massat)

III. Archives Ecclesiastiques de Pamiers (Pamiers)

Dossier Latour-Ladorte

IV. Archives départementales de la Haute-Garonne (ADHG) Toulouse

B (Eaux et forêts, jusques en 1790)

464–467 (Saint-Gaudens, XVII–XVIIIs)

1045, 1050, 1653 [examples of charivaris, 1681–1762]
10B 10C (Comminges)
P (Eaux et forêts, 1790-)
  P 334–335, 371, 380–387, 386, 395/1, 401, 406, 464–467

V. Archives Nationales de France (AN) Paris

Series BB (18)
  7–8 (Ariège)
  1308–1309: Demoiselles, 1829–1862
Series C: C* I, 232–233
Series G: 7 (1336)
Series H: 714 (Pays de Foix, états, 1688–1782); 722/1–3
  (Affaires diverses, Foix, 1718–1788)
Series K: 1162
Series Q (1): 50 (Ariège, 1674–1786); 252
Series D: IV 6; XIV 1–8; XVIII/1
Series F:
  F(1a) 3 18–19
  F(1c) III
  F(7) 6767 (Esprit public) 10 Ariège, 1822–1830
  F(9) 158 1–12 (Conscription, 1801–1832)
  F(10) 403, 1645, 1656, 1664 (Cantonnements)
  F(20) 163–164 (Statistiques, tableaux . . . Ariège, 1793–1813)
  F(21) 976 [Censorship of theaters, 1829–1830]

VI. Archives Nationales de la Marine

Series D(3) 11–15: Bois des Pyrénées

VII. Archives du Ministère de la Guerre, Armée de la Terre

Series E(5) [Military correspondence on the War of the Demoiselles, 1829–1832]
Series M (Mémoires et reconnaissances): 1224 (Ariège)

Printed Materials

Abbreviations

AM *Annales du Midi*
AESC *Annales: Economies, sociétés, civilisations*
BSA *Bulletin de la société ariégeoise des sciences, lettres, et arts*
RGPSO *Revue de géographie des Pyrénées et du Sud-Ouest*

Agulhon, Maurice. 1966. *La sociabilité méridionale: Confréries et associa-tions de la vie collective en Provence occidentale à la fin du XVIIIe siècle,* 2 vols. Aix.

————1968. *Pénitents et franc-maçons de l'ancienne Provence.* Paris.

————1981. *Marianne into Battle: Republican Imagery and Symbolism in France, 1789–1800.* Trans. Janet Lloyd. Cambridge.

————1982. *The Republic in the Village: The People of the Var from the French Revolution to the Second Republic.* Trans. Janet Lloyd. Cambridge.

Alford, Violet. 1959. "Rough Music or *Charivari.*" *Folklore,* 70: 505–519.

Alibert, L., and R. Nelli. 1942. "Les croyances populaire en Languedoc au XVIIe siècle." *Folklore* (Aude): 76–90.

Allan, D. G. C. 1972. "The Rising of the West, 1628–1631." *Economic History Review,* 5: 76–85.

Antonetti, Georges. 1963. "Le partage des forêts usagères ou communales entre les seigneurs et les communautés d'habitants." *Revue historique du droit français et étranger:* 238–286; 418–442; 592–634.

Arbanère. 1828. *Tableau des Pyrénées françaises,* 2 vols. Paris.

Des arbres et des hommes. 1980. Bibliothèque des ruralistes en collaboration avec Actes Sud.

Ariès, Philippe. 1948. *Histoire des populations françaises et de leurs atti-tudes devant la vie depuis le XVIIIe siècle.* Paris.

Armengaud, André. 1951. "Les débuts de la dépopulation dans les cam-pagnes toulousanes." *AESC,* 6: 172–178.

————1953. "La fin des forges catalanes dans les pays ariégeois." *AESC,* 8: 62–66.

————1961. *Populations de l'Est-Aquitain au début de l'époque contempo-raine.* Paris.

Arnaud, G. 1904. *Histoire de la Révolution française dans le département de l'Ariège, 1789–1795.* Toulouse.

Augé, Marc. 1978. "Quand les signes s'inverse." *Communications,* 28: 55–69.

Ayala, P. Giovanni, and M. Boiteux. 1988. *Carnavals et mascarades.* Paris.

Azéman, T. 1883. "Le XVIIIe siècle à Massat." *Revue de Gascogne,* 24: 322–337; 533–550.

Babcock, Barbara, ed. 1978. *The Reversible World.* Ithaca.

Baby, E. 1934. "La répression politique en Ariège de 1815 à 1818." *BSA,* 20: 169–193.

Baby, François. 1972. *La guerre des Demoiselles en Ariège, 1829–1872.* Montbel, Ariège.

————1981. "L'invective et la satire en languedocien ariégeois: Chansons, libelles, et placards, 1783–1890." *Via Domitia,* 1: 29–50.

Bakhtin, Mikhail. 1968. *Rabelais and His World.* Trans. H. Iswolsky. Cambridge, Mass.

Bamford, Paul. 1955. "French Forest Legislation and Administration, 1660–1789." *Agricultural History,* 29: 97–107.

Barousse, Prosper. 1839. "Les Demoiselles," *La mosaique du Midi:* 1–9.

Barrier, Philippe. 1991. *Forêt légendaire: Contes, légendes, coutumes, anecdotes sur les forêts de France.* Paris.

Bechmann, Roland. 1984. *Des arbres et des hommes: La forêt au moyen âge.* Paris.

Bechtel, Edwin de T. 1982. *Freedom of the Press and "L'Association Mensuelle": Philipon versus Louis Philippe.* New York.

Belmont, Nicole. 1973. *Mythes et croyances de l'ancienne France.* Paris.

Bercé, Yves-Marie. 1976. *Fête et révolte: Des mentalités populaires du XVIe au XVIIIe siècles.* Paris.

———1980. *History of Peasant Revolts.* Trans. Amanda Whitmore. Ithaca.

Berges, M. C. 1839. *Lectures morales suivies de la description du département de l'Ariège.* Foix.

Berrong, Richard. 1986. *Rabelais and Bakhtin: Popular Culture in Gargantua and Pantagruel.* Lincoln, Nebr.

Besche-Commenge, Bruno. 1977. *Le savoir des bergers de Casabède, Sentenac d'Oust (Ariège),* 2 vols. Toulouse.

Bianchi, Serge. 1985. "Les mascarades de l'an II dans la région parisienne," in Jean Nicolas, ed., *Mouvements populaires et conscience sociale, XVI–XIXe siècles.* Actes du colloque de Paris, 24–26 May 1984: 149–158. Paris.

Biros, Marc Casimin. 1974. *Soulan en Couserans.* Foix.

Birot, Pierre. 1937. *Etude comparée de la vie rurale pyrénéenne dans le pays de Pallars et de Couserans.* Paris.

Bladé, Jean-François. 1881. "Seize superstitions populaires de la Gascogne." *Revue Agenais,* 9: 14–159; 255–288.

Blazy, Abbé Louis. 1934. "Le carnaval à Foix en 1492." *Bulletin historique du diocèse de Pamiers, Mirepois, Couserans,* 8: 193–194.

———1945. "Mélanges d'histoire révolutionnaire dans l'Ariège." Special issue of *Bulletin historique* (Castillon-en-Couserans).

Bloch, Marc. 1966. *French Rural History: An Essay on Its Basic Characteristics.* Trans. J. Sondheimer. Berkeley.

Blum, André. 1920. "La caricature politique sous la Monarchie de Juillet." *Gazette des beaux-arts:* 257–277.

Boiteux, M. 1977. "Carnaval-Annexe." *AESC,* 32: 356–380.

Bonhôte, Jérome. 1986. "Forges à la catalane et grandes essences forestières: Éléments pour une histoire des forêts de l'Ariège." RGPSO, 57: 395–402.

——— 1987. "La destruction des forêts par les forges à la catalane en Ariège: Problèmes de methodes et sources." *Lettre d'information, institut d'histoire moderne et contemporaine,* 11: 31–35.

Bonnain, Rolande. 1986. "Droit écrit, coutume pyrénéenne, et pratiques successorales dans les baronnies, 1769–1836," in *Les baronnies des Pyrénées:* 157–177, vol. 2 of *Maisons, espace, famille.* Paris.

Bonnain-Moerdyx, Rolande, and D. Moerdyx. 1977. "A propos du charivari: Discours bourgeois et coutumes populaires." *AESC,* 32: 381–399.

Boudou, Jean. 1987. *Les Demoiselles: L'homme que j'étais.* Trans. from the Occitan by Pierre Canivenc. Rodez.

Bourderon, Henri. 1954. "Recherches sur les mouvement populaires dans la généralité de Languedoc au XVIIIe siècle," in *Actes du 78e congrès nationale des sociétés savantes:* 103–118. Paris.

Bourdette, J. 1897. "La maîtrise des eaux et forêts de Comminges avant 1789." *Revue de Comminges:* 249–272.

Bourdieu, Pierre. 1972. "Les stratégies matrimoniales." *AESC,* 27: 1025–1127.

———1977. *Outline of a Theory of Practice.* Trans. R. Nice. Cambridge.

Bourgin, Georges. 1989. *La Révolution, l'agriculture, la forêt* (1st ed. 1909). Paris.

Bourliaguet, Louis. 1947. *La guerre des Demoiselles.* Paris.

Boyer-Mas, A. 1939. "Documents episcopaux de l'ancien régime: Source manuscripte de l'étude du folklore." *Folklore* (Aude): 138–160.

Bozonnet, Jean-Paul. 1992. *Des monts et des mythes: L'imaginaire sociale de la montagne.* Grenoble.

Brazer and Carmouche. 1830. *Les Demoiselles: Pièce en deux actes.* Paris.

Briggs, K. M. 1967. *The Fairies in Tradition and Literature.* London.

Briggs, R. 1989. *Communities of Belief: Cultural and Social Tensions in Early Modern France.* Oxford.

Brillon, Pierre-Jacques. 1711. *Dictionnaire des arrêts, ou jurisprudence universelle des parlements de France et autres tribuneaux,* 3 vols. Paris.

Bristol, Michael. 1985. *Carnival and Theater: Plebeian Culture and the Structure of Authority in Renaissance England.* London.

Brosse, Jacques. 1989. *La mythologie des arbres.* Paris.

Brosselin, Arlette. 1977. "Pour une histoire de la forêt française au XIXe siècle." *Revue d'histoire économique et sociale:* 92–111.

Brousse, M. 1827. *Le code forestier (1827) avec l'exposé des motifs, la discussion des deux chambres, . . .* Paris.

Burguière, André. 1981. "Pratique du charivari et répression religieuse dans la France d'ancien régime en Languedoc," in Jacques Le Goff and Jean-Claude Schmitt, eds., *Le Charivari: Actes de la table ronde:* 179–196. Paris.

Burke, Peter. 1978. *Popular Culture in Early Modern Europe.* New York.

———1983. "The Virgin of Carmine and the Revolt of Masaniello." *Past and Present,* 99: 3–21.

Callois, Roger. 1958. *Les jeux et les hommes.* Paris.

Campagne, Albert. 1912. *Les forêts pyrénéennes.* Luchon.

Le carnaval, la fête, et la communication: Actes des premières rencontres internationales. 1985. Nice.

Caro Baroja, Julio. 1965. *El Carnaval.* Madrid.

Casanova, Antoine. 1973. "Culture populaire et société rurale traditionnelle: Les problèmes du carnaval," in *Hommage à G. Fournier:* 87–188. Paris.

Casteras, C., and G. Tougne. 1972–1973. *Forêts et paturages du Couserans occidental.* Thèse de maîtrise, Université de Toulouse-Le Mirail.

Casteras, Paul de, ed. 1899. *Les Pyrénées centrales au XVIIe siècle: Lettres ecrites par M. de Froidour.* Auch.

———1911. *Révolutionnaires et terroristes du département de l'Ariège, 1789–an VIII.* Paris.

Castillon, Henri. 1852. *Histoire du comté de Foix.* Toulouse.

Cau-Durban, Abbé. 1891–1894. "La période révolutionnaire à Castelnau-Durban, 1790–1802." *BSA,* 5: 28–83.

Cau-Durban, David. 1987. *Vallée de Bethmal en Ariège.* Toulouse.

Cavaillès, Henri. 1931. *La vie pastorale et agricole dans les Pyrénées des Gaves, de l'Adour, et des Nestes.* Paris.

Certeau, Michel de, Dominique Julia, and Jacques Revel. 1970. "La beauté du mort: Le concept de 'culture populaire.'" *Politique aujourd'hui,* December: 3–23.

Cervini de Macerata, J. A. 1826–1830. *Voyage pittoresques dans les Pyrénées.* Paris.

"Les charivaris dans le Castillonais en 1857." 1914. *Ariège pittoresque,* 87: 3.

Charrière, Georges. 1975. "La femme et l'équidé dans la mythologie française." *Revue historique des religions,* 188: 129–188.

Chartier, Roger. 1981. "La culture populaire en question." *Histoire,* 8: 85–96.

———1987. *The Cultural Uses of Print in Early Modern France.* Trans. Lydia G. Cochrane. Princeton.

———1988. *Cultural History: Between Practices and Representations.* Trans. Lydia G. Cochrane. Ithaca.

———1989. ed., *A History of Private Life,* vol. 3: *Passions of the Renaissance.* Trans. A. Goldhammer. Cambridge, Mass.

Chevalier, M. 1837. "La vallée de l'Ariège et la république d'Andorre." *Revue des deux mondes,* 4: 618–642.

Chevalier, Michel. 1956. *La vie humaine dans les Pyrénées ariégeoises au XIXe siècle.* Paris.

Chevalier, P. 1985. "Le vote du code forestier de 1827 et ses implications politiques," in *Actes du colloque de Lyon de l'association française des historiens des idées politiques:* 73–84. Lyon.

Clarenc, Louis. 1963. "Délits forestiers et troubles politiques dans les Pyrénées centrale de 1827 à 1851." Thesis, Faculté des Lettres de Toulouse.

———1965. "Le code de 1827 et les troubles forestiers dans les Pyrénées centrales au milieu du XIXe siècle." *AM,* 77: 293–317.

———1967. "Riches et pauvres dans le conflit forestier des Pyrénées centrales au milieu du XIXe siècle." *AM,* 79: 307–315.

Clark, Stuart. 1980. "Inversion, Misrule, and the Meaning of Witchcraft." *Past and Present,* 87: 98–127.

———1983. "French Historians and Early Modern Popular Culture." *Past and Present,* 100: 62–99.

Cobb, Richard. 1970. *The Police and the People, 1789–1820.* Oxford.

Cocula, Anne-Marie. 1981. "Trois siècles de carnaval à Sarlat." *AM,* 93: 5–16.

Collingham, H. A. C., with R. S. Alexander. 1988. *The July Monarchy: A Political History of France, 1830–1848.* London.

Collins, Irene. 1959. *The Government and the Newspaper Press in France, 1814–1881.* Oxford.

Combes, L. 1931. "Les circonscriptions territoriales et administratives de l'Ariège depuis la Révolution." *BSA,* 17: 343–349.

———1932. "L'esprit publique en Ariège au lendemain de la Révolution de 1830." *BSA,* 18: 24–36.

Coquerelle, S. 1953. "Les droits collectifs et les troubles agraires dans les Pyrénées, 1848," in *Actes du 78e congrès des sociétés savante:* 345–356. Paris.

Corvol, Andrée. 1984. *L'homme et l'arbre sous l'ancien régime.* Paris.

———1987. *L'homme aux bois: Histoire des relations de l'homme et de la forêt, XVIIe–XXe siècle.* Paris.

———1990. "The Transformation of a Political Symbol: Tree Festivals in France from the Eighteenth to the Twentieth Century." *French History,* 4: 455–486.

Crampon, Maurice. 1936. "Le culte de l'arbre et de la forêt: Essai sur le folklore Picard." *Mémoires de la société antiquaires de Picardie,* 46.

Crubellier, Maurice. 1974. *Histoire culturelle de la France.* Paris.

Cuno, James. 1983. "Charles Philipon, La Maison Aubert, and the Business of Caricature in Paris, 1829–1841." *Art Journal,* Winter: 347–354.

———1985. "Charles Philipon and La Maison Aubert: The Business, Politics, and Public of Caricature in Paris." Ph.D. diss., Harvard University, Cambridge, Mass.

Daneau, Lambert. [1584]. *Traicté contre les baccanales ou mardigras: Auquel tous les chrestiens sont exhortez de s'abstenir des bandquets dudict mardigras et des masques et mommeries.* La Rochelle.

Daniels, Stephen. 1988. "The Political Iconography of Woodland in Later Georgian England," in D. Cosgrove and S. Daniels, eds., *The Iconography of Landscape:* 43–82. Cambridge.

Daremberg, M. 1875. *Dictionnaire des antiquités Grecques et Romains.* Paris.

Darnton, Robert. 1985. *The Great Cat Massacre and Other Episodes in French Cultural History.* New York.

Daubrée, Lucien. 1910. *Statistique et atlas des forêts de France.* Paris.

Daugé, Abbé C. 1916. *Le mariage et la famille en Gascogne d'après les proverbes,* 3 vols. Paris.

———1923. "Le mystère de la nuit en Gascogne," in *Comptes rendus, 47eme congrès de l'association française pour l'avancement des sciences:* 733–751. Bordeaux.

Dauzat, Albert. 1941. *Le village et le paysan de la France.* Paris.

Davies, Douglas. 1988. "The Evocative Symbolism of Trees," in D. Cosgrove and S. Daniels, eds., *The Iconography of Landscape:* 32–42. Cambridge.

Davis, Natalie Zemon. 1975. *Society and Culture in Early Modern France.* Stanford.

———1976. "The Historian and Popular Culture," in J. Beauroy, M. Bertrand, and E. T. Gargan, eds., *The Wolf and the Lamb: Popular Culture in France from the Old Regime to the Twentieth Century:* 9–16. Saratoga, Calif.

———1984. "Charivari, Honor, and Community in Seventeeth-Century Lyon and Geneva," in J. MacAloon, ed., *Rite, Drama, Festival, Spectacle: Rehearsals toward a Theory of Cultural Performance:* 42–57. Philadelphia.

Davis, Natalie Zemon, and Arlette Farge, eds. 1993. *A History of Women: Renaissance and Enlightenment Paradoxes.* Cambridge, Mass.

Deffontaines, Pierre. 1963. *L'homme et la forêt.* Paris.

Dekker, Rudolf M. 1987. "Women in Revolt: Popular Protest and Its Social Basis in Holland in the Seventeenth and Eighteenth Centuries." *Theory and Society,* 16: 337–362.

Dekker, Rudolf M., and Lotte C. van de Pol. 1989. *The Tradition of Female Transvestism in Early Modern Europe.* New York.

Delaye, J. 1936. "Comment, autrefois, on fêtait le carnaval à Pamiers." *Tribune ariégeois,* March 2, 9, 16.

Descartes, René. 1980. *Discourse on Method.* Trans. Donald A. Cress. Indianapolis.

Des Monts, K. 1876. *Les légendes des Pyrénées.* Paris.

Desplat, Christian. 1982. *Charivaris en Gascogne: La "morale des peuples" du XVIe au XXe siècles.* Paris.

Devèze, Michel. 1982. *La forêt et les communautés rurales, XVI–XVIIIe siècles.* Paris.

Dotenville, Henri. 1970. *Histoire et géographie mythiques de la France.* Paris.

——1988. *La France mythologique.* Paris.

Douglas, Mary. 1966. *Purity and Danger.* London.

Dralet, Etienne François. 1812. *Traité de l'aménagement des bois et forêts.* Toulouse.

——1812a. *Traité du régime forestier.* Paris.

——1813. *Description des Pyrénées,* 2 vols. Paris.

——1818. *Traité des délits, des peines, et des procédures en matière d'eaux et forêts,* 4th ed. Toulouse.

——1824. *Traité du hêtre.* Toulouse.

Dubédat, Marcel. 1899–1900. "Le procès des Demoiselles: Résistance à l'application du code forestier dans les montagnes de l'Ariège, 1828–1830." *BSA,* 7: 281–296.

Duclos, Abbé H. 1881–1887. *Histoire des ariégeois.* Toulouse.

Duhamel, H. 1909. *Un village paradoxale: Moeurs, costume, histoire de Béthmale Ariège.* Pau.

Du Mège, Alexandre. 1828–1829. *Statistique générale des départements pyrénéennes,* 2 vols. Paris.

Dumézil, Georges. 1988. *Mitra Varuna: An Essay on Two Indo-European Representations of Sovereignty.* Trans. Derek Coltman. New York.

Dupont, René. 1930. "Les forêts du Saint-Gironnais avant la guerre des demoiselles, 1829–1831." *RGPSO,* 3: 281–296.

——1933. *La guerre des demoiselles dans les forêts de l'Ariège, 1829–1831.* Toulouse.

Durand Barthez, M. 1937. "La maîtrise des eaux et forêts de Comminges avant 1789." Thesis, Ecole Nationale de Chartes.

Du Tilliot, M. 1751. *Mémoires pour servir à l'histoire des fêtes des Fous.* Lausanne.

Duval, M. 1954. *Forêt et civilisation dans l'Ouest, XVIIIe siècle.* Rennes.

——1954a. *La Révolution et les droits d'usage en Bretagne.* Rennes.

Duvignaud, A. J. 1974. *Fêtes et civilisations.* Paris.

Les eaux et forêts du 12e au 20e siècle. 1987. Paris.

Ehrard, Jean. 1963. *L'idée de nature en France dans la première moitié du XVIIIe siècle.* Paris.

Eliade, Mercea. 1954. *The Myth of the Eternal Return: Cosmos and History.* Princeton.

Elias, Norbert. 1978. *The History of Manners,* vol. 1 of *The Civilizing Process.* Trans. Edmund Jephcott. New York.

Esler, A. 1972. "Youth in Revolt: The French Generation of 1830," in R. Bezucha, ed., *Modern European Social History:* 301–334. Lexington, Mass.

Estoile, Pierre de l'. 1958. *The Paris of Henry of Navarre as Seen by Pierre de l'Estoile . . .,* ed. N. L. Roelker. New York.

Fabre, Daniel. 1976. "Le monde du carnaval." *AESC,* 31: 389–407.

———1977. *La fête en Languedoc: Regards sur le carnaval aujourd'hui.* Toulouse.

———1989. "Families: Privacy versus Custom," in R. Chartier, ed., *History of Private Life,* vol. 3: *Passions of the Renaissance:* 531–570. Trans. A. Goldhammer. Cambridge, Mass.

Fabre, Daniel, and Jacques Lacroix. 1973. *La vie quotidienne des paysans du Languedoc au XIXe siècle.* Paris.

Fabre, Daniel, and Jacques Lacroix, eds. 1975. *Communautés du Sud,* 2 vols. Paris.

Farcy, J. C. 1992. "Jeunesses rurales dans la France du XIXe siècle," in *1848 Révolutions et mutations au XIXe siècle:* 19–39.

Farge, Arlette. 1993. "Protesters Plain to See," in Natalie Zemon Davis and Arlette Farge, eds., *A History of Women in the West: Renaissance and Enlightenment Paradoxes:* 489–506. Cambridge, Mass.

Faure, Alain. 1978. *Paris carême-prenant: Du carnaval à Paris au XIXe siècle.* Paris.

Febvre, Lucien. 1962. "Folklore et folkloristes: Problèmes et bilans," in *Pour une histoire à part entière:* 607–619. Paris.

"Festivals and Carnivals: The Major Traditions"; "Festivals and Cultures." 1976. *Cultures,* vol. 3, nos. 1–2. Paris.

"Fêtes locales des diverses communes de l'Ariège." 1877. *Annuaire du département de l'Ariège.* Foix.

Feuillet, Michel. 1991. *Le Carnaval.* Paris.

Fortes, Myer. 1936. "Ritual Festivals and Social Cohesion in the Hinterland of the Gold Coast." *American Anthropologist,* 35: 590–604.

Fortier-Beaulieu, P. 1940. "Le charivari dans le Roman de Fauvel." *Revue de folklore français et du folklore colonial,* 11: 1–19.

———1940a. "Le charivari aux veufs: Matériaux et documents." *Revue de folklore français et du folklore coloniale,* 11.

Foucault, Michel. 1985. *The Use of Pleasure: The History of Sexuality,* vol. 2. Trans. Robert Hurley. New York, France.

Founée, J., ed. 1875. "Enquête sur le folklore de la forêt et de l'arbre en Normandie." *Cahiers Léopold Delisle,* 24: 1–79.

Frazer, Sir James George. 1913. *The Golden Bough: A Study in Magic and*

Religion, 12 vols. London. One volume abridged edition, 1922, New York.

Fritz, G. 1988. *L'idée de peuple en France du XVIIe au XIXe siècle.* Strasbourg.

Froidour, Louis de. 1683. *Ordonnances des eaux et forêts . . . mises en ordres par Mr. de Froidour . . . avec des nottes et des observations à la marge . . . et un traité pour l'instruction des mêmes gardes . . .* Toulouse.

Fruhauf, Christian. 1980. *Forêt et société: De la forêt paysanne à la forêt capitaliste en pays de Sault sous l'ancien régime (vers 1670–1791).* Paris.

Gadrat, François. 1924. "La vie du montagnard ariégeois au début du XIXe siècle." *BSA,* 16: 125–132.

———1938. "Le mouvement de la population en Ariège au début du XIXe siècle." *RGPSO,* 7: 5–45.

Gaignebet, Claude. 1972. "Le combat de carnaval et de carême de P. Breughel, 1559." *AESC,* 27: 313–343.

———1975. "Le cycle annuel des fêtes à Rouen au milieu du XVIe siècle," in J. Jacquot, ed., *Les fêtes de la Renaissance,* 3 vols., iii: 569–578. Paris.

Gaignebet, Claude, and Marie-Claude Florentin. 1974. *Le Carnaval: Essai de mythologie populaire.* Paris.

Galy-Gasparrou, G. H. 1900. *La vérité sur la question des montagnes de Massat.* Foix.

Gastineau, B. 1855. *Le Carnaval.* Paris.

Gaussen, Henri. 1930. "La question forestière aux Pyrénées," *RGPSO,* 1: 205–214.

———1937. "Les forêts de l'Ariège et du Salat," *RGPSO,* 8: 364–375.

Gauvard, C., and A. Gokalp. 1974. "Les conduites de bruit et leur signification à la fin du moyen âge: Le Charivari." *AESC,* 29: 693–704.

Geertz, Clifford. 1973. *The Interpretation of Cultures.* New York.

Ginzburg, Carlo. 1991. "Ritual Pillages: A Preface to Research in Progress," in Edward Muir and Guido Ruggiero, eds., *Microhistory and the Lost Peoples of Europe:* 20–41. Trans. E. Branch. Baltimore.

Glassie, H. 1975. *All Silver and No Brass.* Bloomington, Indiana.

Glotz, Samuel, ed. *Le masque dans la tradition européenne.* Musée international du carnaval et du masque. 1975.

Gluckman, Max. 1954. *Rituals of Rebellion in South-East Africa.* Manchester.

———1965. *Custom and Conflict in Africa.* Oxford.

Goldstein, Robert. 1989. *Censorship of Political Caricature in Nineteenth-Century France.* Kent, Ohio.

Gonnet, Paul. 1955. "Esquisse de la crise économique en France de 1827 à 1832." *Revue d'histoire économique et sociale,* 33: 249–292.

Gratacos, Isabelle. 1987. *Fées et gestes—femmes pyrénéennes: Un statut social exceptionnel en Europe.* Toulouse.

Gresset, Maurice. 1985. "Identité provinciale et mouvements populaires en Franche-Comté de 1661 à 1789," in Jean Nicolas, ed., *Mouvements populaires et conscience sociale, XVI-XIXe siècles.* Actes du colloque de Paris, 24–26 May 1984: 319–324. Paris.

Grinberg, Martine. 1974. "Carnaval et société urbaine, XIV–XVIe siècles: Le royaume dans la ville." *Ethnologie française,* 4: 215–245.

Gros, J. 1910. "La petite eglise, 1803–1850 d'après des documents inédits." *BSA,* 12: 133–150.

Gubernatis, Alexandre de. 1878–1882. *La mythologie des plantes ou la légende du regne végétale,* 2 vols. Paris.

La guerre des Demoiselles en Ariège, 1829–1831. 1982. Exposition itinérante réalisée par les archives départementales de l'Ariège: Catalogue et commentaires. Foix.

Guesquin, M. F. 1976. "Le masque dans la tradition européenne." *Ethnologie française,* 6: 95–102.

Gutton, Jean Pierre. 1975. "Reinages, abbayes de jeunesse, et confréries dans les villages de l'ancienne France." *Cahiers d'histoire,* 20: 443–453.

Harf-Lancner, L. 1984. *Les fées au moyen âge: Morgane et Mélusine—la naissance des fées.* Paris: Librairie Honoré Champion.

Harrison, Robert Pogue. 1992. *Forests: The Shadow of Civilization.* Chicago.

Heers, Jacques. 1971. *Fêtes, jeux, et joutes dans les sociétés d'occident à la fin du moyen âge.* Montreal.

———1983. *Fêtes des fous et carnavals.* Paris.

Heusch, Luc de. 1962. *Le pouvoir et le sacré.* Paris.

Histoire des forêts françaises: Guide de recherche. 1982. Groupe d'histoire des forêts françaises. Paris.

Hobsbawm, E. J. 1959. *Primitive Rebels: Studies in Archaic Forms of Social Movement in the Nineteenth and Twentieth Centuries.* New York.

Hours, Henri. 1970. "Les fayettes de Saint Just d'Avray: Puissance et limites du sentiment de solidarité dans une commune rurale en 1774." *Bulletin de l'académie de Villefranche en Beaujolais:* 83–90.

Huffel, Georges. 1910. *L'économie forestière,* 3 vols. Paris.

Hufton, Olwen. 1971. "Women and the French Revolution, 1789–1799." *Past and Present,* 53: 90–108.

Hugo, Abel. 1835. *La France pittoresque,* 3 vols. Paris.

Iablokoff, C. 1974. "Masques et charivaris chez les Yoruba du Bas-Niger." *Bulletin de la société de mythologie française,* 92: 8–15.

Images de la Révolution française en Ariège. 1989. Foix, Ariège.

Jalby, R. 1971. *Le folklore du Languedoc: Ariège, Aude Lauraguais, Tarn.* Paris.

James, E. O. 1961. *Seasonal Feasts and Festivals*. New York.

———1966. *The Tree of Life: An Archaeological Study*. Leiden.

Joisten, Charles. 1962. "Les êtres fantastiques dans le folklore de l'Ariège." *Via Domitia*, 9: 15–82.

———1965. *Contes populaires de l'Ariège*. Paris.

Jones, David J. V. 1992. *Rebecca's Children: A Study of Rural Society, Crime, and Protest*. Oxford.

Kalaora, B. 1988. *La forêt pacifiée*. Paris.

Kastner, G. 1866. *La parémologie musicale de la langue française*. Paris.

Kertzer, David I. 1988. *Ritual, Politics, and Power*. New Haven.

Kinser, Samuel. 1990. *Rabelais's Carnival: Text, Context, Metatext*. Berkeley.

Kleineg de Zwaan, J. P. 1924. "L'échange de vêtements entre les hommes et les femmes, signification de cette coutume." *Revue anthropologique*, 34: 102–114.

Kligman, Gail. 1981. *Călus: Symbolic Transformation in Romanian Ritual*. Chicago.

Klotz, Pauline. 1987. *Le Théâtre de la Gaité de 1808 à 1835*, 3 vols. Thesis, Ecole Nationale des Chartes.

Laboulinère, P. 1825. *Itinéraire descriptif des Hautes Pyrénées françaises*, 3 vols. Paris.

Lahondes, J. 1884. "Impression de voyage de Louis de Froidour dans le Couserans en 1667." *BSA*, 1: 251–271; 287–294.

Laisnel de la Salle. 1875. *Croyances et légendes du centre de la France*. Paris.

Lalou, Henri. 1904. "Des charivaris et de leurs répressions dans le midi de la France." *Revue des Pyrénées*, 16: 493–514.

Latour, Philip de. 1979. "D'un ancien féminisme du côté des Pyrénées et d'un anti-féminisme venu d'ailleurs." *Revue de Comminges, Pyrénées centrales*.

Latour de Saint-Ybars. 1849. *De la question forestière en Ariège*. Toulouse.

Lavalley, Gaston. 1914. "L'art du charivari en 1831." *Académie nationale des sciences, arts, et belles lettres de Caen. Mémoires*: 165–185.

Lavergne, Adrien. 1880. "Les vierges blanches, superstitions populaires." *Revue de Gascogne*, 21: 78–79.

Le Bondidier, M. 1932. "Le charivari dans les Hautes Pyrénées." *Revue du folklore français et du folklore colonial*, 2: 40.

Lebovics, Herman. 1992. *True France: The Wars over Cultural Identity, 1900–1945*. Ithaca.

Le Goff, Jacques, and Jean-Claude Schmitt, eds. 1981. *Le Charivari: Actes de la table ronde organisée à Paris*. Paris.

Le Goffic, Charles. 1911. *Fêtes et coutumes populaires*. Paris.

Le Roy Ladurie, Emmanuel. 1974. *The Peasants of Languedoc*. Trans. J. Day. Urbana.

————1979. *The Territory of the Historian*. Trans. Ben and Sian Reynolds. Chicago.

————1978. *Montaillou: The Promised Land of Error*. Trans. B. Bray. New York.

————1979. *Carnival in Romans: A People's Uprising, 1579–1580*. Trans. Mary Feeney. New York.

Lévi-Strauss, Claude. 1952. "Le Père Noël supplicié." *Les temps modernes*, 77: 1572–1590.

————1966. *The Savage Mind*. Chicago.

————1975. *The Raw and the Cooked: Introduction to a Science of Mythology*, vol. 1. Trans. John and Doreen Weightman. New York.

Lincoln, Bruce. 1989. *Discourse and the Construction of Society: Comparative Studies of Myth, Ritual, and Classification*. New York.

Lobet, Camille. 1965. "La guerre des Demoiselles." *Gendarmerie nationale*, 63: 53–59.

Mandrou, Robert. 1964. *De la culture populaire au XVIIe et XVIIIe siècles: La bibliothèque bleue de Troyes*. Paris.

Margadant, Ted W. 1984. "Tradition and Modernity in Rural France during the Nineteenth Century." *Journal of Modern History*, 56: 667–697.

Margolin, J. C. 1975. "Charivari et mariage ridicule au temps de la Renaissance," in J. Jacquot and E. Konigson, eds., *Les fêtes de la Renaissance*: iii, 579–601. Paris.

Markale, Jean. 1983. *Mélusine*. Paris.

Marrus, Michael R. 1977. "Folklore as an Ethnographic Source: A 'Mise au Point,' " in Jacques Beauroy, Marc Bertrand, and Edward T. Gargan, eds., *The Wolf and the Lamb: Popular Culture in France from the Old Regime to the Twentieth Century*: 109–125. Saratoga, Calif.

Marshall, J. M. 1987. "Fairies," in M. Smith, ed., *Mythical and Fabulous Creatures: A Source Book and Research Guide*: 325–348. New York.

Marx, Karl. 1964. *The Class Struggles in France, 1848–1850*. New York.

Maunier, R. 1938. *Introduction au folklore juridique*. Paris.

Maureille, Paul. 1932. "La vallée de Massat: Etude de géographie humaine." *RGPSO*, 3: 415–462.

Maurin, C. 1989. "Le rôle des femmes dans les émotions populaires dans les campagnes de la généralité de Lyon de 1665 à 1789," in *Révolte et société: Histoire du présent*, 3 vols: ii, 134–140. Paris.

Maury, Alfred. 1860. *Les forêts de la France*. Mémoires presentés par divers savants à l'académie des inscriptions et belles lettres, series 2, vol. 4, pt. 1. Paris.

————1896. *Croyances et légendes du moyen age*. Paris.

Mauss, Marcel. 1968. *Oeuvres*, 3 vols., ed. V. Karady. Paris.

Mauss, Marcel, and Emile Durkheim. 1963. *Primitive Classification*. Trans. R. Needham. Chicago.

Mazoyer, Louis. 1938. "La jeunesse villageoise du Bas-Languedoc et des Cévennes en 1830." *Annales d'histoire économique et sociale,* 10: 502–507.

McPhee, Peter. 1978. "Popular Culture, Symbolism, and Rural Radicalism in Nineteenth-Century France." *Australian Journal of Politics and History,* 5: 238–253.

———1992. *The Politics of Rural Life: Political Mobilization in the French Countryside, 1846–1852.* Oxford.

Mercader. an IX [1801]. *Ebauche d'une description abrégée du département de l'Ariège.* Foix.

Merchant, Carolyn. 1989. *The Death of Nature: Women, Ecology, and the Scientific Revolution.* New York.

Mercier, André-Louis. 1945–1952. "Enquête sur les végétaux dans le folklore et l'ethnographie." *L'Ethnographie,* vols. 38, 39, 41, 43, 46–55.

Merriman, John. 1975. "The *Demoiselles* of the Ariège, 1829–1831," in J. Merriman, ed., *1830 in France:* 87–118. New York.

Merriman, John, ed. 1978. *1830 in France.* New York.

Mesnil, Marianne. 1974. *Trois essais sur la fête: Du folklore à l'ethno-sémiotique.* Brussels.

Meyrac, Albert. 1896. *La forêt des Ardennes: Légendes, coutumes, souvenirs.* Chaleville.

Modi, J. J. 1925. "A Note on the Custom of the Interchange of Dress between Males and Females." *Man in India,* 5: 138–141.

Morère, Philippe. 1912–1916. "Notes sur l'Ariège avant le régime démocratique: Le Paysan." *BSA,* 12: 87–97; 14: 201–223; 353–375.

———1918. "La Révolution de 1848 dans un pays forestier." *BSA,* 15: 81–103.

Morère, Philippe, and E. Pelissier. 1914. *L'Ariège historique.* Pamiers.

Mormiche, A. 1984. "La notion d'aménagement forestier." *RGPSO,* 55: 129–140.

Moulin, Annie. 1991. *Peasantry and Society in France since 1789.* Trans. M. C. and M. F. Cleary. Cambridge.

Moulis, Adelin. 1965. "Mariages et fiançailles en Ariège." *BSA,* 21: 33–63.

———1972. *Légendaire de l'Ariège: Contribution au folklore pyrénéenne.* Vernoille, Foix.

———1972a. *Traditions et coutumes de mon terroir: Comté de Foix.* Vernoille, Foix.

———1975. *Croyances, superstitions, observations en comté de Foix.* Vernoille, Foix.

Moulis, Arthur. 1939. "Le carnaval à Vernajoul autrefois." *l'Avenir,* Feb. 23–26.

Muchembled, Robert. 1985. *Popular Culture and Elite Culture in France, 1400–1750.* Trans. Lydia A. Cochran. Baton Rouge, La.

Nelli, René. 1950. "Carnaval-Carême en Languedoc." *Folklore:* 3–12.

———1958. *Le Languedoc et le comté de Foix, le Roussillon.* Paris.

Neumann, Erich. 1955. *The Great Mother: An Analysis of the Archetype.* Princeton.

Newman, E. L. 1973. "What the Crowd Wanted in the French Revolution of 1830," in J. Merriman, ed., *1830 in France:* 320–338. New York.

Noirot, Claude. 1609. *L'origine des masques, mommeries, bernez, et revennez es iours gras de caresme prenant . . .* Langres. Reprinted in C. Leber, ed., 1838. *Collection des meilleurs dissertations . . . relatifs à l'histoire de France,* 9: 50–53. Paris.

Norbeck, Edmund. 1963. "African Rituals of Conflict." *American Anthropologist,* 65: 1254–1279.

Nore, A. de. 1846. *Coutumes, mythes, et traditions des provinces de France.* Paris.

"Notes et Mentions pour l'histoire du Couserans au moyen âge." 1921. *BSA,* 9: 225–238.

Ordonnances des eaux et forêts . . . mises en ordres par Mr. de Froidour . . . avec des nottes et des observations à la marge . . . et un traité pour l'instruction des mêmes gardes . . . 1683. Toulouse.

Ourliac, Paul. 1956. "La famille pyrénéenne au moyen âge." *Revue d'études sociales, Fréderic Le Play.*

Ozouf, Mona. 1975. "Du mai de liberté à l'arbre de la liberté: Symbolisme révolutionnaire et tradition paysan." *Ethnologie française,* 5: 9–34.

———1988. *Festivals of the French Revolution.* Trans. Alan Sheridan. Cambridge, Mass.

Pacques, Vivianne. 1975. "Carnaval, fête du mariage et de la mort." *Revue des sciences sociales de la France de l'Est,* 4: 276–294.

Pasquier, Félix. 1890. "Un épisode du carnaval à Belesta Ariège en 1753." *BSA,* 4: 379–380.

———1895. *Documents sur la période révolutionnaire dans l'Ariège: Cahiers de voeux et doléances pour les états généraux de 1789.* Foix.

Pays de l'Ariège. 1961. Auch.

Peignot, Gabriel [Docteur Calybariat]. 1833. *Histoire morale, civile, politique, et littéraire du charivari, depuis son origine vers le IVe siècle.* Paris.

Pellegrin, Nicole. 1982. *Les Bachelleries: Organisations et fêtes de la jeunesse dans le Centre-Ouest, XVe-XVIIIe siècles.* Poitiers.

Perreux, Gabriel. 1931. *Au temps des sociétés secretes: La propagande républicaine au début de la Monarchie de Juillet, 1830–1835.* Paris.

Philpot, J. H. 1897. *The Sacred Tree in Religion and Myth.* London.

Pilbeam, Pamela. 1976. "Popular Violence in Provincial France after the 1830 Revolution." *English Historical Review,* 91: 278–297.

———1991. *The 1830 Revolution in France.* New York.

Piniès, Jean-Pierre. 1978. *Récits et contes populaires des Pyrénées.* Paris.

Pinkney, David. 1982. *The French Revolution of 1830.* Princeton.

Plaisance, Georges. 1963. *Guide des forêts de France.* Paris.

Plamenatz, J. 1952. *The Revolutionary Movement in France, 1815–1871.* London.

Polge, Henri. 1975. "Le dimanche et le lundi." *AM,* 87: 15–36.

Poole, R. L. 1934. *Studies in Chronology and History.* Oxford.

Pouleigh, J. 1952. *Le folklore des pays d'Oc.* Paris.

Poumarède, Jean. 1972. *Les successions dans le Sud-Ouest de la France au moyen âge.* Paris.

Pouthas, Charles. 1956. *La population française pendant la première moitié du XIXe siècle.* Paris.

Price, Roger. 1971. "Popular Disturbances in the French Provinces after the July Revolution." *European Studies Review,* 1: 323–350.

———1975. *The Economic Modernization of France, 1730–1880.* London.

Procès du charivari à grand orchestre donné en l'honneur de M. Fossau-Colombel, chef de bataillon de la guarde nationale des Batignoles. 1832. Paris.

Procès du charivari, donné a M. le Baron de Talleyrand, prefet du Pas-de-Calais, tribunal d'appel d'Arras. 1832. Arras.

Pujol, Louis. 1989. *Le temps des fleurs.* Miglos, Ariège.

Pythian-Adams, Charles. 1989. "Ceremony and the Citizen: The Communal Year at Coventry, 1450–1550," in Stuart Clark and Paul Slack, eds., *Crisis and Order in English Towns, 1500–1700: Essays in Urban History:* 57–85. Toronto.

Raepsaet, Jean-Joseph. 1827. *Anecdote sur l'origine et la nature du carnaval.* Brussels.

Reiter, Rayna R. 1975. "Men and Women in the South of France: Public and Private Domains," in Rayna R. Reiter, ed., *Toward an Anthropology of Women:* 252–282. New York.

Revel, Jacques. 1984. "Forms of Expertise: Intellectuals and 'Popular' Culture in France, 1650–1800," in S. Kaplan, ed., *Understanding Popular Culture: Europe from the Middle Ages to the Nineteenth Century:* 255–274. Berlin.

Rey-Flaud, Henri. 1985. *Le Charivari: Les rituels fondamentaux de la sexualité.* Paris.

Rivière, Georges Henri, and Marcel Maget. 1943. "Fêtes et cérémonies de la communauté villageoise," in Jean Charbonnier et al., *Agriculture et communauté:* 75–95. Paris.

Rogers, Susan. 1975. "Female Forms of Power and the Myth of Male Dominance: A Model of Female/Male Interaction in Peasant Society." *American Ethnologist,* 2: 727–756.

————1985. "Gender in Southwestern France: The Myth of Male Dominance Revisited." *Anthropology,* 9: 65–86.

Rolland, Eugène. 1896–1904. *Flore populaire de la France.*

Rossiaud, Jacques. 1976. "Fraternités de jeunesse et niveaux de culture dans les villes du Sud-Est à la fin du moyen âge." *Cahiers d'histoire,* 21: 67–102.

Roubin, Lucienne A. 1970. "Espace masculin, espace féminin en communauté provençale." *AESC,* 25: 537–560.

Rousset, Antonin. 1871. *Dictionnaire générale des forêts. Première partie: Législation et administration depuis 1672 à 1871.* Nice.

Ruffié, N., and M. Pasquier. 1889. *Massat: Chansons, dances, usages, et charte communale.* Foix.

Sabatier, Gérard. 1985. "De la révolte de Roure (1670) aux masques armés (1783): La mutation du phénomène contestataire en Vivarais," in Jean Nicolas, ed., *Mouvements populaires et conscience sociale, XVI-XIXe siècles:* 121–148. Paris: Actes du colloque de Paris, 24–26 May 1984.

Sabean, David. 1976. "The Communal Basis of Peasant Uprisings." *Comparative Politics,* 8: 355–364.

Sahlins, Marshall. 1985. *Islands of History:* 73–103. Chicago.

Sahlins, Marshall, and Patrick V. Kirch. 1992. *Anahulu: The Anthropology of History in the Kingdom of Hawaii,* vol. 1: *Historical Ethnography.* Chicago.

Sahlins, Peter. 1980. "The 'War of the *Demoiselles*' in Ariège, France, 1829–1867." Senior thesis, Harvard College, Cambridge, Mass.

————1989. *Boundaries: The Making of France and Spain in the Pyrenees.* Berkeley.

————1993. "Deep Play in the Forest: Peasant Culture and Protest in Nineteenth-Century France," in Barbara Dieffendorf and Carla Hesse, eds., *Culture and Identity in Early Modern France, 1500–1800.* Ann Arbor.

Saintyves, Paul. 1919. "Les rondes et les quêtes de carnaval." *Revue des traditions populaires,* 34: 30–42; 49–69; 121–148.

————1929. "Le mercredi des cendres." *Revue anthropologique,* 39: 178–196.

————1935. "Le charivari de l'adultère et les courses à corps nus." *L'Ethnographie:* 7–36.

————1937. *L'astrologie populaire.* Paris.

————1937a. *Manuel de folklore.* Paris.

Salvador, Jean. 1930. "L'aménagement et l'exploitation des forêts pyrénéennes françaises." *RGPSO,* 1: 58–71.

Savaron, Jean. 1608. *Traitté contre les masques.* Paris.

Schrenk, K. 1980. "Le mouvement artistique au sein de l'opposition de la

Monarchie de Juillet." *Histoire et critique des arts et les dessins de presse:* 67–96. Paris.

Scott, James C. 1990. *Domination and the Arts of Resistance: Hidden Transcripts.* New Haven.

Sébillot, Paul. 1888. "Des usages du mois de mai." *Revue des traditions populaires,* 3: 246–251.

———1898–1899. "Légendes des forêts de France." *Revue des traditions populaires,* 8 (1898): 641–661; 14 (1899): 72–81.

———1904–1907. *Folklore de France,* 4 vols. Paris.

———1985. *La Flore.* Paris.

———1985a. *La terre et le monde souterrain.* Paris.

Segalen, Martine. 1975. "Le mariage et la femme dans les proverbes du Sud de la France." *AM,* 87: 265–288.

———1975–1976. "Le mariage, l'amour, et les femmes dans les proverbes populaires français." *Ethnologie française,* 5 (1975): 119–162; 6 (1976): 33–38.

———1983. *Love and Power in the Peasant Family: Rural France in the Nineteenth Century.* Trans. S. Matthews. Chicago.

Seignolle, Claude. 1960. *Le folklore du Languedoc.* Paris.

Servat, J. M. 1936. *Histoire de Massat.* Foix.

Sire, P., and H. Féraud. 1941. "La femme selon la sagesse populaire languedocienne." *Folklore* (Aude): 177–189.

Sirgant, A. 1933. "Contribution à l'étude du commerce dans l'Ariège sous le premier empire: Les Foires." *BSA,* 18: 139–150.

———1934. "La culture du lin et du chanvre dans les arrondissements de Foix et de Saint-Girons sous le premier empire." *BSA,* 18: 194–199.

———1934a. "L'élevage dans l'Ariège sous le premier empire: Chevaux, bêtes à laine, bêtes à grosse corne." *BSA,* 18: 277–293.

Smith, A. W. 1967. "Some Folklore Elements in Movements of Social Protest." *Folklore* (London), 77: 241–252.

Soboul, Albert. 1956. "The French Rural Community in the Eighteenth and Nineteenth Centuries." *Past and Present,* 10: 78–95.

———1968. "Survivances 'féodales' dans la société française au XIXe siècle." *AESC,* 23: 965–986.

Sonenscher, M. 1972. "La révolte des masques armés dans le Vivarais." *Vivarais et Languedoc: Actes du XLIVe congrès de la fédération historique de Languedoc méditerranéen et du Roussillon:* 243–267. Montpellier.

Soriano, Marc. 1977. *Les contes de Perrault: Culture savante et traditions populaires.* Paris.

Soulet, Jean-François. 1974. *La vie quotidienne dans les Pyrénées sous l'ancien régime du XVIe au XVIIIe siècles.* Paris.

———1987. *Les Pyrénées au XIXe siècle,* 2 vols. Toulouse.

Sourioux, Jean-Louis. 1961. "Le Charivari: Etude de sociologie criminelle." *L'année sociologique*, 3rd series: 401–414.

Stallybrass, Peter, and Alain White. 1986. *The Politics and Poetics of Transgression*. Ithaca.

Statistique forestière. 1878–1879, 2 vols. Paris.

Swain, B. 1932. *Fools and Folly during the Middle Ages and the Renaissance*. New York.

Tchernoff, I. 1901. *Le parti républicain sous la Monarchie de Juillet: Formation et évolution de la doctrine républicaine*. Paris.

Teissier, Octave. 1896. *Le prince d'amour et les abbés de la jeunesse*. Marseilles.

Terdiman, Richard. 1985. *Discourse/Counter-Discourse: The Theory and Practice of Symbolic Resistance in Nineteenth-Century France*. Ithaca.

Thiers, Abbé. 1679. *Traité des superstitions*. Paris.

Thomas, Keith. 1983. *Man and the Natural World: Changing Attitudes in England, 1500–1800*. London.

Thompson, E. P. 1972. "Le charivari anglais." *AESC*, 27: 285–312.

———1974. "Patrician Society, Plebeian Culture." *Journal of Social History*, 7: 382–405.

———1975. *Whigs and Hunters: The Origin of the Black Act*. London.

Tilly, Charles. 1979. "Did the Cake of Custom Break?" in John Merriman, ed., *Consciousness and Class Experience in Nineteenth-Century Europe*: 17–41. New York.

———1981. "Charivaris, Repertoires, and Urban Politics," in John Merriman, ed., *French Cities in the Nineteenth Century*: 73–91. New York.

———1986. *The Contentious French*. Cambridge, Mass.

Traer, J. F. 1980. *Marriage and the Family in Eighteenth-Century France*. Ithaca.

Traver, E. 1933. *Les Bachelleries*. Melle.

Tricoire, Jean. 1942. "Magie et traditions populaires dans la vallée de Montségur." *Folklore* (Aude): 120–127.

Tricoire, Jean, and Raymond Tricoire. 1942. *Folklore du pays de Montségur Ariège*. Paris.

Turner, Victor. 1967. *The Forest of Symbols*. Ithaca.

———1969. *The Ritual Process*. Ithaca.

———1974. *Dramas, Fields, and Metaphors*. Ithaca.

Valérie, Valério. 1985. *Kingship and Sacrifice: Ritual and Society in Ancient Hawaii*. Chicago.

Van Gennep, Arnold. 1937–1945. *Manuel de folklore français contemporain*, 4 vols. Paris.

———1942. "Coutumes et mariage dans l'Ariège." *Visages du monde*, 72.

———1960. *The Rites of Passage*. Trans. M. B. Vizedom and G. L. Caffee. Chicago.

Varagnac, André. 1945. "Folklore et histoire des civilisations: Cultures dissociées et cultures homogènes." *Annales d'histoire sociale*, 8: 95–102.

———1948. *Civilisation traditionnelle et genres de vie*. Paris.

Vassal, Guy. 1975. *La guerre des Demoiselles*. Paris.

Vaultier, Roger. 1965. *Le folklore pendant la guerre de cent ans d'après les lettres de rémission*. Paris.

Verdier, Yvonne. 1979. *Façons de dire, façons de faire: La laveuse, la couturière, la cuisinière*. Paris.

Vidalenc, Jean. 1970. *La société française de 1815 à 1849: Le peuple des campagnes*. Paris.

Villadary, Agnès. 1968. *Fête et vie quotidienne*. Paris.

Vincent, P. 1968. *Daumier and His World*. Evanston, Illinois.

Vloberg, Maurice. 1936. *Les fêtes de France*. Grenoble.

Vovelle, Michel. 1976. *Les métamorphoses de la fête en Provence de 1750 à 1820*. Paris.

Walter, Georges. 1963. *Histoire des paysans de France*. Paris.

Weber, Eugen. 1976. *Peasants into Frenchmen: The Modernization of Rural France, 1870–1914*. Stanford.

Weill, Georges. 1899–1900. "Les républicains français en 1830." *Revue d'histoire moderne et contemporaine*, 1: 321–351.

———1900. *Histoire du parti républicain en France de 1814 à 1870*. Paris.

Weisberg, Gabriel P. 1989. "The Coded Image: Agitation in Aspects of Political and Social Caricature," in *The Art of the July Monarchy in France, 1830 to 1848*: 148–191. Columbia, Missouri.

Welsford, E. 1937. *The Fool: His Social and Literary History*. London.

Whited, Tamara. 1994. "The Struggle for the Forest in the French Alps and Pyrenees, 1860–1940." Ph.D. diss., University of California, Berkeley.

Williams, David. 1955. *The Rebecca Riots*. Cardiff, New York.

Wolf, Eric. 1982. *Europe and the People without History*. Berkeley.

Woronoff, Denis. 1989. *La Révolution et l'espace forestière*. Paris.

Wylie, Laurence. 1975. *Village in the Vaucluse*. Cambridge, Mass.

Zink, Anne. 1993. *L'héritier de la maison: Géographie coutumière du Sud-Ouest de la France sous l'ancien régime*. Paris.

Zonabend, Françoise. 1984. *The Enduring Memory: Time and History in a French Village*. Trans. Anthony Foster. Manchester.

ACKNOWLEDGMENTS

This book's first material form was an undergraduate thesis at Harvard College in 1980, inspired by John Bohstedt's seminar on collective violence in the fall of 1978. I had pursued the Demoiselles in the Ariège archives during the summer of 1979, my research funded by the Center for European Studies at Harvard. Then, after a long diversion in a neighboring valley in the Pyrenees, I undertook further archival research in 1989 and 1991, generously supported by the History Department of the University of California, Berkeley. My debts over these years are numerous. David Eddy, Forest Reinhardt, and Sooni Taraporevala were there at the beginning. Michael Donnelly's careful supervision of the initial thesis greatly improved its clarity. James Fernandez and John Merriman offered valuable criticisms. The work and example of Natalie Zemon Davis consistently advanced my interpretations of the Demoiselles, as is evident in the text. In more recent years, many friends have carefully read through sections of the manuscript: I would especially like to thank Susanna Barrows, Marjorie Beale, David Eaton, Charlotte Eyerman, Stephen Greenblatt, Timothy Hampton, Christian Jouhaud, Thomas Laqueur, Irwin Scheiner, Lynn Sharp, Anne Wagner, and Tamara Whited for their (too often unheeded) critical comments. James Amelang, James Boyden, Robin Einhorn, Ruth Harris, Jacques Revel, Marshall Sahlins, and Randolph Starn read the entire manuscript, preventing numerous errors of fact and dated formulations from making their appearance in print. Most of all, Ramona Naddaff read through the manuscript at critical moments, and especially helped it all make sense.

Parts of Chapters 1 and 2 were presented at the symposium "Dialogues with the Past" at Boston University in November 1990, and at the Agrarian Studies Seminar at Yale University in January 1992.

I thank the organizers and participants in these seminars for their timely and critical comments. A version of the talk was published as "Deep Play in the Forest: The 'War of the *Demoiselles*' in the Ariège (1829–1831)," in Barbara Dieffendorf and Carla Hesse, eds., *Culture and Identity in Early Modern France, 1500–1800* (Ann Arbor: University of Michigan Press, 1993): 159–177. Permission from the publisher to reproduce materials drawn from this article is gratefully acknowledged.

INDEX